Understanding God's World

Laurel Hicks
Dawn Mereness

A Beka Book.
A MINISTRY OF
PENSACOLA CHRISTIAN COLLEGE
PENSACOLA, FLORIDA 32523-9160

Contributing writers: Wilfred Gunderson, Matilda Nordtvedt, Julie Rickard, Judy Hull Moore, George T. Thompson, Pam Tisdale

A Beka Book Science and Health

Science	*Health*
God's World	
Discovering God's World	Health, Safety, and Manners 1
Enjoying God's World	Health, Safety, and Manners 2
Exploring God's World	Health, Safety, and Manners 3
Understanding God's World	Developing Good Health
Investigating God's World	Enjoying Good Health
Observing God's World	Choosing Good Health
Science: Order and Reality	A Healthier You
Science: Matter and Motion	Let's Be Healthy
Science of the Physical Creation	
Biology: God's Living Creation	
Chemistry: Precision and Design	
Physics: The Foundational Science	

Designer: **Michael Petty**

Illustrators: Frank Hicks
Todd Knowlton
Michael Petty

Copyright© 1989 *A Beka Book* Publications
All rights reserved. Printed in U.S.A.

CONTENTS

Chapter   **Page**

1 SCIENCE: Let's Find Out   3

   1.1   Stop, Look, and Wonder   3
   1.2   Learn to Observe   8
   1.3   Observing North American Birds and Flowers   13

Something to Do
      Observing life in the soil   7
      Growing plants from seeds   11

Special Features
      Birds and flowers of the fifty states   14
      Canada's floral emblems   18

2 INSECTS: Miniature Marvels of Creation   20

   2.1   Ten Million Designs   20
   2.2   An Insect Zoo   24
   2.3   Learning about Insect Life Cycles   29
   2.4   Designer Heads   32
   2.5   Designed for Motion   35
   2.6   Crickets and Grasshoppers   38
   2.7   How Insects Defend Themselves   41
   2.8   How Insects Communicate   44
   2.9   Where Insects Live   47
   2.10   Dwellings of Social Insects   51
   2.11   Jean Henri Fabre: Explorer of Backyard Wonders   56

Science Concepts
      Incomplete metamorphosis   40

Special Features
      Butterflies and moths you should know   26
      Consider the ladybug   50

CHAPTER CHECK-UP   **58**

3 PLANTS: Provision for Man and Beast   62

    3.1   Designed to Produce   62
    3.2   Needleleaf Trees   65
    3.3   Broadleaf Trees and Palms   68
    3.4   Observing Flowers   70
    3.5   Seed Design   77
    3.6   Traveling Seeds   79
    3.7   Germination   82
    3.8   Poisonous Plants   84
    3.9   Plants: Helpful and Beautiful   89
    3.10   George Washington Carver: The Plant Doctor   92

Something to Do
    State and provincial flowers   72
    Observing the parts of a seed   78
    Observing germination   84

Special Features
    Wildflowers you should know   74
    Garden flowers you should know   76

CHAPTER CHECK-UP   94

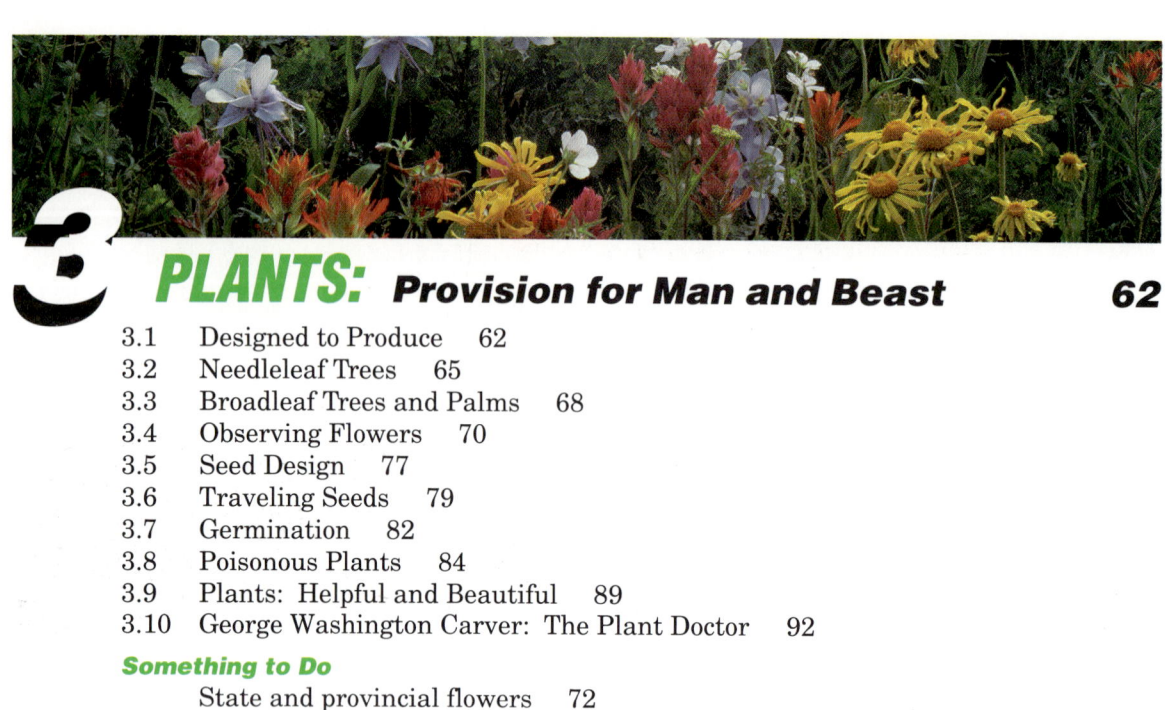

4 BIRDS: Winged Wonders   98

    4.1   Birds in Your Back Yard   98
    4.2   More Backyard Birds   103
    4.3   Recognizing Birds   108
    4.4   Feeding the Birds   110
    4.5   Birdbaths and Birdhouses   113
    4.6   Birds of the Forest   117
    4.7   Designer Birds   120
    4.8   Designed for Flight   125
    4.9   The Jack Miner Bird Sanctuary   129

      How do birds sing?   106
      Why should a birdbath not be made of metal?   116
      How do a bird's feathers keep it warm?   129

Something to Do
      Observing lift   126

CHAPTER CHECK-UP   *131*

5 MATTER: Water, Air, and Weather   134

  5.1   God's Gift of Water   134
  5.2   Water for Life   137
  5.3   Water, Steam, and Ice   140
  5.4   Water Changes State   142
  5.5   Water's Energy   144
  5.6   The Atmosphere: An Ocean of Air   147
  5.7   Air's Weight and Pressure   149
  5.8   Wind: Moving Air   152
  5.9   Water in the Air   154
  5.10 Condensation and Precipitation   157
  5.11 Kinds of Precipitation and Clouds   159
  5.12 Weather Forecasting   161
  5.13 Robert Boyle: Father of Chemistry   163

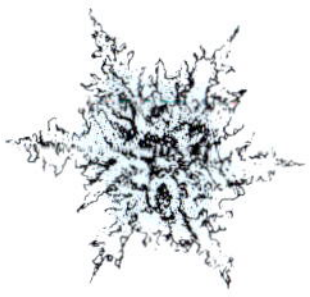

Something to Do
      Observing surface tension and dissolving substances   142
      Making a water wheel   146
      The weight of air   150
      Observing air pressure   150
      The power of moving air   154
      Evaporation and heat   156
      Observing condensation   158

Science Concepts
      Why is the sky blue?   149

CHAPTER CHECK-UP   *165*

6 ENERGY: Sound and Hearing 168

    6.1   Sounds All around Us   168
    6.2   Making Sound   173
    6.3   Receiving Sound   176
    6.4   High and Low Sounds   181
    6.5   Sounds That Bounce Back   184
    6.6   Preserving Sound   187
    6.7   Alexander Graham Bell: Inventor of the Telephone   190

Something to Do
    Observing sound travel   172
    Observing sound vibrations   180
    Tin can telephone   180
    Make a straw instrument   183
    High and low sounds   183
    Bouncing energy   185
    Sound difference   189

Special Feature
    The American manual alphabet   174

CHAPTER CHECK-UP   192

7 GEOLOGY: Planet Earth 194

    7.1   Our Home, the Earth   194
    7.2   The Earth's Motion   197
    7.3   The Oceans and Continents of the Earth   201
    7.4   Soil and the Earth's Layers   205
    7.5   Water and Soil   210
    7.6   Rocks   213

Something to Do
    Measuring the earth   196
    The cause of day and night   197
    Why winter is cold   200
    Making a compass   204
    Making crystals   207
    Rock collections   217
CHAPTER CHECK-UP   218

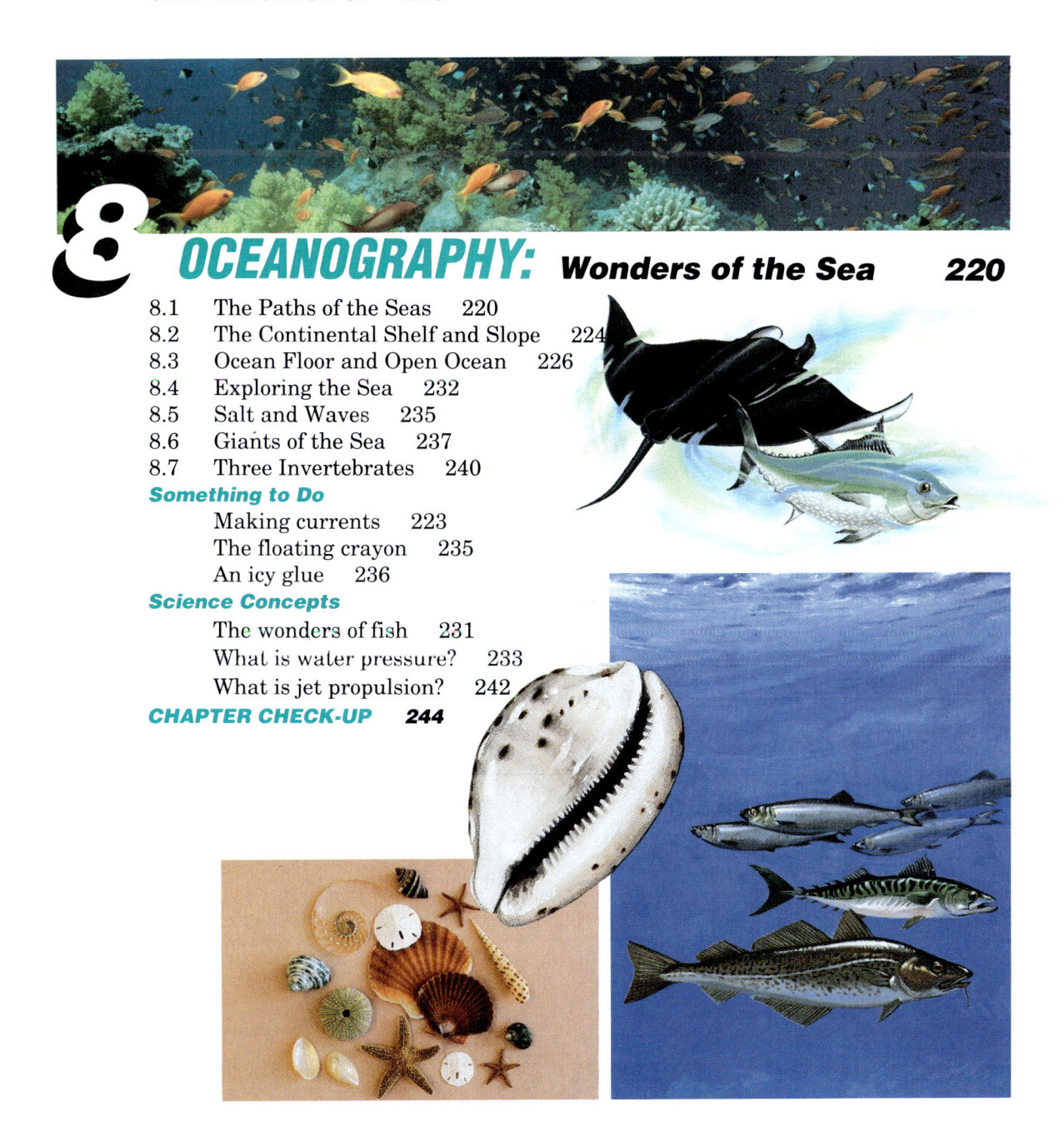

8 OCEANOGRAPHY: Wonders of the Sea   220

  8.1   The Paths of the Seas   220
  8.2   The Continental Shelf and Slope   224
  8.3   Ocean Floor and Open Ocean   226
  8.4   Exploring the Sea   232
  8.5   Salt and Waves   235
  8.6   Giants of the Sea   237
  8.7   Three Invertebrates   240

Something to Do
    Making currents   223
    The floating crayon   235
    An icy glue   236

Science Concepts
    The wonders of fish   231
    What is water pressure?   233
    What is jet propulsion?   242

CHAPTER CHECK-UP   244

9 ASTRONOMY: Consider the Heavens 246

9.1 Wonders of the Night Sky 246
9.2 Seasons, Days, and Years 252
9.3 Pictures in the Sky 255
9.4 The Sun: The Greater Light 262
9.5 The Moon: The Lesser Light 265
9.6 The Origin of the Universe 269

Something to Do
Making a star viewer 260
Stars in sunlight 261

Science Concepts
A dark shirt on a hot day 263
The movements of the sun 264
Why does the moon shine if it cannot produce light? 266

CHAPTER CHECK-UP 273

Glossary 276
Index 287
Scripture Index 294
Credits 295

God, who made the earth,
    The air, the sky, the sea,
Who gave the light its birth,
    Careth for me.

God, who made the grass,
    The flower, the fruit, the tree,
The day and night to pass,
    Careth for me.

O Lord, how manifold are thy works!
in wisdom hast thou made them all:
the earth is full of thy riches.
Psalm 104:24

1 SCIENCE:
Let's Find Out

1.1 Stop, Look, and Wonder

Did you ever wonder how snowflakes are formed? Do you know where the North Pole is and which plants and animals live near it?

Do you know how a jet engine works? Do you know what happens to the oceans as the moon moves around the earth?

Do you know how air can be used to make work easier and how birds fly through the air?

Do you know how many times your heart beats each day and how to keep your heart healthy? Do you know the names of the flowers, birds, and insects that you see every day?

These questions and many others can be answered through a study of science.

It is fun to think about puzzling questions and to try to figure out how things work. God made us curious. This is one of many good reasons for studying science.

Why we study science

God created us with minds that are able to learn about Him and His world. He gave us the ability to enjoy His world and to use it wisely.

God also gave us a desire to help others. Many scientists have worked for years trying to find ways to help other people. They have thought of ways to prevent or cure disease. They have learned how to make hard jobs easier. They have found ways to make people comfortable.

These are just a few reasons for studying science. Can you think of some others?

1. God made us curious.

2. God gave us good minds.

3. God gave us the ability to enjoy His world and use it wisely.

4. God gave us a desire to help others.

What science is

Science is *the study of the wonders of the universe.* A **scientist** is *a person who spends time trying to learn about things God has made.*

There is a huge museum in New Zealand that has many displays of animals and birds from all over the world. Above the entrance is a Bible text from Job 26:14: "Lo, these are parts of his ways: but how little a portion is heard of him!"

Even the greatest scientists understand only a small part of the wonderful things God has made.

How do scientists learn?

Scientists learn in the same ways as other people.
1. They look carefully. They observe.
2. They gather information and try to think clearly.
3. They try to make sensible guesses, or hypotheses.
4. They test their hypotheses with experiments to see whether they are correct.

Lo, these are parts of his ways: but how little a portion is heard of him!

Let's Find Out

Observation

In this chapter, we shall think about observation, or observing. **Observation** is *looking carefully at something.* We can learn thousands of facts by observing.

One of the best places to begin your observation of the world around you is in your own back yard. There are many interesting things there that you may have never thought about before. Perhaps you can dig up a scoop of soil and look for living, moving things in it. Do you know their names? Look at the soil itself. Is it sandy, or is it reddish and sticky like clay or a rich, brown color? Observe the grass. Is it green and growing, or has it dried out? Can you find what look like several different grass plants? Slowly pull up one grass plant so you can observe its roots. They are all about the same size, and they grow in a tangled mass. The tangled roots of grass help hold soil particles together so the soil does not wash away.

You will probably be able to find several different kinds of insects and other creatures crawling through the soil, walking across a blade of grass, or flying in the air. Can you name the animals that you see? Do you know how to catch them and keep them for observation? In chapter 2 you will meet many common insects and learn how to make an insect zoo.

Are there any trees in your back yard? Can you name them? Do you know how they change through the seasons? Do you know the names of the birds, mammals, reptiles, and amphibians that live in or around them? Once you learn to look closely at the marvels of God's creation and to try to find out more about the world around you, you will realize that there are many interesting things to see, do, and think about no matter where you are.

6 ■ Understanding God's World

SOMETHING TO DO   *Observing life in the soil*

You would be amazed to find out how many tiny creatures make their home in just a scoop of soil. Here is a way to bring these creatures out of the soil so you can observe them more easily.

You will need a metal can, a can opener, a piece of cloth screen (hardware cloth) which is larger than the bottom of the can, a funnel, a large glass or plastic jar with a wide mouth, black construction paper to wrap around the sides of the jar, tape, paper towels, and something with which to scoop up dirt.

Tape the black paper around the jar. Place several moist paper towels inside the wide-mouthed jar. Line the funnel with the cloth screen and place it in the mouth of the jar. Be sure the funnel does not touch the bottom of the jar. Remove both ends from the metal can and place it inside the funnel. Scoop up some dirt and fill the metal can with it.

Place the funnel in bright sunlight or under an electric light. The little creatures in the soil will move away from the light, tunneling deeper into the soil, and then they will fall through the funnel to the paper towels in the jar below. This process may take a day or two.

Remove the paper towels and observe the creatures you have caught. Did you find any of these?

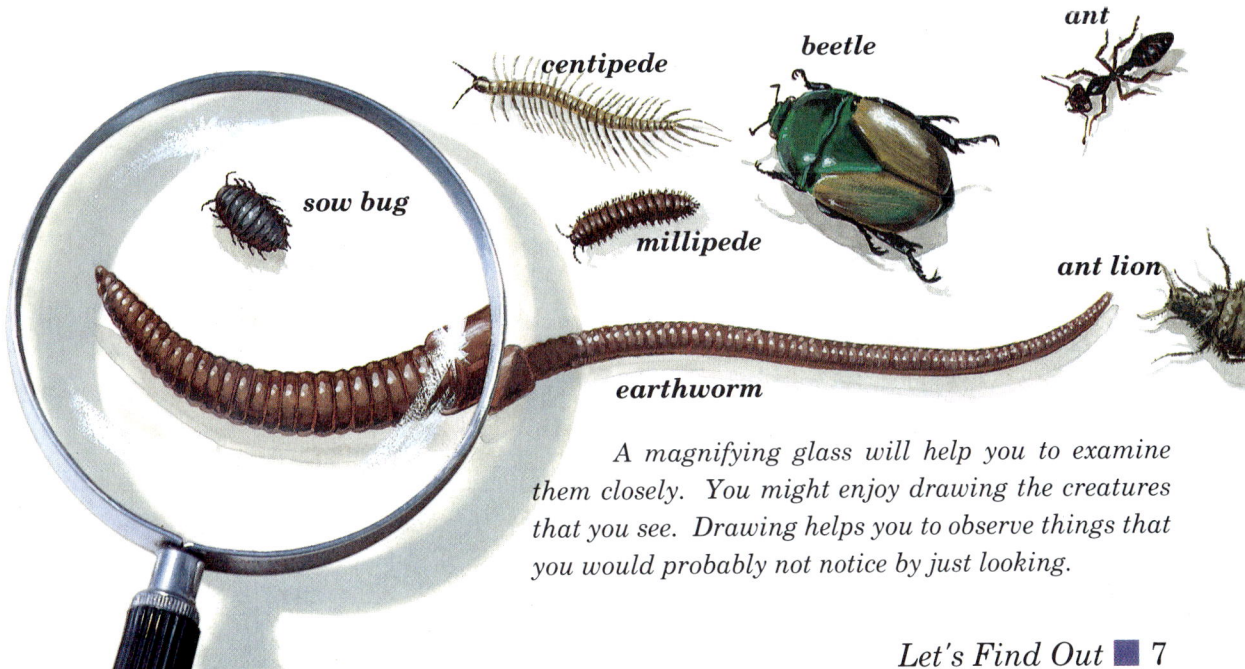

centipede **beetle** **ant**
sow bug
millipede
ant lion
earthworm

A magnifying glass will help you to examine them closely. You might enjoy drawing the creatures that you see. Drawing helps you to observe things that you would probably not notice by just looking.

Let's Find Out ■ 7

Comprehension Check 1.1 (Answer orally.)
1. Give four good reasons for studying science.
2. Name four ways that scientists (and other people) learn.
3. What is **observation?**

1.2 Learn To Observe

What is it?

Look for something interesting or unusual in your back yard, in your neighborhood, or in the schoolyard. It should be something that you would like to know more about — perhaps a feather, an old bird's nest, a rock, a shell, a flower (ask before you pick!), a beetle, a seed, a cone, or a leaf. Make a "What is it?" sign for the classroom and put your object under the sign. Then see who in the class can find the answer.

The answer might be somewhere in this book. Check the table of contents, the glossary, and the index, and then look through the book to familiarize yourself with it. You might want to make a list of things in the book that you especially want to learn.

Field guides are helpful for finding the answer to "What is it?" questions. Look in your school library for books with titles like these:

Birds of North America
Field Guide to Reptiles and Amphibians
Field Guide to Wildflowers
How to Know the Mammals
Field Guide to the Stars

Perhaps your teacher will check out some of these for use in your classroom. If you start a nature collection, perhaps a collection of feathers, leaves, rocks, shells, or seeds, you will find field guides to be very helpful.

As you make observations and ask questions, you will come to a greater understanding of the fascinating world of science.

What to look for

Leaves   Notice the colors and shapes of the leaves you see around you as they change color in the fall. Maple leaves usually turn brilliant red or orange. Leaves from poplars and cottonwoods become bright yellow. Oak leaves become deep red before they turn golden.

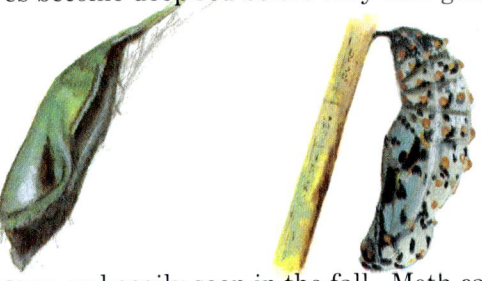

Caterpillars   Caterpillars are large and easily seen in the fall. Moth caterpillars are preparing to spin their cocoons, and butterfly caterpillars are ready to be encased in a chrysalis. Look for them on trees, on buildings, and on the ground.

Shells   If you live near the beach or a pond, you might enjoy collecting shells. After you use a field guide to identify the shell, you could read a book about the animal that used to make that shell its home.

Fruits   Hawthorns, chokecherries, apples, wild grapes, and wild cranberries are among the many fruits that ripen in the fall. Be sure not to eat any fruit until you know it can be eaten safely and has been washed thoroughly.

Let's Find Out   ■ 9

Rocks   If you walk through a stony field, a gravel pit, beside a pond, or along the seashore, you will enjoy examining the different kinds of rocks to be found.

Feathers   Fall is an especially good time to look for feathers, because many birds are replacing their old feathers with new ones. Large feathers come from large birds such as owls, eagles, and hawks. Smaller feathers come from the smaller songbirds. The colors, patterns, and shape of the feather indicate which bird it came from. An all-red feather probably came from a cardinal. A bright blue tail feather streaked with black was lost by a blue jay. A feather which seems black at first glance, but which sparkles with a rainbow of colors in the sunlight, probably came from a starling. Wash your hands after handling feathers.

Animal tracks   If you take a walk after a rainfall, be alert to animal tracks in the moist soil. Deer tracks are narrow and heart-shaped. Rabbits and squirrels run by putting their hind feet ahead of their forefeet. The prints of the red fox look like those of a dog, except the fox's tracks run in a straight line while the dog's tracks are side by side. Mice and rats make very tiny tracks; sometimes you can see the dragging marks made by their tails.

10 *Understanding God's World*

Seeds   A seed is a marvelous package containing a baby plant just waiting to reach the right place for it to grow. Some seeds are carried to their new homes by the wind. Look for milkweed and dandelion seeds being blown by the breeze. Other seeds will find you! Burdocks, cockleburs, beggar's ticks, and tick trefoil will hitch a ride on any person or animal that brushes by. Acorns, the seeds of the oak tree, are plentiful in the fall. If an acorn feels soft, there are probably young acorn weevils (a kind of insect) inside. If you find a small hole in the acorn, the weevils have left the acorn. You might also find some chewed-on acorns that tell you that squirrels are nearby.

SOMETHING TO DO   *Growing plants from seeds*

Seeds take time to grow. Plant some seeds in your classroom now, and they will be plants for you to observe by the time you are ready to study chapter 3. *You will need several containers to use as planters; potting soil; a large plastic bag for each planter; a tray to set the planters on; black construction paper; tape; and seeds. If your classroom does not get good sunlight, a plant light will help.* Some seeds that grow well are beans, cucumbers, pumpkins, acorn squash, dwarf marigolds, dwarf zinnias, Tiny Tim tomatoes, and morning glories. You could also plant wildflower seeds either indoors or outdoors.

Let's Find Out 11

Poke a few small holes in the bottom of each planter for drainage. Place a pebble over each hole to allow extra water to drain out while keeping the soil in. Plants need water, but if they get too much water they will rot. Fill the planters with potting soil. Sprinkle the seeds on the soil and mix them into the top layer of dirt with your hands. Sprinkle the soil with water, put each planter inside a plastic bag, and tie the end of each bag shut. Check the moisture of the soil occasionally. Do not let it become dry and crumbly or wet and soggy. When the seeds sprout, remove the bag. Water when necessary, and be sure the plants get sufficient light.

Lima bean

ZINNIA

SQUASH

MARIGOLD

Scarlet runner bean

MORNING GLORY

CUCUMBER

PUMPKIN

BUSH BEAN

Cucumber

Zinnia

Marigold

Morning glory

Observe the plants as they continue to grow. Plants grown from kidney beans and lima beans may become mature enough to produce seeds if the plants receive enough light. Scarlet runner beans grow beautiful, flowering vines. Lovely vines will also grow from pumpkin, acorn squash, and cucumber seeds. Cucumber vines often produce little cucumbers, and if you are patient you can get little tomatoes from your Tiny Tim tomato seeds. Marigolds and zinnias will flower if given enough light. Morning glory plants grown from seeds will produce new seeds in about three months.

12 ■ *Understanding God's World*

1.3 Observing North American Birds and Flowers

Every state in the United States has chosen a bird and a flower as two of its state emblems. Each province and territory of Canada also has an official flower, but only a few provinces have provincial birds. **On pages 14 and 15 are postage stamps showing the official bird and flower of each state.** To test your powers of observation, study the stamps and then try to answer the following questions. You may look at the stamps again as you work on the answers. Answer orally.

1. How many states have chosen the cardinal as their state bird?
2. Name and describe your state's official bird and flower.
3. What do the bird and the flower of Maryland have in common?
4. What makes the state bird of Louisiana unusual?
5. What makes the state bird of California unusual?
6. What is the difference between the mountain bluebird and the eastern bluebird?
7. What do the eastern bluebird and the robin have in common? How are they different?
8. What is unusual about the chickadee?
9. What is unusual about the state bird of Oklahoma?
10. What two states have chickens as their state bird?
11. What is unusual about the state flower of Mississippi?
12. How many states have a rose as their official flower?
13. Name the state flowers that are yellow or yellow-orange.
14. Which state flowers are blue or violet?

You could make up more questions to ask your classmates.

Let's Find Out

Birds and flowers

of the fifty states

15

Bird of the week

State bird project

There are fifty states in the United States but only twenty-five state birds. This is because some birds have been chosen to represent more than one state. Do you remember how many states chose the cardinal as their state bird? Other popular birds include the bluebird, the goldfinch, the meadowlark, the robin, and the mockingbird. **This year you should learn to recognize each of the twenty-five state birds and be able to tell several interesting facts about its appearance and behavior.** This will be easy if you learn one new bird each week.

Your first bird is the robin, which is probably the most familiar of all North American birds. Locate the robin card on the top right-hand corner of the next page. How many interesting traits of robins can you name? You will learn even more about this cheerful bird when you read chapter 4 Beside the picture of the robin is a little map of North America. This is called a **range map**, because it shows the **range** of the animal, or the part of the continent where it usually can be found. The range map shows the robin's summer range in red and its winter range in blue. Like many other birds, the robin **migrates** to the warmer southern regions in the fall and returns north in the spring.

There are twenty-five state-bird cards throughout this book that provide a picture of the bird, a range map, and interesting facts about the bird. They are all on the top right-hand corner of right-hand pages of your book.

Canadian birds

If you live in Canada, you will still want to learn most of the state birds, because all but a very few of them can be seen in Canada. Some state birds are more widespread in Canada than in the United States; the field maps will show you which ones. The three provincial birds are as follows:

    Prince Edward Island—**blue jay**
    Saskatchewan—**sharp-tailed grouse**
    Alberta—**owl**

You will find information about the blue jay in chapter 4. The sharp-tailed grouse, a favorite game bird, is similar to Pennsylvania's ruffed grouse, but its tail is short and pointed rather than fan-shaped. You probably already know many interesting facts about owls.

1 Robin

summer
winter
both

The cheerful robin can be found all across North America from Alaska and Canada to southern Mexico. It is one of the last birds to migrate south in the fall. Some robins stay in the north throughout the winter, but most of them spend the winter south of Canada. The return of the robin is considered a sign of the coming spring in many northern areas. The robin's sweet, clear song of "cheer-up, cheerily" is a welcome sound.

Robins seem to enjoy being around people. Because they also enjoy bathing, a birdbath in your back yard is almost sure to attract them.

The male robin is easily recognized by its gray back and bright reddish breast. The female is not as brightly colored, and the juveniles (young) have speckled breasts. The robin is a medium-sized bird, about ten inches long.

Go on a "bird hunt" through your book right now to see how many you can locate. Then see how much you can recall about the robin.

Canadian floral emblems project

Each province and territory of Canada has a beautiful floral emblem. Read about them on pages 18 and 19 and begin now to learn to identify them. Work on this project as you study chapters 1–3. You will want to learn these flowers whether you live in Canada or not, because they have been carefully chosen for their beauty or for some unusual feature, and half of them are also the official flower of one or more states. One of Canada's official flowers traps and eats insects. Do you know which one?

Let's Find Out 17

Canada's floral emblems

Newfoundland
pitcher plant

The hollow, pitcher-shaped leaves of this interesting plant have sweet juice at the "spout" that attracts insects. Hairs on the spout keep the insect from escaping, and it slides down into the pitcher, which is filled with rainwater. Once trapped inside the leaf, the insects become food for the plant. Plants that feed on animals are called *carnivorous plants*.

Northwest Territories
mountain avens

The mountain avens is a sturdy plant with short, woody stems and small, white flowers. It is designed to grow high in the mountains, where it forms a mat of shrubbery over rocky places.

Quebec
white garden lily

The white lily is a lovely garden flower with large, sweet-smelling blossoms. Most lilies have trumpet-shaped blossoms, long, narrow leaves, and petals in groups of three or six.

Saskatchewan
prairie lily

Many people believe that the prairie lily, which grows in bogs and in the rich prairie soil, is the most beautiful wild lily. Its deep scarlet-orange flower cup opens upward, revealing a yellowish base flecked with deep purple spots.

Ontario
white trillium

The trillium, a kind of lily, is a common woodland flower which is sometimes called the wake-robin because it blooms very early in the spring. The three petals and three leaves remind many people of the Trinity.

Yukon Territory
fireweed

This tall plant with a spike of light purplish-red flowers got its name because it is one of the first flowers to grow in an area which has been burned over by a forest fire.

Understanding God's World

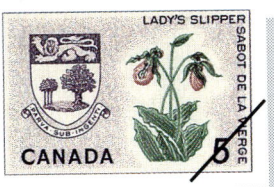

Prince Edward Island
lady's slipper

The lady's slipper is an orchid which is sometimes called the moccasin flower because each blossom is shaped like a tiny moccasin or slipper. Many insects, especially bees, are attracted to the flower because it produces a large amount of nectar.

Nova Scotia
trailing arbutus

The trailing arbutus, or mayflower, is a creeping plant with five-petaled pink or white blossoms which grow in clusters. It is protected by law in many places because it is scarce.

New Brunswick
purple violet

The purple violet grows in damp meadows and woods. Each of its dainty, pansylike flowers grows on its own slender stem, surrounded by heart-shaped leaves.

Manitoba
pasqueflower

The pasqueflower, or prairie crocus, has purple or blue cup-shaped flowers. The stalks, leaves, and seeds are covered with silky hairs. The flower's name means "Easter flower."

British Columbia
flowering dogwood

The flowers of the dogwood tree are very small and greenish-white, but they are surrounded by from four to six large pink or white bracts, or special leaves, which make the flowering dogwood a breathtaking sight in early spring.

Alberta
wild rose

The wild rose is a five-petaled white or pink flower which has been popular for hundreds of years. A wild rose bush, which may grow to be 9 feet tall and 9 feet wide, can produce a large number of flowers each spring.

Let's Find Out ■ 19

2 INSECTS: Miniature Marvels of Creation

2.1 Ten Million Designs

As you walk across a field, through the woods, or even in your own yard, you are surrounded by thousands of tiny creatures. Insects crawl through the grass and soil, dart about among the trees and flowers, and even find their way into your home. Some are so small that you can barely see them. Some buzz or hum, while others make no sound. You admire beautiful insects such as the butterfly and shy away from ugly ones like the silverfish or the roach. Beautiful or ugly, they are all creations of God, designed to do special tasks in His world.

About half of all the animals in the world are insects. Scientists have identified 800,000 different kinds of insects, but they think there are many others that have not been found yet.

Every year, from 7,000 to 10,000 new kinds of insects are discovered and named. This leads entomologists (scientists who study insects and similar creatures) to think that there may be more than **ten million kinds of insects,** each with its own unique features and purposes. Could you think of ten million different designs for insects? God did. What makes it even more wonderful is that each difference in design is for a special purpose.

Special characteristics of insects

For an animal to be classified as an insect, it must have three special characteristics:
1. an outside skeleton, or exoskeleton
2. three body parts
3. six jointed legs

Most insects also have several other common characteristics, such as antennae, compound eyes, and wings.

Exoskeleton

You may remember that there are two main groups of animals: vertebrates and invertebrates. *Vertebrates* are animals with backbones, such as dogs, birds, fish, frogs, and lizards. Vertebrates have skeletons of bone inside their bodies to support them.

Worms, spiders, jellyfish, starfish, and many other creatures are *invertebrates*, or animals without backbones. Insects are invertebrates. Insects belong to a group of invertebrates that have a skeleton—not an internal (inside) skeleton, like vertebrates, but an external (outside) skeleton. This hard coat of armor that protects the tiny body parts of insects is called an **exoskeleton** (*exo-* means "outside").

An insect's exoskeleton is lighter and stronger than bone. As you grow, your bones grow, but an insect's exoskeleton cannot grow with the insect.

Insects

When the insect outgrows its exoskeleton, it grows a new exoskeleton under the old one and then crawls out of the old skeleton. This process is called **molting**. Beetles, grasshoppers, and true bugs have thick, tough exoskeletons, but bees, flies, and butterflies have thinner, softer exoskeletons.

Three body parts

All insects have three body parts: head, thorax, and abdomen. The **head** contains the insect's brain, antennae, eyes, and mouth parts. The two antennae are the insect's "feelers." The **thorax** is the middle body part where the wings and legs are attached. The **abdomen**, the last body part, contains the insect's heart and stomach. The head, thorax, and abdomen are labeled on the *grasshopper* below. Can you identify the body parts of the *housefly?* On some insects it is not easy to see where the thorax ends and the abdomen begins. You would have to look inside the insect to tell.

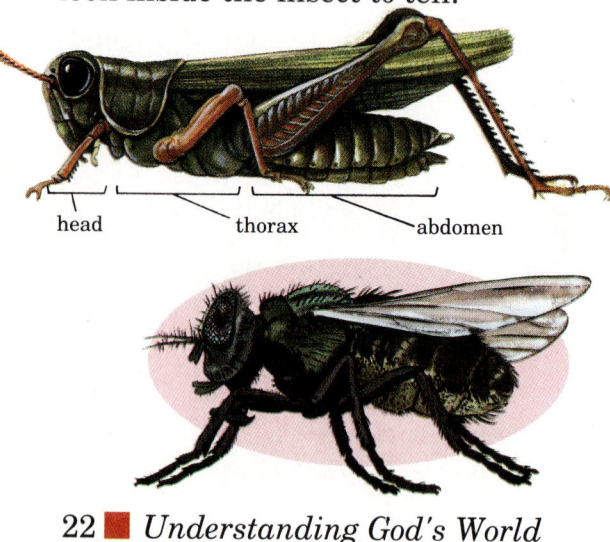

head   thorax   abdomen

Molting dragonfly

The bodies of insects vary to a wondrous degree. Some, like the *walking stick* (1), are long and narrow. Others, like the *ladybug* (2), are wide and thick. Some are soft like the body of the *gnat* (3), while others are hard like that of the *grasshopper* (4). The females of some, like the *cricket* (5), have a long, narrow, egg-laying part called the **ovipositor**. The ovipositor is not as noticeable on others. Some, such as *honeybees* (6), *hornets* (7), and *yellow jackets* (8), have stingers for protection. Insects' bodies vary in size from the one-hundredth of an inch *fairy fly* (9) to the four-inch-long *Goliath beetle* (10), which is **the largest insect.**

Breathing tubes

Insects do not have lungs as people do. Instead, God has designed them with breathing tubes which carry air containing oxygen to their body tissues. The air enters the tubes through tiny holes called **spiracles** that are found along the side of the body. Find the spiracles on the labeled grasshopper.

Understanding God's World

O Lord, How manifold are thy works!

ovipositor

In wisdom hast thou made them all.
Psalm 104:24

All of the insects above except the gnat and the fairy fly are shown their actual size. Use a ruler to figure out how long each is.

Insects ■ 23

Comprehension Check 2.1

1. Define these terms: *vertebrate, invertebrate, exoskeleton, molting, spiracles, ovipositor.*
2. Name the three special characteristics of insects.
3. List the three body parts of insects.
4. Learn the name of each insect pictured in this section and at least one fact about it.

Thought Question
How do you suppose the Goliath beetle got its name?

2.2 An Insect Zoo

Andy's zoo

Because Andy lived in an apartment where it was against the rules to keep pets such as cats or dogs, he decided to keep insects instead. His parents gave their permission, but Andy had to promise to keep his insects confined to jars and in his room. Andy spent many interesting hours setting up his zoo and observing the insects. He learned a lot, too.

Your zoo

To make an insect zoo, you will need this equipment:

- *jars or clear plastic containers (the bigger the better)*
- *lids with holes punched in them for the bigger insects*
- *fine screen, gauze, or cheesecloth for covers for tiny insects*
- *a small shovel for scooping dirt*
- *newspaper or an old sheet*
- *a net (not essential, but helpful for catching some insects)*
- *a magnifying glass, if available*

24 ■ Understanding God's World

An old sheet or a newspaper can be a handy tool for collecting insects. Spread out the sheet or the newspaper on the ground beside a bush or some tall plants. Gently bend the stems and leaves of the plant over the sheet. Shake the plant carefully. Insects and other small animals will land on the sheet. You will be able to see them clearly and choose the ones you would like for your zoo. Be sure to collect some leaves from the plant, also. Since insects are small and plentiful, you could have many different kinds in your zoo. In fact, there may be a thousand different kinds of insects just in your back yard! Some of them you will be able to identify by looking at the pictures in this book. You will need to use a field guide for others. Here are some insects that make good pets: crickets, grasshoppers, caterpillars, ladybugs and other beetles, ants, and praying mantises. If you would like to take an insect to school for the class insect zoo, put it into a plastic container for safety rather than in a glass jar.

Mockingbird

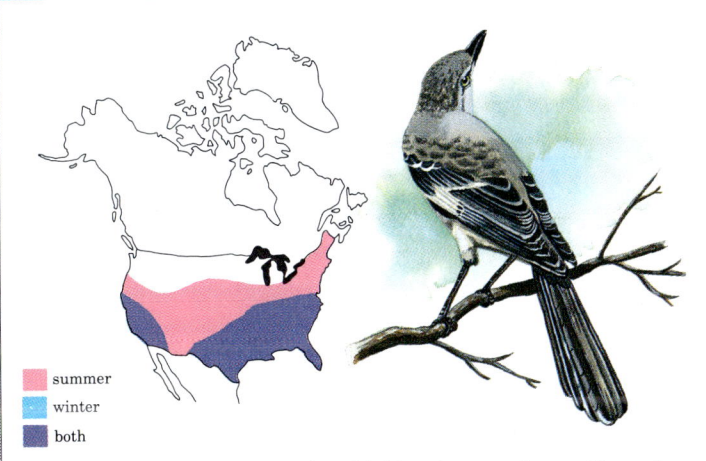

- summer
- winter
- both

The slender, gray mockingbird is a famous singer. Not only is its own song beautiful, but it is also an expert mimic of other birds. One mockingbird was heard imitating 36 other kinds of birds.

The musical mockingbird is also a helpful bird because it eats many harmful insects. It can often be seen strolling over grassy areas in search of a meal. Sometimes the mockingbird flashes its wings as it walks. Perhaps it does this to scare insects out into the open where they can be easily seen and devoured.

The mockingbird can be found throughout North and South America. It lives in areas where it can find open, grassy places to feed, thick shrubbery to hide its nest, and high perches from which to sing. The mockingbird is often found around farms, villages, and city parks.

Butterflies and moths you should know

Painted lady butterfly ⬇

The painted lady is probably the most widespread butterfly in the world. Every year, painted ladies migrate from California to Hawaii, from North Africa to Iceland, and from New Zealand to Australia or the Fiji Islands. Only our wise, caring God could give the delicate creatures their keen sense of direction. Because the caterpillar feeds on **thistle plants,** the painted lady is sometimes called the thistle butterfly.

Isabella moth and woolly bear ⬇

The Isabella moth is a small moth with a fat body and golden yellow wings. The caterpillar, which is called the **woolly bear,** is covered with a thick, hairy coat divided into three bands of color, black on each end and reddish-brown in the middle. The woolly bear eats a variety of grassy plants and is especially fond of plantain leaves. The woolly bear curls up into a tight ball if it is disturbed. It spends the winter curled up under a rock or a log.

Black swallowtail butterfly ➡

This beautiful butterfly is often seen fluttering close to the ground in fields and flower gardens. It has yellow spots around the edge of each wing and also spots of blue and orange on the hind wing. Can you see the "tails"? It lays its eggs on the leaves of **Queen Anne's lace,** parsley, celery, and carrots, which all are similar in appearance. The caterpillar is bright green with black bands and yellow or orange spots.

26 ■ Understanding God's World

NOTE: *The eggs are shown much larger than they actually are in proportion to the caterpillars and adults.*

← Monarch butterfly

The monarch is a large butterfly with a wingspan of 3 1/2 to 4 inches. Because the caterpillar feeds solely on **milkweed** leaves, the monarch has an unpleasant taste, and birds leave it alone. The monarch is famous for its yearly migrations.

Fall webworm moth ➡

The fall webworm moth is very small, with a 1- to 1 1/2-inch wingspan. Some of the moths are pure white; others are speckled with black. Colonies of webworm caterpillars live together in webs which they spin over the branches of trees. Apple, ash, and oak trees are their favorites, and they can do a great deal of damage to these trees. Webworm caterpillars leave the nest in the late fall, spend the winter in cocoons, and hatch in the spring.

⬆ Cabbage butterfly

The cabbage butterfly is small, with a wingspan of only 1 1/4 to 2 inches. It is mostly white, with black-tipped forewings and a few black spots. The caterpillar is small and solid green. Because it feeds on the leaves of **cabbages,** it is considered a garden pest. The cabbage butterfly is one of the first butterflies to appear each spring.

Insects 27

Butterflies and moths in the making

Two of the most interesting insects to observe are butterflies and moths in the making. It will not be hard for you to find a **caterpillar** in your back yard or garden. Scientists call a caterpillar a **larva**.

Place your caterpillar into a jar with some of the leaves upon which you found it. This is important, because most caterpillars will eat only one kind of plant. The plant on which you find your caterpillar can be a clue to which butterfly or moth it will become. Keep the jar covered with screening. Moisten the leaves each day with a few drops of water, and add new leaves of the same kind when needed. Put twigs in the jar, because caterpillars like to climb.

When the caterpillar has turned into a **pupa,** it will no longer eat. It still needs some moisture, however; so keep a piece of wet paper towel in the jar.

It will take from several weeks to several months for the **adult** insect to emerge. If you are patient, one day you will see either a beautiful butterfly or a moth in your jar. What a miracle!

You will want to keep the lovely creature in the jar, but please don't. When its wings are dry, it would like so very much to escape from the jar and fly away. Wouldn't you if you were a butterfly or a moth?

Butterfly or moth?

Here are some ways to tell whether your caterpillar has become a butterfly or a moth:

1. Butterflies fly about by day, but moths prefer to fly at night; that is, they are nocturnal.
2. Butterflies fold their wings together when they rest, but moths rest with their wings spread out.
3. The butterfly's antennae are thin with a knob at each end; a moth's antennae are feathery.
4. A butterfly's body is usually not as thick as a moth's.

"Will I be a butterfly or a moth?"

28 ■ *Understanding God's World*

Comprehension Check 2.2

1. What do scientists call a caterpillar?
2. What does a caterpillar become before it turns into an adult?
3. Is the insect in the picture above a butterfly or a moth? How can you tell? What are some other differences between butterflies and moths?
4. Learn to recognize the butterflies, moths, caterpillars, and food plants on pages 26 and 27.

2.3 Learning about Insect Life Cycles

Complete metamorphosis

Many insects go through a number of striking changes before they become adults. We call this change in form **metamorphosis**.

Nearly all insects lay eggs. If the insect goes through the *four stages* of **complete metamorphosis,** the **eggs** (1) hatch into **larvae** (2) [lär´ vē; singular is *larva*]. The larvae can be either **caterpillars, grubs,** or **maggots.** The larvae are always hungry and spend most of their time eating. As they grow, they have to molt, because the exoskeleton cannot grow or stretch as our skin does.

After molting a number of times, the larvae are ready for a rest. A moth larva spins a cozy little silk case, or **cocoon**, for itself. The butterfly larva grows a hard shell covering called a **chrysalis**. Now the insect is a **pupa** (3). Hidden in its case, the pupa goes through a miraculous transformation.

1

2

3

Insects 29

One day the case splits open, and out crawls an **adult** (4) insect which looks entirely different from the larva that went into the case. Miracle of miracles, the caterpillar has changed into a glorious butterfly or moth! After resting for a few minutes to allow its wings to dry, it flies lightly away. Butterflies and moths are not the only insects that go through complete metamorphosis; beetles, flies, mosquitoes, bees, and wasps do, also.

4 Monarch butterfly

Francesco Redi's famous experiment

Scientists have not always understood that caterpillars become butterflies or moths, grubs become beetles, wasps, or bees, and maggots become flies. In ancient times and during the Middle Ages, many people thought that living things could come from nonliving things. Even during the time of Christopher Columbus, people believed that rats came from old rags sprinkled with wheat, that mud could turn into frogs, and that spoiled meat turned into maggots.

Of course, we know today that maggots are the larvae of flies, but this was not understood until an Italian scientist named Francesco Redi performed some experiments to test the old idea, or hypothesis, of spontaneous generation, the false belief that living things can come from nonliving things. In science, a **hypothesis** is a reasonable or sensible explanation of something based on observations of that thing. To find whether a hypothesis is true, scientists seek a way to test it. An **experiment** is a planned way to test a hypothesis.

Four hundred years ago, about one hundred years after the time of Christopher Columbus, Francesco Redi performed his experiments to test whether the hypothesis of spontaneous generation were true. Redi gathered

30 ■ Understanding God's World

some jars and placed meat into each one. He left half of the jars open. The other jars he sealed tightly. According to the law of spontaneous generation, maggots should grow from the rotting meat in every jar.

After a time, Redi found that all the meat had spoiled but no maggots appeared in the sealed jars. Nor were these jars visited by flies. In the open jars, flies were crawling everywhere, and the meat was covered by maggots.

As Redi looked closely, he observed that the flies were laying eggs on the meat in the open jars. The eggs hatched into white maggots, and the maggots later became flies.

Redi thought about what had happened, and he reached these conclusions.

1. Flies lay eggs on spoiled meat.
2. The eggs hatch into maggots, or larvae.
3. The maggots eventually become flies. (They go through a pupal stage first.)
4. If the flies cannot get to the meat to lay eggs, there will be no maggots in the meat.
5. Maggots do not come from spoiled meat. They come from the eggs that flies lay.

Other scientists started doing experiments to test spontaneous generation. They all came to the same conclusions. After performing many careful experiments for many years, scientists believe the law of biogenesis. The **law of biogenesis** says that *life can only come from other life*. This law is in agreement with the Bible, which states that living things were created by the living God and that He told living things to reproduce other living things after their kind, or like themselves.

Comprehension Check 2.3

1. Name in order the four stages of complete metamorphosis.
2. Name five insects that go through complete metamorphosis.
3. Define these terms: *metamorphosis, larva, chrysalis, cocoon, pupa, hypothesis, experiment*.
4. State the law of biogenesis.

Insects 31

2.4 Designer Heads

God created each kind of insect with special head gear—antennae, mouth parts, and eyes—exactly designed to fit its needs.

Two antennae

Two **antennae,** or feelers, branch out from an insect's head. (The singular word is *antenna:* one antenna, two antennae.) Antennae are marvelously designed sense organs that allow an insect to taste, smell, touch, keep its balance, and find direction.

If you look at the antennae of several insects through a magnifying glass, you can see how they are all designed differently. The *painted lady butterfly* (1) has very long antennae with knobs at the end. It uses its antennae to smell flowers and perhaps to hear. The male *polyphemus moth* (2) has feathery antennae that enable it to smell a female polyphemus moth more than a mile away. The *housefly* (3) has two thick, short antennae between its eyes. It uses them to feel changes in the movement of the air or to smell rotting meat and garbage, its favorite foods. The female *mosquito's* (4) antennae are long and threadlike. One way she finds her dinner is by feeling the heat of a warm-blooded animal or person with her antennae. She also hears with her antennae.

Understanding God's World

Sensilla

Most antennae are covered with tiny sense organs called **sensilla.** (Sensilla is a plural word; one of these sense organs is a *sensillum*). Some sensilla look like tiny hairs. The sensilla give insects their senses of touch, balance, hearing, smell, taste, and temperature. The sensilla on the antennae help the insect with its senses of smell, taste, and touch. Although the antennae are considered to be the insect's main sense organs, they are not the only organs with sensilla. Some insects are covered with them. Some have taste sensilla on their legs. That is why a butterfly or a housefly can "taste" the food it walks over.

Eyes

Most insects have a pair of **compound eyes,** large eyes which are made up of many small eyes. These enable insects to see in almost all directions at once. Insects also usually have several **simple eyes** in between their large ones. With these they can see light and movement. Locate the two compound eyes and three simple eyes on the yellow jacket on page 54. Since insects have no eyelids, their eyes stay open at all times.

The eyes of insects vary according to their needs. An insect that spends most of its time on the ground feeding on vegetable matter has smaller eyes than does an insect that eats other insects. The *dragonfly* (5), one of the fastest insects, has especially large eyes, which enable it to catch insects while it and its prey are in flight. The dragonfly can see moving insects eighteen feet away. The *whirligig beetle* (6) has two pairs of compound eyes. The upper eyes are designed for seeing above water and the lower for seeing under the water. The whirligig can look up and down at the same time!

Insects 33

Mouth parts

God designed a wide variety of mouth parts for insects, depending on the kind of food they eat. *Grasshoppers* (7) and *crickets* (8) need a **chewing mouth** in order to chew plants. *Beetles* (9), whose name means "biters," use their chewing mouths to chew plants and other insects. *Termites* and *cockroaches* also have chewing mouth parts.

The long **sucking mouth** of the *butterfly* (10) and *moth* is especially designed as a "straw" for reaching the nectar in flowers. The insect coils up its straw when it is not drinking. *Caterpillars* (11), which spend most of their time eating, have chewing mouth parts.

Some insects have a **piercing-sucking mouth.** The *weevil's* (12) mouth is at the end of a long, slender snout. This enables the weevil to make deep, narrow holes in fruits, grains, and nuts. The *large milkweed bug* (13) uses its tubelike mouth to pierce milkweed pods. It injects a special saliva into the pod and sucks out the dissolved contents. *Flies* and *mosquitoes* (14) have tiny lances around their sucking tube. The male mosquito eats the juices of plants and flowers, but female mosquitoes would rather eat you!

The *bee* (15) has a **chewing-lapping mouth.** Its long, daggerlike tongue unrolls only as far as necessary to reach the nectar the bee desires.

34 ■ *Understanding God's World*

Comprehension Check 2.4
1. Define these terms: *sensilla, compound eyes*.
2. Name the four kinds of insect mouths and at least one insect for each.
3. Be able to identify each insect pictured in this section and to tell at least one fact about it.

2.5 Designed for Motion

An insect's thorax is its "engine room." The legs and wings are attached to this middle section of the insect's body.

Six jointed legs

Every adult insect has six legs attached to its thorax. The legs are jointed like your elbow or wrist so they can bend. Creatures that have more than six legs, such as the spider or the centipede, are not classified as insects. Are earthworms insects? How do you know?

Insect legs are marvels of design. When pursued by an enemy, the *mole cricket* (1) uses its strong forelegs as shovels for burrowing quickly into the ground and making its escape. The forelegs of the mole cricket also have a pair of "scissors" for cutting through small roots in the earth. The *water boatman* (2) uses its hind legs for oars and its two front legs as spoons for scooping up bits of plants for dinner as it rows about. *Bees* have special "baskets" on their legs for collecting pollen and carrying it back to their hive (3).

Insects 35

The *grasshopper's* very powerful legs enable it to jump as far as 30 inches. The strong legs of a *flea* (4) allow this creature to jump 100 times its own height. The *praying mantis* (5), which holds its forelegs in what looks like a position of prayer, is actually holding them ready to grab insects to eat. God has given each insect the kind of legs it needs for the job it has to do.

Wings

Besides three pairs of legs, most insects also have one or two pairs of wings attached to the thorax. Insect wings come in different shapes and sizes, but they are all made up of membrane supported by a network of ribs or veins. A membrane is a thin, soft layer of tissue. The vein pattern of insect wings differs from one species to another. You can see some of these patterns by looking at insect wings under a magnifying glass. The veins are used mainly for support. A set of muscles in the insect's thorax moves the thorax up and down, and the wings move with the thorax. Other muscles directly attached to the wings from the thorax control the direction of flight.

Scientists have named many of the groups of insects for their wing characteristics. *Flies* and *mosquitoes* have only one pair of wings (two wings), and their wings are usually clear and transparent. Most insects, including butterflies, moths, bees, dragonflies, most beetles, most true bugs, aphids, and crickets, have two pairs of wings (four wings). When an insect has four wings, the two wings on each side usually work together like one large wing. *Dragonflies* (6) have clear wings. The wings of *butterflies* and *moths* (7) are covered with very small scales. *Beetles* (8) have a pair of hard wings that cover and protect the regular

7 Polyphemus moth

36 ■ *Understanding God's World*

wings. A few insects, such as *silverfish* (9), *springtails*, *fleas,* and *lice*, have no wings at all. Some winged insects do not have wings during certain stages in their life cycle. Wings are important because adult insects often must travel long distances to get food or to find the right place to lay their eggs.

Migration

A few insects, such as butterflies and locusts, migrate, or move from one part of the world to another. *Ladybugs* go on short migrations. *Locusts* (migrating grasshoppers) travel in large groups and eat all the green things they can find along the way. During the 1800s, many farmers in the United States had their crops destroyed by large bands of young migrating locusts. One swarm of the insects was reported to be 70 miles long and 23 miles wide. You can see how such a large band of insects could easily strip the land of every green plant.

A plague of locusts

In Proverbs 30:27, the Bible says, "The locusts have no king, yet go forth all of them by bands." This verse means that locusts know how to work together, even though they have no leader to direct them. God is pleased with us when we work together to accomplish goals which bring honor to Him.

The Bible also tells us that God sometimes used locusts to punish people who were disobedient. He sent a plague of locusts upon the Egyptians when Pharaoh refused to let the Israelites go (Exodus 11:12–15). God later sent locusts to destroy the crops in the land of Judah because the people were worshiping false gods (Joel 1:4). God sent the locusts to get the attention of the people. He wanted them to leave their idols and return to Him.

The *monarch butterfly* migrates all the way from Canada to southern California, Florida, or Mexico to spend the winter and returns in the spring. She may travel over 1,800 miles each way. She has no map or compass, yet always finds her way. Her offspring do the same. God has given them an inner compass. *Painted lady butterflies* go on even longer migrations than the monarchs.

Insects 37

> **Comprehension Check 2.5**
>
> 1. Why is a spider not an insect?
> 2. To which section of its body are an insect's wings attached?
> 3. Why are wings important to insects?
> 4. Name two insects which migrate.
>
> **Thought Question**
>
> Although wings are very important to most insects, fleas and some kinds of grasshoppers do not have wings. Why do you think wings are not necessary for these particular insects?

2.6 Crickets and Grasshoppers

A cricket for your zoo

Crickets are excellent insects to observe. If you would like to go cricket hunting, first you need to put some moist sand in the bottom of a jar so the cricket you find will have a home. Add a rock, some twigs, and a few leaves to make it feel at home. Crickets are most active after dark; that is, they are **nocturnal.** Some evening in late summer or fall, sit outside with your flashlight ready. Listen. If you hear a cricket chirping, move slowly toward the sound. You don't want to frighten it away. (If you hear a cricket chirping, it will be a male; female crickets do not have wings designed to produce the special chirping sound that male crickets make.)

It may not be easy to find the cricket that you hear. Crickets are little ventriloquists: they can make it sound as if they are some place that they are not! Shine your flashlight around slowly. If you find the cricket, capture it quickly by cupping the palm of your hand over it. Be very gentle. You want to be careful not to do it any harm as you transfer it to the jar that you have prepared. It is not wise to try to keep two male or two female crickets in the same jar. They will probably fight until one has killed and eaten the other. You can identify the female by her long ovipositor (page 23).

Of course, your cricket will need food. Almost anything that *you* eat will do, such as bits of fruit, vegetables, or meat. Keep your cricket's home moist but not soggy. Putting a piece of wet cotton in the jar will keep the soil just about right.

Grasshopper or cricket?

You may want to capture a grasshopper for your zoo. Or you may not be sure if the insect you have is a grasshopper or a cricket. Here are some things to look for. When a grasshopper is not flying, its wings meet in a peak on the grasshopper's back like the roof of a house. A cricket's wings lie flat, one wing on top of the other. The cricket's antennae are very long and slender. Often they are longer than the cricket's body. Grasshoppers may have long or short antennae. If you find a cricketlike creature with long antennae, check its wings. Also notice when your insect is the most active. Crickets are busy after dark; grasshoppers are usually quiet at night and active during the day.

Grasshoppers

Crickets

Observing your cricket

After you have captured your cricket, you may want to take it to school so the whole class can enjoy observing it. Bring along some of its favorite food so you can watch it eat. What kind of mouth parts does a cricket have? Notice the way the mouth parts move. Our mouths work up and down, but the mouth parts of a cricket work from side to side.

Observe the way it breathes. You have lungs; the cricket takes in air through the spiracles on the sides of its abdomen. There may also be a few spiracles on the thorax. If you have a magnifying glass, use it to look for the spiracles. Notice how the segments (parts) of the abdomen move very regularly in an accordian fashion as the cricket breathes.

Crickets, like all other insects, are **coldblooded.** This means that a cricket's *body temperature changes as the outside temperature changes.* Notice the effect this has on your cricket. What happens when your classroom gets warm? Your cricket will be more lively and chirp more when the air around him is warm. You can even estimate the temperature of the air by counting the number of chirps. You will need a watch with a second hand. Count the number of times your cricket chirps in fourteen seconds. Then add forty to the number of chirps. The sum of those numbers will be very close to the temperature on the Fahrenheit scale.

Insects 39

SCIENCE CONCEPTS *Incomplete Metamorphosis*

You have learned that butterflies, moths, beetles, bees, wasps, and flies go through complete metamorphosis, or four stages of growth. Nearly nine out of ten insects undergo complete metamorphosis. Most of the others, including crickets, grasshoppers, cockroaches, mantises, dragonflies, cicadas, bugs, and termites, go through what is known as **incomplete metamorphosis**, or *three stages of growth.* They change from an **egg** (1) to a **nymph** (2) (a baby insect that looks almost like its parents), and from a nymph into an **adult** (3).

3 Large milkweed bug

The grasshopper is one of the insects that goes through three stages of growth. Grasshoppers lay their eggs right in the soil. When the egg hatches in the spring, out crawls the nymph, looking like a tiny grasshopper without wings. It can jump, and it can eat. How it can eat! It feeds on plants and grows bigger and bigger. As the nymph grows, its hard exoskeleton becomes too small, so it splits open and the grasshopper discards it. The grasshopper molts like this about five times, each time looking a little more like an adult, until finally it is fully grown with a handsome pair of wings.

A few insects do not go through either complete or incomplete metamorphosis. They change very little after they hatch except in size. Among these are silverfish and the springtails. A newly hatched silverfish looks like a miniature adult silverfish.

Comprehension Check 2.6

1. Give three ways of telling the difference between a cricket and a grasshopper.
2. How can you tell a male cricket from a female cricket?
3. Use the pictures to the right to describe the incomplete metamorphosis of the grasshopper.

Understanding God's World

2.7 How Insects Defend Themselves

Most insects are no match in size for the larger animals and birds that desire to eat them for dinner. God has given them other ways to protect themselves from predators, however. (A **predator** is an animal that captures and feeds upon other animals.)

Valiant fighters

The *Jerusalem cricket* (1) has strong spiked legs. When attacked, it turns over on its back and kicks its enemy. The *giant waterbug* (2) defends itself with its bearlike mouth parts. Some *beetles* bite when frightened. An *earwig* (3) has two pincers at the end of its abdomen for defense. *Bees* and *wasps* protect themselves by the stingers at the end of their abdomen. Other insects, such as the *grasshopper*, escape enemies by jumping great distances. Still others play dead. Many insects use their wings to fly away from danger.

Chemical warfare

Many insects that are not strong enough to protect themselves any other way resort to chemical warfare. When disturbed, they secrete a burning acid or spray an irritating gas or liquid on their enemies. Some of these chemicals are made in the insect's body; others come from the food the insect eats. A *termite soldier* (4) shoots a disagreeable liquid out of a horn on the front of its head to discourage enemies from invading the nest. The *bombardier beetle* (5) has a truly unusual defense. Inside its body, it has a special storage space for three chemicals. When an enemy approaches, the chemicals are combined to form a hot, bad-smelling acid which the bombardier beetle blasts from a hole in its abdomen. God has given the bombardier beetle the ability to aim its "cannon" in all directions with great accuracy. Bombardier beetles have been known to shoot out as many as twenty-nine "acid bombs" within four minutes. *Stinkbugs* (6), *lacewings* (7), and *carrion beetles* (8) also release a foul odor that keeps enemies at a distance. Insects do not like bad smells any more than we do.

The *monarch butterfly* and the *milkweed beetle* (9) do not need to hide from their enemies, because they taste just like the bitter milkweed on which they feed. Most milkweed eaters are bright orange. This color serves as a warning to all around them. Because birds and other creatures that eat milkweed eaters become violently ill, they soon learn to leave milkweed eaters alone.

Scare tactics

Some insects are so ugly they scare predators away. The *tiger swallowtail caterpillar's* (10) large eyes make the insect look like a monster from outer space. But don't be fooled. Those startling eyes are only patches of color. The real eyes are quite small and hidden beneath the ugly head. Most of us would not like to be ugly, but the swallowtail caterpillar doesn't mind. Its ugliness is its protection. Besides, after going through metamorphosis, it will be a beautiful butterfly.

Insect disguises

Camouflage. During wartime, soldiers who are fighting in jungles wear brown clothing with a pattern of green leaves which helps them to blend in with the trees, bushes, and grass and not be seen by the enemy. A disguise that causes people or animals to blend in with their surroundings is called **camouflage.**

As a *dead leaf butterfly* (11) sails through the air, a bird spots her bright wings. Swooping down, it is about to snatch her for dinner when she suddenly disappears. The bird is mystified. Where has his dinner gone? She is still there, sitting on a leaf, but the bird cannot see her. When she folds her wings and stays very still, she looks like a leaf instead of a butterfly because the undersides of her wings are the same color and shape as a dead leaf.

The coloring of many moths blends so well with the bark of trees that when they flatten themselves against a tree trunk, they cannot be seen. Notice how the green and brown *measuring worm moth* (12) of New Guinea blends in with the tree trunk. It becomes almost invisible when it rests on the green lichen that grows on the tree.

A kind of praying mantis that lives in Thailand (13) looks like part of the flower on which it lives. By hiding as a flower it escapes detection by both its enemies and the insects it preys on. Who but God could have thought of such a beautiful way to hide?

Mimicry. Do you remember why predators avoid the beautiful *monarch butterfly* (14)? God has given the *viceroy butterfly* (15) a way to take advantage of the monarch's bitter taste. The viceroy looks very much like the monarch butterfly but is a little smaller. You can tell them apart by looking at the hind wings.

The hind wings of both butterflies have black borders, but the viceroy's has an extra black line going across the middle. You can tell the difference, but birds cannot. The viceroy does not feed on milkweed and have a bitter taste, but because it resembles the monarch butterfly so closely, birds are afraid to eat it. When a harmless animal looks like a harmful one, this is called **mimicry.**

Comprehension Check 2.7
1. Name one insect which uses each method of protection.
   a. *bad taste* b. *camouflage* c. *bad odor* d. *jumping* e. *chemical defense*
2. Name two insects that defend themselves with parts of their body.
3. How does the viceroy butterfly escape its enemies?
4. What is the defense of the swallowtail caterpillar?
5. Define these words: *predator, camouflage, mimicry.*

Thought Question
The syrphid fly at the right looks very much like a yellow jacket. What kind of protective design is this? How does it help the fly?

2.8 How Insects Communicate

All insects have ways of communicating with other insects of their own kind. This is important for food finding, for defending the nest, and especially for finding a mate.

Sight

Female firefly from below (top) and above (right)

Scientists believe that *dragonflies* with their big eyes can recognize females by their color. The males of the American dragonfly are blue and green, while the females are yellow-green with brown stripes. Female *fireflies* see the flashing lights of the males that are looking for them and flash a reply. Each of the one hundred species of fireflies has its own secret code.

Understanding God's World

Smell

Because many insects are very small, they are not able to find their mates by sight. Their highly developed sense of smell comes to their rescue. When an insect wishes to attract a mate, it usually gives off a chemical from its glands that produces a certain odor. The insects pick up these odors by the sensilla on their antennae and on other parts of their bodies.

3 Meadowlark

summer
winter
both

The meadowlark, known for its beautiful whistling tunes, is a chunky bird about the size of a robin. Two kinds of meadowlarks live throughout Canada and the United States. Eastern and western meadowlarks look very much alike, but the western bird is the better singer.

The meadowlark is at home in fields, meadows, and prairies. It makes a nest of grass and weed stems in a thick clump of grass. The female usually weaves a clump of grass over the top to protect the nest. Often the nest is entered through a tunnel made at the side.

The cheerful meadowlark is beneficial to farmers because its main food is insects. It is especially fond of cutworms, the caterpillars of a certain kind of moth. It also eats grasshoppers, wild grass seeds, and waste grain.

Touch

Some insects produce a chemical but do not release it into the air. In such cases the insect that wishes to receive a message does so by touching the other insect with its antennae. *Ants* communicate in this way.

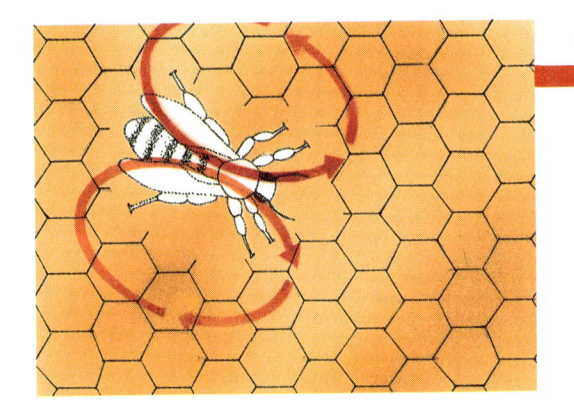

Dancing

When *honeybees* find a good source of food, they come back to the hive and share this information with the other bees by doing a dance. A round dance means the source of food is nearby. A waggle dance, done in a figure eight, means that the food is farther away.

Insects 45

Sound

Although many insects are silent, others relay messages by sounds. You have heard crickets and cicadas [sĭ-kā´dəz] singing, haven't you? The males are calling to the females, telling them they are ready to mate.

Most insects produce sound by rubbing one part of their body against another. *Cicadas* (1) produce sound by contracting their muscles against a drumlike organ at the base of their abdomen.

Crickets and *katydids* (2) vibrate their wing covers. Males of some *fruit flies* strike their wings against bristles on their abdomen to make sounds like a flute.

Some *male mosquitoes* have antennae so sensitive that they can sense the wing vibrations of a female mosquito.

The hearing organs of some insects, such as many kinds of *moths, grasshoppers,* and *cicadas,* are on their abdomen. Other insects, such as some kinds of *crickets, bees, ants,* and *termites,* have their "ears" on their legs.

The sensilla, the tiny hairs on their bodies, help many insects to pick up sound vibrations. You will remember that the sensilla also give insects their senses of taste, smell, touch, balance, and temperature.

File and scraper on katydid wings

Comprehension Check 2.8
1. Name five ways that insects communicate.
2. How do honeybees tell their fellow bees where to find a good food supply?

46 ■ Understanding God's World

2.9 Where Insects Live

Everybody needs a home, even a tiny insect. Insects make their homes in trees, bushes, soil, wood, water, or even in our homes as uninvited tenants.

The insect motorhome

The *caddis worm* (1) is the larva of an aquatic (water-dwelling) insect, the caddis fly. The caddis worm makes itself a very comfortable little home right in the water where it hatches. First it makes a sticky tube. Then it puts tiny sticks on the tube to build a cozy little log cabin. Other caddis worms use tiny stones or leaves for building their homes. Some caddis worms make their houses round, and others make theirs square, oblong, or in the shape of a snail shell. The handy thing about the caddis worm's house is that the insect can take it along wherever it wants to go. The caddis worm simply sticks its head and feet out the front door, and away it goes! We might say it has an "insect motorhome"!

Home is where the food is!

God has given insects instincts to know how to provide for their young. (An **instinct** is a God-given ability or behavior that is inherited rather than learned. Animals are born with many instincts that help them survive.) Insects usually lay their eggs on, in, or near a food supply so the young can immediately become hearty eaters. The *monarch butterfly* always lays her eggs on milkweed leaves, because that is the food her offspring needs. When the caterpillars hatch from the eggs, their food supply is right there so they can begin feeding at once. How is that for an instant breakfast?

Acorn weevils insert their eggs into acorns. The baby weevils feed on the acorns as soon as they hatch. Many kinds of beetles lay their eggs in the bark or wood of trees. The larvae have a safe place to grow and plenty of wood tissue to eat.

The *burying beetle* (2) (also called sexton beetle) looks for a dead mouse or bird to bury. Working very hard, the tiny insect, usually aided by another, digs a shallow grave for the dead animal. Then they move the animal, which is much larger than themselves, bit by bit to the gravesite, where it sinks into the ground and is covered with loose soil. The insects then dig a tunnel for themselves near the dead animal, and the female lays her eggs. When the eggs hatch into larvae, the beetle parents do not need to go grocery shopping. The larvae just feed on the dead animal in their back yard!

A **parasite** is an animal or plant that attaches itself to another animal or plant and feeds on it. The animal or plant on which the parasite feeds is called its **host**. Many insect parasites lay their eggs on other insects. When the young hatch, they feed on the insects upon which they were born. *Parasitic wasps* that lay their eggs on caterpillars are one example of insect parasites. Their young get free room and board, but what about the poor host? It will be greatly weakened and probably die. The *mud dauber wasp* (3) builds a little house of mud and saliva. She then paralyzes a number of spiders with her sting and drops them into her nest. Finally she lays her eggs and closes the lid of her mud house. When the eggs hatch, the young are surrounded by fresh food.

48 ■ *Understanding God's World*

Lice (4) are homebodies, traveling only one or two inches during their entire lifetime. They are attached to their home, which is an animal's feather or fur or in the hair of a human upon which they feed. Some eat their host's blood. They do not need to travel—all the food they need is right where they live!

Other places eggs are laid

The *praying mantis* finds a suitable branch and secretes foam from her body onto it. She lays her eggs in the foam, and then covers the eggs with more foam. The foam hardens into a snug little case (5), a safe, warm place for the eggs to stay until they are ready to hatch. We might wish she were as caring of her husband—she usually eats him!

Mosquitoes lay their eggs (6) on plants growing in or near the water. The larvae live in the water of ponds, stagnant pools, mud puddles, or even old water-filled cans. Sometimes mosquitoes can be controlled by filling in ponds and pools, thus destroying their nurseries. Often this is not practical, however, and the larvae must be killed by applying an insecticide to the breeding area. (An **insecticide** is a chemical used to kill insects.) Mosquito control is important, because mosquitoes are carriers of many diseases.

The *giant water bug* (7) lays her eggs in a most interesting place. She glues them on the back of her mate, forcing him to be responsible for the family whether he wants to or not!

Insects 49

Eggs
Larva
Pupa
Adult feeding on aphids

CONSIDER THE LADYBUG

Have you ever watched a ladybug crawling along the stem of a plant? The ladybug, or ladybird beetle, was probably hard at work. This insect is one of man's best friends because it preys on harmful insects, including aphids, greenflies, and scale insects. Scale insects are very tiny creatures that live on plants and suck the juices from them. Although scale insects are small, they can do a great deal of damage to fruit trees and other crops. Aphids multiply very rapidly and do tremendous harm to plants with their piercing-sucking mouth parts. A ladybug larva can eat 500 aphids each day. What a help to farmers and gardeners!

Because the ladybug has such a large appetite, gardeners and farmers often buy ladybugs to help control insect pests. How can they get the insects from one place to another? Many kinds of ladybugs migrate to mountain canyons to **hibernate** (go into a long, deep sleep) for the winter. Ladybug hunters know where to look for the insects, because for many generations they choose the same spot to hibernate. One prospector found about 750 million ladybugs in one place! The sleeping ladybugs are packed carefully in sacks of straw and refrigerated until spring. Then they are shipped out in boxes of pine cones; this gives the ladybugs a safe place to travel in. Farmers and gardeners buy the ladybugs by the ounce. Two ounces of ladybugs will take care of the pests on one acre of land. Surely the little ladybug is a wonderful provision of God for man's well-being!

Comprehension Check 2.9
Answer **true** or **false**.
1. The giant waterbug builds a house which it can carry about with him.
2. Many insects lay their eggs on or near a source of food.
3. Parasites are animals which attach themselves to and get their food from another animal.
4. Lice are parasites.
5. Mosquitoes can sometimes be controlled by filling in ponds and pools.
6. The ladybug is a pest because it destroys crops.

Thought Question
Why are lice wingless?

2.10 Dwellings of Social Insects

Many insects live alone, such as most beetles, flies, butterflies, moths, and parasitic wasps. Other insects, such as honeybees, ants, termites, and paper wasps, live in communities. They are called **social insects** because they live and work closely together. Their colonies are like small cities with thousands of inhabitants.

Leaf-cutting ant carrying a leaf to its underground fungus garden

Carpenter ants tending their larvae. Eggs are not seen in this picture; they are much smaller than the larvae.

Ant nests

Keeping ants. Ants would make interesting pets for your insect zoo. Because they are social insects, you will want to gather many of them from the same location and keep them together in the same container. You can find them under rotting logs or rocks. Dig up some soil and place it on a newspaper that is spread out. Look for adult ants, the small white ant eggs, and small larvae. Try to find the queen, which you can recognize by her large size. Spoon the ants into plastic bags, and later transfer them to a large jar with soil in it. Keep dark paper around the jar so the ants will build tunnels close to the glass. Remove the paper when you want to watch them.

Feed your ants bits of fruit, vegetables, bread crumbs, and meat. Watch how they use their strong jaws to cut, crush, and chew food. Remove spoiled food from the jar, and remember to keep the soil slightly moist.

You will enjoy watching your ants make tunnels. Use a magnifying glass to observe their three main body parts, six legs, and antennae. Notice their large compound eyes. Watch how they work together. You can find many fascinating facts about ants in an encyclopedia or a nature study book.

Insects

Ants around the world.
Ants can live anywhere on earth, but most ants prefer warm climates. Some ants live in trees, but most live underground. Some ants are "cowboys," herding and "milking" aphids for the sweet honeydew they give. Amazon ants kidnap baby ants from enemy ant nests and bring them up as slaves. Driver ants travel in large droves and are so fierce that even elephants run away from them.

Ants in Arizona removing parts of a cactus flower to get at the sweet nectar

Plant ants of New Guinea pulling leaves together to make a nest

Plant-dwelling ants of Asia taking a dead grasshopper to their nest

Red harvester ants carrying seeds through nest entrance to the storage chambers

Harvester ant nest entrance

Ants in the Bible. The Bible tells us we should learn from the hard-working ant. "Go to the ant, thou sluggard; consider her ways and be wise: which having no guide, overseer, or ruler, provideth her meat in the summer, and gathereth her food in the harvest" (Proverbs 6: 6–8). God wants us to be industrious, too. We should work hard at the tasks He sets before us each day. The Bible also says that ants are wise because they prepare for the future. Who gave the ants their wisdom?

Understanding God's World

Honeybees on a nest comb suspended in a tree

Close-up of the same bees

Beehives

Honeybees live together in a hive which consists of many small cells the bees make out of wax. The queen bee lays her eggs in some of these cells; honey and pollen are stored in the others. Bees take good care of their hive, keeping it in repair and stationing soldiers at its entrance to defend it from enemies. Because bees are so helpful to man, beekeepers usually provide wooden hives for their bees.

Side view of brood cells showing the pupae at different stages

Honeybee egg and two larvae in brood cells

Wooden hives built by a beekeeper in Switzerland

Insects

A yellow jacket nest cut open to show the brood cells. The larvae are reared in open cells, and then the cells are capped for the pupae.

Can you find the three simple eyes on this yellow jacket? Notice also the sensilla all over its body.

Paper nests

Social wasps, which we commonly call hornets, yellow jackets, or paper wasps, make paper nests. Some people think that the Chinese invented paper after observing the habits of these amazing insects. A social wasp queen gathers wood fiber from dead trees or posts, chews it well, and forms it into sheets for her nest. She then fills the nest with six-sided cells that she builds from the same material. In these cells she lays her eggs, which hatch into grubs (larvae). The grubs spin cocoons, and later the adult wasps come out. Do you remember what kind of metamorphosis this is? Now there are more workers to gather wood fiber and build more paper walls and cells so there will be room for the queen to lay more eggs and raise more offspring. Long before man learned how to air-condition houses and cars, wasps had "air-conditioned" nests. They just station two or three wasps at the entrance of the hive to beat their wings at high speed to circulate the air. Some tropical wasps put small pieces of mica, a transparent mineral, in their walls as "windows" to admit light.

Understanding God's World

Termite mounds and tunnels

It is amazing what God's tiny insects can do when they all work together in harmony. Consider the industry of the termite. Their homes may usually be found in dry wood above ground or in moist, rotting wood underground. Never venturing into daylight, termites build their houses from the inside. Whenever possible, they tunnel their way into wooden buildings or fences, eating as they go. Wood must be as delicious to termites as chocolate ice cream is to you! The termites cannot digest the wood alone; they must have tiny creatures inside their intestines that do this job for them.

Some species of African termites build waterproof mounds, or nests, of earth, debris, and saliva. They can be 25 to 30 feet high, and as solid as rock. Some large mounds have been used to make roads, tennis courts, and bricks (450,000 bricks have been made from one mound). The large queen stays in her own "bedroom" in this termite nest where she lays up to 36,000 eggs per day for up to 50 years! The central nursery in these mounds always has just the right amount of moisture and temperature whether in the cool of the night or the blazing African sun. One scientist wrote this about the termites: *"When we come to consider the order of these insects, and of their subterranean cities, they will appear foremost on the list of the wonders of the creation."*

Comprehension Check 2.10

1. Name three social insects.
2. What substance do bees use to make the cells of their hives? How do wasps make their nests?
3. Through what kind of metamorphosis do honeybees go? Point out each stage of metamorphosis in the pictures on page 53.

Insects

2.11 Jean Henri Fabre: Explorer of Backyard Wonders

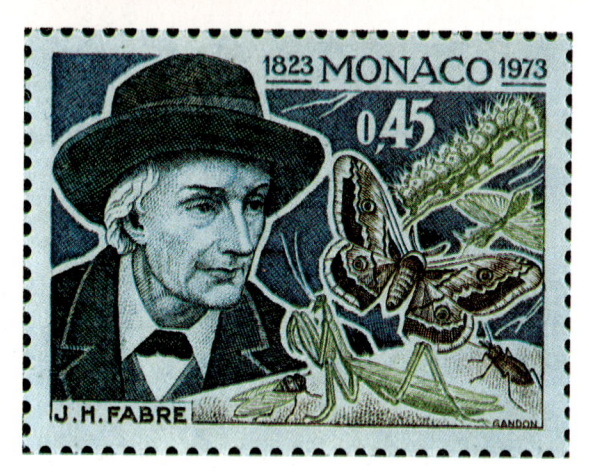

When Jean Henri Fabre was a boy growing up in France over 150 years ago, scientists knew very little about the lives and habits of insects. Many people had made collections of dead insects, but Fabre was the first to devote his life to observing and describing the behavior of living insects in their natural habitats. He wrote ten books for adults describing what he saw in the fields and gardens around his home and also delighted French school children with his famous science textbooks, which combined careful descriptions of nature with testimonies to Fabre's own faith in the God who designed and created the natural world.

Jean Henri Fabre was born in a small village in France to a poor French peasant family. Little Henri was a naturalist (a person who studies nature) from his earliest childhood, keenly observing the world of grasshoppers and sparrows, snails and lizards, and always on the lookout for beetles and waterweeds and bits of fossils. In the icy winter, he and his family had to live in the barn to keep warm by the heat of the animals and of the decaying dung and hay. In the hot summer, it was Henri's job to drive the ducks to the pond each day, giving him time to engage in nature study along the way. His one-room, one-window country schoolhouse was often filled with pigs and chickens that wandered in, but the boy learned to read and write and do arithmetic here and even began the study of Latin. Henri worked his way through high school and college and then taught for many years in the French schools. His students loved him, but he was fired from one teaching job because he allowed girls to attend his science classes!

Throughout his life, Henri Fabre spent every spare moment with the insects that he found so fascinating. He did important research on bees, wasps, beetles, grasshoppers, and crickets. He discovered the importance of instinct in insects and described very carefully how insects behave together. Not until he was almost eighty years old, however, did others recognize the

56 ■ *Understanding God's World*

importance of his scientific work. He is now known as ***the world's greatest entomologist***.

When Henri Fabre was about 35 years old, an English naturalist named Charles Darwin published a book about evolution. Darwin said that God did not create the living world as we know it and as the Bible says. Darwin believed that all living things developed somehow over vast ages of time. He said that invertebrates like insects and jellyfish slowly turned into vertebrates like fish, lizards, and horses. He said that there were no people at first, but then some tree-dwelling, monkeylike creatures with tails, hairy bodies, and pointed ears gradually developed into people.

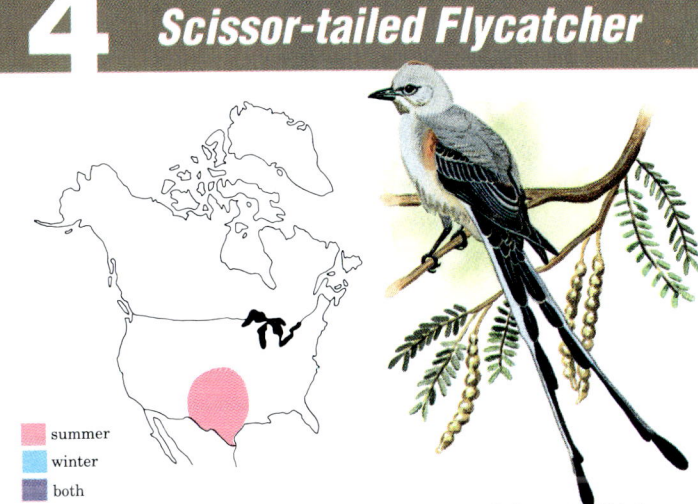

Of course, Henri Fabre knew that this was a false and silly idea; the Bible says that God created everything in the world and that He made the first man, Adam, from the dust of the ground, not from a creature like a monkey. When many other people started believing Charles Darwin, Jean Henri Fabre kept right on believing God instead. Fabre had observed the beautiful design of nature much too closely to believe that it could all be just an accident. He did not think that Darwin's hypothesis was a reasonable or sensible explanation of the wonders we see in the world around us. He declared: "I observe, I experiment, and I let the facts speak for themselves. The facts that I observe are of such a kind that they force me to dissent from [disagree with] Darwin's theories." Although many people of Fabre's day turned away from God, thinking that evolution was true, Jean Henri Fabre, the great scientist, knew better. He testified: *"Without [God] I understand nothing; without Him all is darkness.... You could take my skin from me more easily than my faith in God."*

4. Scissor-tailed Flycatcher

summer
winter
both

The scissor-tailed flycatcher is an extremely beautiful bird of the open country. You may see one perching on its favorite spot—a tree, a bush, a fencepost, or perhaps a wire. Its exceptionally long tail—which may be folded together—its chattering song, or its aggressive behavior will easily attract your attention. The scissor-tailed flycatcher is about 14 inches long; over half of this length is tail.

Flocks of up to 200 scissor-tailed flycatchers have been observed feasting on swarms of insects. This beneficial bird aids the farmer by devouring many insect pests. In the spring scissor-tailed flycatchers put on a spectacular courtship display in which they "sky-dance" very gracefully.

The scissor-tailed flycatcher is found in the south central United States as far north as Missouri and Nebraska. It spends its winters in Mexico, Central America, and the Florida Keys.

Insects 57

Chapter Check-up

A *Make sure you know the name of each insect pictured in this chapter and at least one fact about it.*

B *Match each term with the phrase that identifies it.*

_____ 1. molt
_____ 2. thorax
_____ 3. exoskeleton
_____ 4. spiracles
_____ 5. larva
_____ 6. sensilla
_____ 7. ovipositor
_____ 8. metamorphosis
_____ 9. hibernate
_____ 10. nymph
_____ 11. antennae
_____ 12. abdomen
_____ 13. parasite
_____ 14. pupa
_____ 15. cocoon
_____ 16. predator

A. a silk case
B. an insect in the stage between larval and adult
C. feelers
D. an insect's egg-laying organ
E. holes in an insect's body for breathing
F. an animal that captures and eats other animals
G. the part of the insect's body where wings and legs are attached
H. the hard outer covering of insects
I. to shed the outer covering
J. a sudden change in form
K. to spend the winter sleeping
L. a termite's home
M. tiny hairs for hearing and sensing
N. a caterpillar, maggot, or grub
O. a young insect which looks almost like the adult
P. a plant or animal that lives off another
Q. the part of the insect's body containing the heart and stomach

C *Label the four stages of growth for the hera moth, and number the stages in order.*

58 ■ *Understanding God's World*

D *Name **one** insect that does the following:*

1. Buries dead animals _____

2. Keeps "cows" for the nectar they give _____

3. Has two pairs of compound eyes _____

4. Lays her eggs on her husband's back _____

5. Communicates food sources by doing a dance _____

6. Tastes bitter _____

7. Carries its house around _____

8. Destroys crops _____

E *Name **two** insects that do the following:*

1. Migrate long distances _____

2. Protect themselves by their stings _____

3. Protect themselves by letting off a foul odor _____

4. Chew wood _____

5. Pretend to be harmful _____

F *Name **three** insects that do the following:*

1. Go through complete metamorphosis _____

2. Go through incomplete metamorphosis _____

3. Feed on other insects _____

4. Live in the water _____

5. Live in colonies _____

G Write the letter of the correct answer.

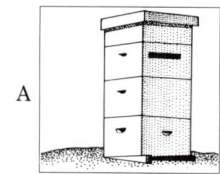

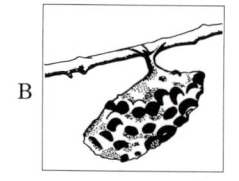

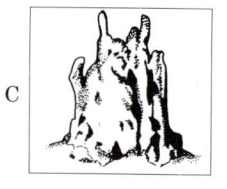

_____ 1. Which of these homes belongs to the termite?

A   B   C   D

_____ 2. Which of these insects lays her eggs in foam from her body?

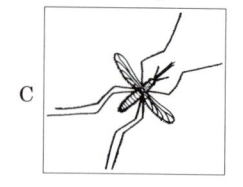

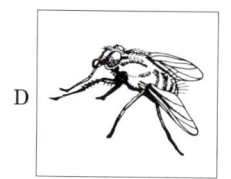

A   B   C   D

_____ 3. Which of these insects damages crops?

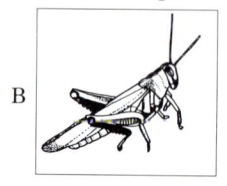

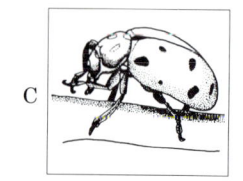

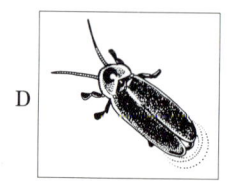

A   B   C   D

_____ 4. Which of these insects has hard front wings?

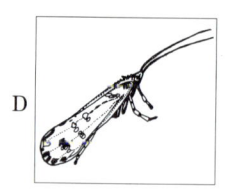

A   B   C   D

_____ 5. Which of these insects does not change after hatching from eggs except in size?

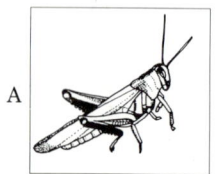

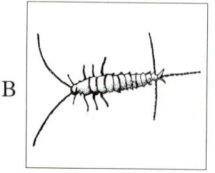

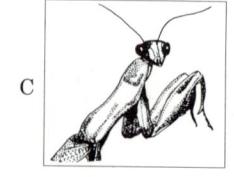

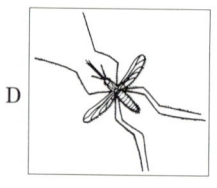

A   B   C   D

_____ 6. Which of these insects is known for its song?

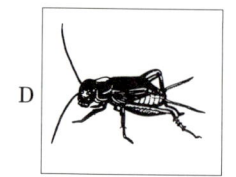

A   B   C   D

60 ■ *Understanding God's World*

H *Match each insect with the phrase that identifies it.*

_____ 1. Termite
_____ 2. Firefly
_____ 3. Driver ant
_____ 4. Bombardier beetle
_____ 5. Flea
_____ 6. Cicada
_____ 7. Ant
_____ 8. Amazon ant
_____ 9. Ladybug
_____ 10. Field cricket
_____ 11. Caddis worm

A. hears with its knees
B. jumps 100 times its height
C. has a drumlike organ on its abdomen which produces sound
D. gets honeydew from aphids
E. kidnaps and enslaves baby ants
F. builds a small house around itself
G. buries dead insects
H. eats wood
I. flashes a secret code
J. benefits fruit growers
K. scares even elephants
L. shoots "acid bombs" from a hole in its abdomen

I *Draw a line from the name of the insect part to its location on the yellow jacket.*

1. Compound eye
2. Simple eye
3. Mouth parts
4. Antennae

5. Abdomen
6. Wing
7. Leg
8. Thorax

Insects 61

3 PLANTS: Provision for Man and Beast

3.1 Designed to Produce

Almost anywhere you go on earth, you will find plants. Some are able to grow in hot deserts; others live in the icy arctic regions of the earth. Some even live inside the bodies of animals. There are more than 350,000 different kinds of plants. There are also far more individual plants than individual animals and people. (Think of a grass plant and you will understand why this is true.) The biggest living things on earth are plants, the *giant sequoia trees* of California. Some of the smallest living things are also plants. One very tiny kind of plant, the *diatom*, is so small that about 500 diatoms can live in one drop of water.

All plants were created by God for man to use. In fact, if there were no green plants on earth, we could not survive. Plants produce food and provide oxygen, shelter, fuel, medicine, and many other things that we need or enjoy.

Plants produce food

Photosynthesis. Living things on earth depend on green plants for food. This is because green plants are able to make food, something that no animal or human can do. Green plants contain **chlorophyll,** a green coloring matter that makes it possible for them to manufacture their own food. Green plants use the energy of sunlight to change water and carbon dioxide into sugars. This process is called **photosynthesis.** People, animals, and plants without chlorophyll depend on green plants as the source for all their food. Two thirds of the food we eat comes directly from plants; the remaining one third comes from animals, which also depend on plants.

The plants we eat. Think of all the ways we use plants for food. We eat the **seeds** of *wheat, rice,* and *corn* plants. We also grind those seeds to make bread. We use some seeds, like those of the *sunflower* and the *soybean*, to obtain *oil* used in cooking. Have you eaten any **roots** lately? If you had *beets, carrots,* or *sweet*

Plants 63

potatoes for supper last night, you have! Think of all the **leaves** we eat, such as *lettuce, spinach, cabbage, beet greens,* and *watercress*. We munch the crunchy **stems** of *celery* and cook *rhubarb* stems to use in delicious desserts. Your french fries came from the underground stem of a *potato* plant. We even eat some **flowers,** such as *broccoli* and *cauliflower*. Probably some of your favorite plant products are the **fruits** of some plants, such as crisp *apples*, mellow *bananas,* and juicy *berries*.

Plants improve the air

Take a deep breath and fill up your lungs with the air that your body must have in order to live. With every breath, you are removing oxygen from the air. Think of all the people who have lived since God created Adam and Eve, the first man and woman. They and all the animals have taken oxygen from the air or water with each breath, also. How is it that there is any oxygen left for us to breathe? God planned a wonderful way to resupply the air with oxygen. When a green plant makes its food by photosynthesis, it takes **carbon dioxide** from the air and puts **oxygen** back into the air for you to breathe. When you breathe, you return carbon dioxide to the air for the plants to use.

Trees, the largest plants, help to control the amount of moisture in the air and in the soil. When there is not enough rain, the trees take moisture from deep within the earth and release that moisture into the air.

Plants improve the soil

Fallen leaves decay and provide a layer of rich, moist soil. The leaves that remain on the trees shade the earth and keep the soil from receiving too much heat from the sun's rays. The leaves also help to keep the earth from becoming too cold at night. By providing a layer of insulation, the leaves help the soil to retain some of the heat it absorbed during the day.

Comprehension Check 3.1
1. All living things depend on ? for food.
2. The green coloring matter in green plants that enables them to make food is called ? .
3. We use certain parts of different plants for food. Name a particular food for each of the following plant parts.
   a. seed   b. stem   c. leaf   d. root   e. flower   f. fruit
4. How does oxygen get back into the air?

Understanding God's World

3.2 Needleleaf Trees

The tallest plants on earth are trees. Trees are also the oldest living things on earth. There are bristlecone pines in California that may be 4,000 years old!

What makes a plant a tree? Scientists usually agree that all trees have the following characteristics. A tree is a plant with one woody stem that is at least fifteen feet tall when mature. The stem, or trunk, is able to stand upright on its own and is at least three to four inches thick.

Bristlecone pine

Parts of a tree

As you observe trees around you, notice that each has three main parts. The **crown** of the tree is its leaves and branches. The leaves are very important because they make food for the entire plant. At certain times of the year, you will also find flowers or fruit in the crowns of most trees. The stem of the tree is its **trunk,** which is made of woody fiber. A protective layer called the *bark* covers the outside of the trunk. You usually cannot see the third main part of the tree, the **roots,** but the roots perform very important tasks. They anchor the tree in the ground. They also absorb water and minerals that the tree needs in order to produce its food. How large do you think a tree's root system is? Look at the crown of a tree. Every tree's root system is at least as large as the spread of the crown.

Many trees grow a new layer of wood each year. If the tree is cut down, you can see the layers of wood, which are called **annual rings.** By counting the annual rings, you can tell how old a tree is. The width of each annual ring also tells something about the conditions under which the tree grew each year. If during one year the tree did not get enough water or sunlight, the annual ring for that year will be thin. In a year when there was plenty of water and sunlight, the annual ring will be thicker.

Plants 65

Identifying trees

Although trees are alike in these important ways, there are also many interesting differences. Learn to identify several of the most common trees in your area by observing them carefully and looking them up in field guides. Make a collection of tree leaves and see who in your class can find the largest variety of leaves. Most of the trees that grow in North America can be divided into two main groups, needleleaf trees and broadleaf trees. Palms belong to a third group of trees.

Needleleaf trees

Trees that have very narrow leaves that are needlelike or scalelike are called **needleleaf trees.** Pines, firs, spruces, hemlocks, larches, redwoods, cedars, and junipers are all needleleaf trees. Most needleleaf trees that live in regions that have changing seasons are **evergreen.** This means that the trees do not lose all their leaves each year. Old needles turn brown and fall off a few at a time, but they are constantly being replaced with new needles. Most needleleaf trees are also **conifers.** Conifers are trees that produce seeds in **cones** instead of flowers. You might enjoy seeing how many different kinds of cones you can find and identify.

By examining its needles and cones you will be able to tell which family a needleleaf tree belongs to. **Pines** (1) have long, thin needles that grow in bundles of two to five. The number of needles in a bundle will tell you what kind of pine it is. **Hemlocks** (2) have very short, flat needles growing on little stalks on each branch. Each needle is dark green on the top side and lighter green underneath. **Fir trees** (3) have single needles that grow directly on the twig, not on a stalk. Notice how the cones grow on a fir tree. They grow only on the top side of the branch, pointing upward. The short, four-sided needles of **spruce trees** (4) grow in spirals on stalks. Spruce cones grow on the bottom side of the branch, pointing down.

Comprehension Check 3.2

1. List and describe the three main parts of a tree.
2. What is an annual ring?
3. What are three main groups of trees?
4. What are conifers?
5. List four kinds of needleleaf trees and explain how to tell them apart.
6. What kind of tree is pictured at the right?

Plants 67

3.3 Broadleaf Trees and Palms

Broadleaf trees

A second main group of trees is known as the **broadleaf** trees. Oaks, maples, ashes, elms, walnuts, and willows are just some of the broadleaf trees. They are also called **deciduous** trees because, in regions that have changing seasons, most of them lose their leaves in the fall. Deciduous means *falling down*. Most broadleaf trees have flowers and form seeds. Some, like the magnolia, dogwood, cherry, and apple, have very attractive flowers which can help you identify the tree. Most tree flowers, however, are very tiny and dull colored.

Oak trees. Oak trees are most easily distinguished from other trees by their fruits, which are called **acorns.** Acorns are hard-shelled fruits topped with scaly caps. Most oaks have leaves which are deeply divided along the edges, but the shape of oak leaves varies greatly, even among leaves growing on the same tree. Some kind of oak trees are evergreen, keeping their leaves through the winter. When new leaves develop in the spring, the old leaves are pushed off the tree. Oak leaves do not grow opposite each other on the branch; rather, they grow in an alternate pattern, with a leaf on one side of the branch, a space, and then a leaf on the other side of the branch.

Elm trees. Elm trees can also be easily recognized by their fruits, which are small, flat seeds encased in paperlike wings. Oval-shaped elm leaves are toothed, or notched, along the edges.

Understanding God's World

Maple trees. Many varieties of the popular and useful maple tree grow in North America. The shape of the maple leaf is unique; it is a broad leaf which resembles a hand. The leaves grow in pairs that are always opposite each other on the branch. The maple leaf is one of the national emblems of Canada and appears on the Canadian flag. The fruit of the maple is also easy to recognize. Maple trees produce winged fruits called **keys** which grow in pairs, each bearing a seed.

Palms

One kind of tree that is neither a broadleaf nor a needleleaf is the palm. And not all palms are trees; some are shrubs or vines. Palms are similar in many ways to lilies, banana plants, and grasses. Palms do not grow in the same way that other trees do. They do not have annual rings or bark. A bud in the center of the crown controls the palm's growth. If the bud is removed, the palm dies. Most palms are evergreens with fan-shaped or featherlike leaves. The *raphia palm* has the biggest leaf in the world—65 feet long! Palms produce fruits that may be as small as peas or as large as coconuts.

Date palms

Coconut plantation

The *coconut palm* is probably the most useful kind of palm. There are 1,000 uses for its products. People eat the sweet meat of the coconut. Dried coconut meat is also processed into an oil which is used in cooking and to make such products as soap and margarine. The *date palm* is also important for the delicious fruit it produces. Two native American palms are the *sabal palm* and the *Washington palm*.

Plants 69

State trees

Many states have chosen a particular kind of tree as one of their state emblems. Find out about your state tree. Your teacher can help you find books that will tell you many interesting facts. Try to find out what birds, insects, and other animals benefit from, help, or harm the tree. Look for specimens of your state tree growing in your community, and try to draw one. An excellent way to observe your state tree is to make a special collection of its leaves, twigs, seeds, and flowers or cones. A photograph or drawing of the tree will make your collection complete.

Comprehension Check 3.3
1. List six kinds of broadleaf trees.
2. What does *deciduous* mean?
3. Name each of these trees. Tell how you identified each.
4. What controls the growth of a palm tree?
5. List four kinds of palms.

3.4 Observing Flowers

No matter what time of the year it is, there are flowers blooming somewhere in our country. Do you know the names of the flowers that are blooming where you live? Do you know which flowers are most common in your area? Take a good look at a flower that is growing in a field or garden. How tall is the plant on which the flower grows? Is it growing in rich, moist soil or sandy, dry soil? What color, shape, and size are the flowers? After you have observed the flower carefully, find a wildflower or garden flower book and look for the flower in the book. Check your library, or ask your parents or teacher to help you. You will learn many interesting things about the flower. You might learn how it got its name, where it grows, what insects and other animals feed on or near it, and whether it is a native American plant or not. Look especially for the common fall flowers pictured on pages 74–76.

Understanding God's World

Flower parts

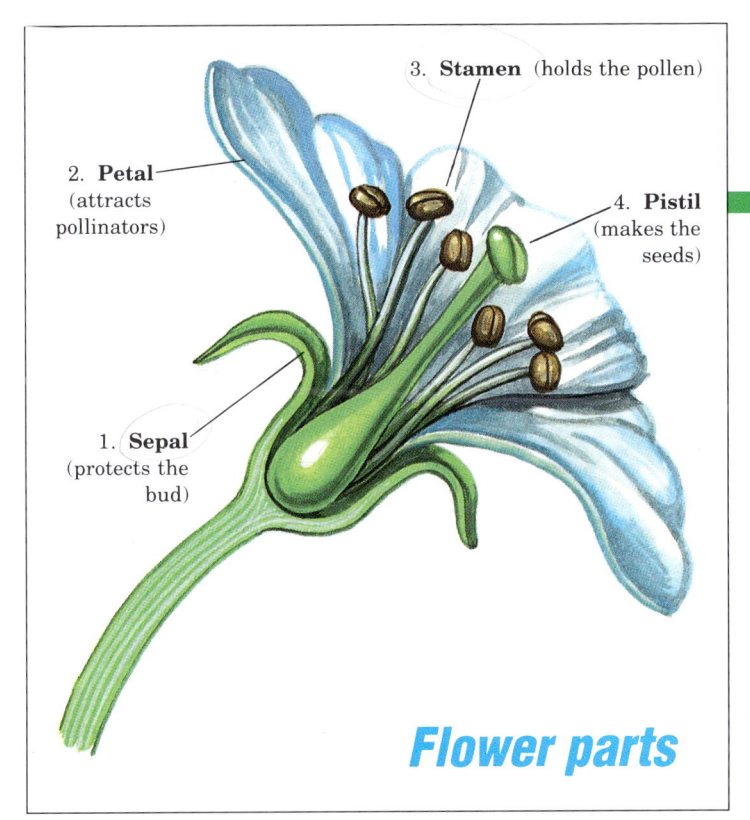

2. **Petal** (attracts pollinators)

3. **Stamen** (holds the pollen)

4. **Pistil** (makes the seeds)

1. **Sepal** (protects the bud)

The parts of a flower

God has created a wide variety of beautiful flowering plants, and yet most of them are variations of the same basic design. This is because all flowers have one purpose for the plant—to produce seeds. The stem that holds up the head of the flower and supplies it with water and food may be short or tall, thick or thin. On the underside of the flower's head are special leaflike structures called **sepals** (1). The sepals enclosed and protected the flower when it was a bud. Above the sepals are the **petals** (2), which help attract birds and insects to the flower. The center of the flower head is made up of **stamens** (3) and **pistils** (4). The stamens make pollen, the fine, yellowish dust you often see on flowers. The pistil contains many undeveloped seeds in the enlarged part down at its base. You can remember the flower parts by starting at the outside and thinking s___, p___, s___, p___. Some flowers have only three of these parts. Some plants, such as the maple tree, have two kinds of flowers. The staminate flowers have only stamens, and the pistillate flowers have only pistils.

Maple: staminate flowers (above) and pistillate flowers (right)

Plants ■ 71

Pollinators

When honeybees, bumblebees, wasps, flies, and other insects visit flowers in search of nectar, pollen brushes from the tips of the stamens onto their bodies. As the insect travels from flower to flower, it moves pollen from the stamens to the pistils. Scientists call this process **pollination.**

Fruit growers are so dependent upon honeybees to pollinate their apple, cherry, plum, and pear trees that they rent hives of honeybees during the time their trees are in blossom. Field crops such as peas, onions, carrots, cabbage, and alfalfa also depend on insects to pollinate them. Gnats, beetles, and ants do their share in pollinating plants. God designed insects to do this important work for man. Some birds and bats are also designed to be pollinators.

After the flower is pollinated, tiny sperm cells in the pollen **fertilize,** or unite with, the undeveloped seeds at the base of the pistil. Now the seeds will be able to grow into new plants, each after its own kind.

Orange-breasted sunbird, South Africa

SOMETHING TO DO — *State and provincial flowers*

How many of Canada's floral emblems do you know now? Try to find your state or provincial flower growing in your area. (See pages 13–19.) Observe it and write down a description. Notice the size of the plant, the leaves, the flowers, when the plant blooms, and where it grows. Then read as much as you can about your flower in an encyclopedia and in books about flowers. Try to find out why your state chose it and if any other state has the same state flower. Write a brief report about what you observe and what you read and make a colored sketch of the flower.

You might also enjoy finding out about the official flowers of your neighboring states or provinces. Those flowers probably grow in your area, also.

Understanding God's World

Weeds

Have you ever wondered why some flowering plants are called weeds? A weed is any plant that grows where it is not wanted. Some weeds arrived in North America accidentally in shipments of other seeds. Other weeds were brought here on purpose. For example, the early colonists brought burdock with them because they ate the root. Burdock root is not a popular food today, but the burdock plant continues to thrive. Most weeds are very tough and easy to grow. The root systems of weeds help prevent soil erosion and break up hard-packed soil. Deep roots also bring minerals that are deep in the earth up near to the surface where other plants can use them. Some weeds are useful as medicines, dyes, or foods. Many weeds produce great quantities of seed. This is very important to the birds that depend on weed seeds for food.

Many flowers in one

Did you know that when you pick a daisy, you are really picking more than one flower? The part of the daisy that we usually call the flower is made up of hundreds of tiny flowers. The white parts that we often call "petals" are not true petals at all. Each one is an individual flower! Since these flowers radiate from the center, they are called *ray flowers*. The yellow disk (center) of the daisy contains many tiny tube-shaped flowers. Because these flowers form a disk, they are called *disk flowers*. Asters, sunflowers, and coneflowers are a few of the other flowers which have both ray flowers and disk flowers. Many of our favorite flowers are in the daisy family, which is also called the sunflower family or composite family. All of the flowers on pages 74–76 with an asterisk (*) before their names are members of the daisy family. How many others can you find?

Daisy

Cut view

Disk flower

Ray flower

Plants 73

Wildflowers you should know

*Daisy (1)

*Aster (2)
Asters are daisy-like flowers with yellow centers and white, blue, or purple ray flowers. There are over one hundred kinds of asters in North America. Most asters bloom in the fall, and some continue to bloom even after a frost. Whereas daisies have a stalk for each bloom, asters have several blooms on a stalk.

*Black-eyed Susan (3)
Black-eyed Susans are sometimes called yellow daisies. They have yellow ray flowers and dark brown or purplish disk flowers on a rounded or cone-shaped center. The plant's leaves are hairy, and its stems are tough and difficult to pick.

Butter-and-eggs *(Toadflax)* (4)
When you see the butter-and-eggs plant, you will know how it got its name, for the flowers are the color of yellow butter and orange egg yolks. The flowers are shaped like those of the snapdragon and are full of nectar, which attracts bumblebees. If you hold a flower up to the light, you will be able to see the liquid nectar at its base.

*Ironweed (5)
The branching stems of this moisture-loving plant support many heads made up of dark purple flowers. It can be a troublesome weed in pastures, because it spreads quickly and is not edible by livestock.

Cardinal flower *(Scarlet lobelia)* (6)
The cardinal flower is a native American plant that grows up to four feet tall. It has narrow, dark green leaves and brilliant red blossoms which attract hummingbirds. The cardinal flower is a kind of lobelia, but most lobelias are blue and attract bumblebees.

74 Understanding God's World

An asterisk (*) indicates a member of the daisy family.

*Goldenrod (7)
Over one hundred kinds of goldenrod grow in North America. Most are tall plants with tough stems and hundreds of tiny, yellow flower heads growing in clusters along the flower stem. The blossoms produce large amounts of pollen and nectar, which attract a wide variety of insects. If you ever want to find some insects, just look for a goldenrod plant.

Jewelweed (*Touch-me-not*) (8)
Jewelweed is a tall plant with many branches which grows in moist places. Only hummingbirds and bumblebees have tongues long enough to reach the nectar deep within the yellow or orange flowers. The jewelweed's ripe seed capsules burst open at the slightest touch, giving the plant its other name, "touch-me-not."

Queen Anne's lace (9)
The flower head of Queen Anne's lace is made up of many small clusters of tiny white flowers, with one dark red or purple flower in the center. The stem is covered with fine hairs, and the leaves look and smell like those of the carrot plant. In late summer, the flower heads curl up, giving the plant its other name, "bird's nest."

Chicory (10)
The pretty blue flowers of chicory are often seen among Queen Anne's lace blooms. The flowers are bright in the morning but begin to wilt by noon. The roots are sometimes ground to make a coffeelike beverage.

*Tansy (11)
The orange-yellow flowers of the tansy plant look like daisies that have had their white ray flowers removed. Tansy is sometimes called "bitter buttons" because the plant has a strong characteristic odor.

*Dandelion (12)
The bright yellow dandelion is just the opposite of the tansy—it has ray flowers but no disk flowers. The flower heads open and close every day. If you pick a closed flower head late in the afternoon and put it in water under a light, you can watch it start to open.

Plants 75

Garden flowers you should know

An asterisk (*) indicates a member of the daisy family.

*Chrysanthemum
The chrysanthemum is one of the most popular garden flowers in the world. Chrysanthemums grow in a variety of shapes and can be white, yellow, pink, or red. The chrysanthemum is a bushy plant; its stems and leaves give off a strong odor when they are touched.

*Cosmos
The cosmos is a tall plant with thin stems and delicate leaves. Its daisylike blossoms are white, orange, pink, or red.

*Dahlia
The dahlia, which originally came from Mexico, is now grown throughout North America and Europe. The flowers are of various colors and may be shaped like daisies or like pompons.

*Sunflower
The wild sunflower is a tall plant with flowers that turn to face the sun. The flower heads have yellow ray flowers and dark brown or purplish disk flowers growing on a flat center. Garden sunflowers grow much taller and produce hundreds of seeds. The head of a garden sunflower may be over a foot wide, and the plant may be fifteen feet tall.

*Marigold
The marigold is a hardy plant that is easily grown. Its flowers are usually yellow or orange. The flowers have a strong odor that some people find unpleasant, but many people enjoy the marigold because it produces a large number of blossoms over a long period of time.

Petunia
The petunia produces large, soft, funnel-shaped flowers in a variety of colors. Some petunias have two-colored flowers. Others have flowers with ruffled petals.

Phlox
The phlox is a tall plant with upright stems and fragrant, brightly colored flowers. The flowers are tube-shaped with five wide lobes each, and they grow in clusters at the tops of the stems.

Salvia
Salvia is a popular garden plant because it is easy to grow and its flowers are long lasting. Clusters of red, purple, blue, yellow, or white flowers grow at the top of each floral stem.

Understanding God's World

Comprehension Check 3.4

1. Name the parts of this tulip flower. What parts are missing? What is the purpose of each part?
2. Why would a farmer call the daisies growing in his hayfield "weeds"?
3. Name two important jobs that weeds do.
4. Learn the names of the wildflowers and garden flowers on pages 74–76 and at least one fact about each.

3.5 Seed Design

Flowers have four main purposes:

1. *to glorify their Creator*
2. *to bring enjoyment to man*
3. *to provide pollen and nectar for insects and other animals*
4. *to produce seeds that provide food for man and animals and a way for the plant to reproduce after its kind*

Seed production is the important purpose of flowers for the plant. The seeds produced by the apple blossom are protected within the delicious fruit. Other seeds are protected by smaller, drier fruits, by cones, or in other ways. The primary purpose of the fruit to the plant is to get the seeds where they need to go.

Seeds come in all sizes and shapes. One kind of coconut tree produces a fifty-pound seed, the largest seed in the world. The tiniest seeds are those of the African witchweed plant. Each of its seeds is only 1/1,000 of an inch long. The size of the seed is not determined by the size of the plant. Redwood trees are the tallest living things, and yet a redwood seed is only 1/16 of an inch long.

Whether a seed is too heavy for you to lift, or so small that you can hardly see it, there is one thing that all seeds have in common.

Every seed contains a new, living plant.

Plants 77

Parts of a seed

Every seed has three main parts:
1. the embryo, or new plant
2. the stored food
3. the seed coat, or covering

The **embryo** is the new plant. An apple seed contains a new apple tree; a corn plant is inside a seed of corn. You will never get corn from apple seeds, nor apples from corn seeds. You can plant apple seeds and corn seeds side by side in the same garden, where they will share the same soil, sunlight, and water, and the apple seed will always grow into an apple tree that produces apple seeds. It will never grow corn, squash, tomatoes, or any other fruit. God determined this at the time of Creation, when He said, "Let the earth bring forth grass, and herb yielding seed, and the fruit tree yielding fruit *after his kind,* whose seed is in itself" (Gen. 1:11).

All seeds also contain **stored food** to nourish the young plant until it is able to make its own food. The third part of the seed is the **seed coat.** The seed coat is a covering that protects the embryo from injury until it is time for the seed to sprout.

SOMETHING TO DO — Observing the parts of a seed

You can observe the three parts of a seed in lima bean seeds which have been soaked overnight in water. The seed coat absorbs enough water to make it easy to remove. Remove the seed coat by carefully splitting it along the outside edge of the seed.

Inside the seed coat is the stored food for the young plant. In lima beans, the food is stored in a special tissue called the **cotyledon** [kŏt′ĭ-lē′dun]. Lima beans have two cotyledons. The two cotyledons will usually separate after the seed coat is removed. If they do not, carefully separate them by splitting the seed along the outside edge.

You will see that the third part of the seed, the embryo, has begun to sprout. Find the parts of the embryo that will someday be the roots and the leaves.

How careful an observer are you? Try sketching the cotyledons and the embryo of your lima bean seed.

78 ■ *Understanding God's World*

Comprehension Check 3.5
1. What are the three main parts of a seed?
2. Why will you never get cherries from radish seeds?
3. Why is the stored food inside the seed important?

3.6 Traveling Seeds

Goldfinch

summer
winter
both

The goldfinch's musical song and bright coloring have earned it the nickname "the wild canary." You may see this friendly fellow swinging from a thistle, chattering away; even when eating or resting he continues to twitter. The goldfinch is a small bird, about five inches long. In the spring, the male is bright lemon yellow with a black cap. The female is a duller olive yellow with no cap. In the winter, the male's plumage turns dull yellow also.

Goldfinches live in southern Canada and most of the United States. They usually do not migrate but remain in the same area year round. You will see goldfinches in orchards and gardens, along roadsides, and in weed-filled fields. Weed seeds are their favorite food, but they will also eat wild fruits, aphids, and caterpillars.

The goldfinch got its name from its color and from the fact that it is a finch, or seed-eating bird.

Fruits are designed in many different ways to help the seed travel to a place where it can sprout and grow. If seeds could not travel away from the parent plant, they would not be able to grow into strong, healthy plants, because the older, taller plant would take the larger share of the sunlight, water, and minerals available in that spot. God designed several ways for fruits to help the seeds move away from the parent plant.

Airborne seeds

Many kinds of seeds are moved by the wind. Seeds that are designed to be spread by the wind are usually lightweight. *Orchids* produce seeds that are as fine as dust. Because orchid seeds are so light, the wind can easily carry them. The beautiful *poppy* (1) flower produces a capsule fruit. After the petals fall off, the capsule splits open in dry weather. The many tiny poppy seeds are released when the capsule shakes in the wind.

Plants 79

Wind

Other airborne seeds are attached to downy tufts or plumes. These fine hairs help the seeds to float on the breeze. *Cattails, dandelions* (2), *milkweed* (3), and *thistles* are a few of the plants that are equipped with downy hairs. Have you ever seen a dandelion that has gone to seed? Each tiny seed has its own little parachute.

Some seeds which are designed to travel through the air have wings. Many *grasses* have small, winged seeds. Each seed in a *pine cone* (4) has one delicate wing that is caught by a gentle breeze. Because *maple seeds* (5) and *elm seeds* are heavier than most other wind-borne seeds, God designed the special wings of these seeds and placed them on very tall plants. There the seeds are better able to catch the wind and travel to a new location. Most winged seeds travel several hundred feet, but one maple seed holds an amazing record. It traveled six miles!

In the central and western parts of the United States, there are several different kinds of plants which are called *tumbleweeds* (6). When their seeds are ripe, tumbleweeds become so dry that they break off from their roots. As the wind carries the plants across the prairie, tumbleweeds scatter their seeds wherever they go.

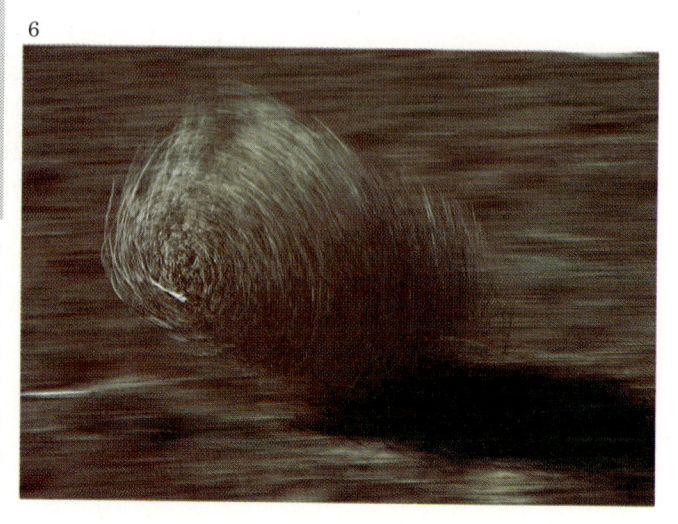

Understanding God's World

Water

Water is another distributor of seeds. Rain washes seeds out of open seed pods and carries them to new locations. Some water-borne seeds are covered with a waxy coating that keeps them from being soaked.

Plants that grow in or near a body of water often depend on it to scatter their seeds. *Pussy willow* seeds are spread when the wind blows them into the water. They float on the surface and wash up on shore. Often they soak up just the right amount of water so that they are able to sprout and grow where they land. *Coconuts* fall into the ocean and float to islands or other shores, where they grow into coconut palm trees. Seeds of the *red mangrove tree* (7) sprout roots while they are still on the tree. When the seeds drop into the salt water where the trees grow, the heavy roots keep them upright in the water. When the rootlet reaches a muddy spot, it anchors there, and the tree grows.

Animals and people

Animals are responsible for moving many seeds. Some seeds are collected by squirrels (8) or blue jays. The animal stores the seeds for food, but sometimes loses or forgets them. When fruits with large seeds are eaten by animals, the seed is dropped to the ground after the animal eats the juicy fruit. When fruits with small seeds, such as blackberries, are eaten, the animal often eats the seeds right along with the fruit. The seeds then pass unharmed through the animal's digestive tract and grow where they are dropped.

Some seeds are designed with little hooks or barbs. These structures help the seeds to latch on to an animal's fur (9), a bird's feathers, or even your sweater or socks (10). *Cockleburs, burdocks,* and *beggar's ticks* are a few of the hitchhiking seeds. Other seeds, such as *flax,* are covered with a sticky substance that helps them to hitch a ride on a passing animal.

People often move seeds deliberately when they travel from one place to another and carry plants or seeds with them.

Plants 81

Other special methods

Some plants are designed to scatter their own seeds. When the fruit of the jewelweed ripens, it explodes, shooting its seeds in all directions. Wisteria and other members of the pea family produce seeds in pods. When the pods dry out, they split, and the seeds are scattered. When the squirting cucumber is ripe, it drops from its stalk, leaving a hole in the end of the fruit. The seeds are shot out of this hole. Some seeds are shot as much as fifteen feet away from the plant.

3.7 Germination

Most seeds ripen and are carried away from the parent plant in the fall. In areas that have cold winters, seeds remain **dormant** throughout the winter. This means that the seeds are alive but not growing. Why do you think God designed seeds to be dormant for a time? What would happen if the seed sprouted and began to grow into a new plant at the end of autumn?

When spring comes and conditions are right, the seed is ready to **germinate,** or sprout. The seed, which looked no more alive than a pebble, begins to change. There are three things that all seeds need in order to germinate.

> **Comprehension Check 3.6**
> 1. Why are seeds designed to travel away from the parent plant?
> 2. List three things which carry seeds away from the parent plant.
> 3. What is unique about the way in which each of the following plants scatters its seeds?
>   a. *tumbleweed*
>   b. *jewelweed*
>   c. *dandelion*
>   d. *flax*

Seeds need water

Seeds absorb water when they are ready to germinate. Some seeds need to be soaked in water; others need only a small amount of water. Water causes changes to take place inside the seed. Water also softens the seed coat so that the tissues inside the seed can swell and break through the seed coat.

The job of the seed coat is now finished, and it dies. But the embryo that was inside the seed coat is very much alive. It is now ready to grow into a new plant that can bring forth fruit. Jesus said, *"Except a corn of wheat fall into the ground and die, it abideth alone: but if it die, it bringeth forth much fruit"* (John 12:24). The death of the seed coat is a lovely picture of the death of Jesus, who gave Himself for us. Just as the grain of wheat brings forth new life, so Jesus' death and resurrection bring new life to those of us who trust Him as Savior.

Seeds need oxygen

You will remember that seeds contain a supply of stored food. Growing seeds, like growing children, need good food to give them plenty of energy for growth. But germinating seeds also need oxygen in order to use the stored food.

Seeds need the right temperature

The third condition for germination is the right temperature. Different kinds of plants need different amounts of heat in order to germinate. Some seeds must also be exposed to just the right amount of light in order to germinate.

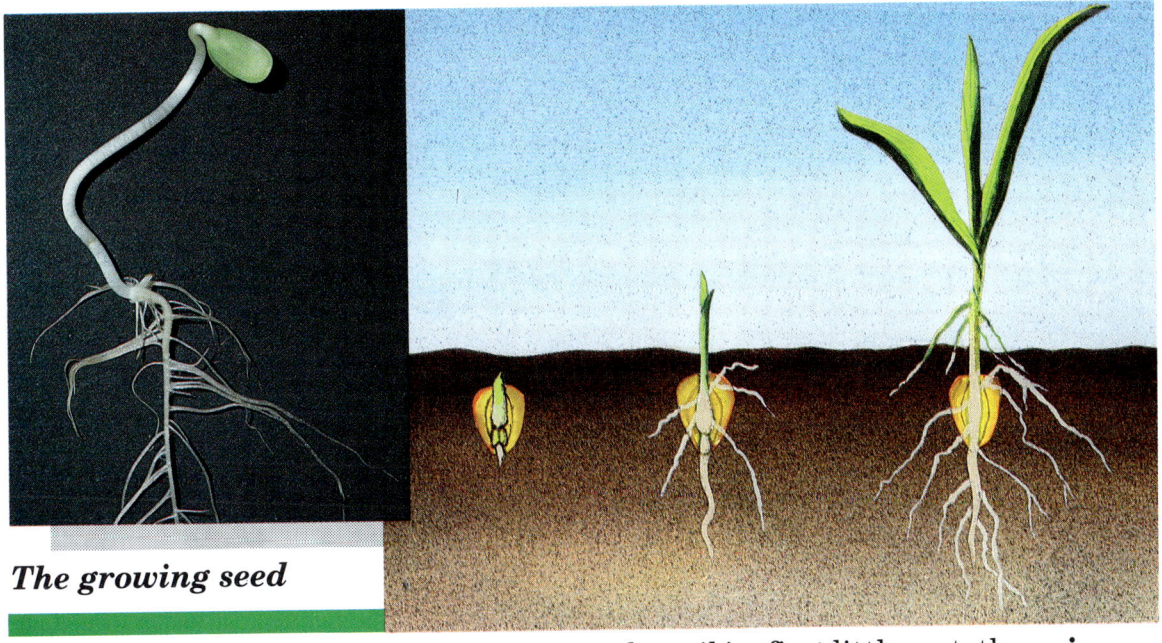

The growing seed

As the seed germinates, it sends into the soil its first little root, the **primary root,** Soon more roots push their way into the soil and a network of roots begins to form. God has designed seeds in such a way that every seed that sprouts sends its roots down into the soil, never up into the air. After the roots grow downward, the stem and the leaves of the plant begin to grow upward. They break through the soil as they continue to grow. The seed is perfectly designed to send its leaves up toward the sun, never down into the soil. When the stored food is gone, the roots and the leaves are ready to do the jobs for which they were created. The roots begin drawing water and minerals from the soil, and the leaves begin making food.

Seeds are a part of God's plan to produce plants needed for man and animals. We depend upon plants for our food, and they also provide medicine, clothing, shelter, and other good things. We have God's promise that "While the earth remaineth, seedtime and harvest . . . shall not cease" (Genesis 8:22).

Plants

SOMETHING TO DO   *Observing germination*

You can observe seeds germinating by making a seed viewer. You will need several different kinds of seeds. Lima bean, corn, squash, pumpkin, apple, orange, and cucumber seeds work well. You will also need two pieces of cardboard (about one foot square each), clear plastic wrap, tape, and a stapler.

Tear off a piece of plastic wrap about the size of one of your pieces of cardboard. Dampen four layers of paper towels and place them on the plastic. Arrange the seeds neatly on the towels, about two to three inches apart. Put another layer of plastic wrap on top of the seeds and towels.

Staple the plastic to the cardboard, keeping the towels and seeds between the layers of plastic. Be sure to pull the plastic wrap firmly before stapling so that the seeds will stay in place. Make a hinge by taping the two pieces of cardboard together at the top.

Stand your seed viewer in a warm place and observe the seeds as they sprout. After they have sprouted, turn the viewer on its side. What happens in a few days?

Comprehension Check 3.7
1. Define *dormant, germinate.*
2. What things must a seed have in order to germinate?
3. What part of the seed dies when the seed germinates? Why?
4. What is the first root which the plant sends out called?

3.8 Poisonous Plants

Scientists have estimated that there are well over 350,000 kinds of plants in our world, but no one knows for sure. Of all these plants, about 700 of the North American ones are known to be poisonous. These poisonous plants are not just rare and exotic plants you would find in some deep, dark jungle or in a scientist's laboratory. Many of them grow in your own back yard or even in your house! It is very important that you learn to recognize them. Many produce food that we eat; we just do not eat the poisonous parts.

Ornamental plants that are poisonous

House plants. Take a look inside your house first to see if you have any ornamental plants (plants used as decorations) that are poisonous. Many people have a house plant called **dumbcane,** or **dieffenbachia** (1). It has big, green leaves with yellow in the center. It is a very beautiful plant, but do not let your baby brother or sister eat any of it! It would cause an intense burning in their mouth and swelling of the tongue. If enough of it is eaten, it could mean death.

Another favorite houseplant is the **philodendron** (2). It is a long, green vine with heart-shaped leaves that are green or green and yellow. Again, it is a very beautiful plant, but eating just one leaf can be fatal (cause death) to a child.

Garden plants. Now look around outside your house. People have died from eating the flowers, leaves, stems, or bulbs of plants like the **hyacinth** (3) and **crocus** (4).

6 Cardinal

summer
winter
both

The cardinal is perhaps one of the best known and most easily recognized songbirds. Cardinals are often called "redbirds" because the male is bright red and the female is reddish brown. Like goldfinches, they are members of the finch family, the large family of seed-eating birds. Unlike most birds, both male and female cardinals sing and whistle throughout the year.

Besides being beautiful and friendly, the cardinal is helpful to man because young cardinals relish insect pests such as boll worms and potato beetles. Adult cardinals eat weed seeds and harmful insects.

Cardinals do not usually migrate. They stay in the same area all year long. Cardinals are found in southeastern Canada, throughout much of the United States, and in Mexico. They make their homes in woodlands, thickets, swamps, and people's back yards.

Plants 85

Even some of our favorite plants like **azaleas** (5), **poinsettias** (6), **daffodils** (7), **irises** (8), **morning glories** (9), **wisteria** (10), and **mistletoe** (11) are poisonous.

Berries. Many plants, such as the **daphne** and **holly** (12) produce berries that are poisonous. *It is never wise to eat berries from any plant unless you are accompanied by an adult who knows for sure that they are harmless. Neither should you chew on any plant—or part of a plant—that you do not know is harmless.*

Edible plants that have poisonous parts

Asparagus (13) is a delicious vegetable, but never eat it raw, and never eat its berries. **Rhubarb** (14) is a very common garden vegetable used in making sauces, cakes, and pies. The stems are sour and good to eat, but you should never eat the leaves. Because of its poisonous leaves, rhubarb is considered one of the most dangerous garden plants.

86 ■ *Understanding God's World*

Even an **apple** can be poisonous if you eat large quantities of its seeds. **White potatoes** (15) and **tomatoes** (16) are members of the nightshade family. The leaves and stem of a tomato plant are poisonous. For many years people would not eat the tomatoes, thinking they were poisonous, too. The leaves, sprouts, and spoiled parts of the white potato plant are poisonous, as well.

Poisonous mushrooms. Another plant which may be dangerous is the **mushroom** (17). There are more than 38,000 kinds of mushrooms. They look like umbrellas, shelves, horns, balls, or cups. Some mushrooms are very delicious, but most are fatal. In fact, only about 1,000 kinds are edible (can be eaten safely). It takes a well-trained person to tell the difference between the poisonous and nonpoisonous ones. You should never eat mushrooms that you pick unless you are with a mushroom expert who says it is all right.

You will find mushrooms in meadows, forests, and lawns, especially after it rains. The main part of the plant grows below ground. The part above the ground is called the fruiting body. Its job is to disperse spores (cells) to make new mushrooms. A mushroom cannot produce food of its own, because it does not contain chlorophyll. Therefore it must get its food from something else. Most mushrooms live off dead plants.

Emergency medical help

If someone you know has swallowed the poisonous part of a plant, you need to get help immediately. It is important for you to stay calm so that you can think clearly. *If the person is conscious,* you should call the **poison control center** or your doctor if one of these numbers is listed at the front of your telephone directory. If you do not know either of these numbers, dial the **emergency number 911** or dial **0** for the operator and ask for the poison control center. Tell the medical person who answers your call your name, the address and telephone number (if you know them) of your location, and the approximate age of the person who swallowed the poisonous plant. Carefully describe the plant. What color and shape are the leaves? Does the plant have flowers? If so, what color are they? How many petals do the

Plants ■ 87

flowers have? Does the plant have berries? If so, what color and size are they? If you are instructed that the person needs to see the doctor or go to the hospital, take part of the plant. This will help the doctor to identify it. Knowing what plants in your area are poisonous can be a great help in emergencies.

If the person is unconscious, is having seizures, or is having trouble breathing, dial the emergency number 911 or dial 0 for the operator and ask for an ambulance or emergency medical help. You will need to state your name, the address and telephone number of your location, and the condition of the poisoned person. Do not hang up the telephone until the person to whom you are talking has all the information he needs. In any emergency, it is important to stay calm so that you can give the necessary information clearly and accurately.

Leaves of three

If you were asked to name a poisonous plant, you would probably say, **"poison ivy"** (18). It is a shrub or vine that climbs trees or grows along the ground. Its leaves are in groups of three leaflets which may vary in shape from plant to plant. In its bushy form it is often called **poison oak** (19). These plants give off an oil when rubbed against. The oil causes an irritation to the skin that can make the skin blister. This oil can spread easily to the rest of the body. If you think you have touched poison ivy or poison oak, do not touch any other part of your body. Immediately wash the affected area thoroughly with soap and cool water. Do not use a washcloth, because it will pick up and spread the poison. Be sure none of the water touches any other part of your body, since that may spread the poison. When you finish washing, rinse the area with rubbing alcohol. You should also wash any clothing which may have the oil on it, because oil on your clothes can get on your body. Putting a special lotion on the rash as it develops will help to relieve the burning and itching. Study the pictures of these poisonous plants so you will learn to avoid them. Remember, the shape of the leaflets may vary. The best way to recognize poison ivy or poison oak is to look for the group of three leaflets and remember this: **"Leaves of three, let it be!"**

Tobacco

Another plant contains a poison that many thousands of people take into their bodies every day. This plant is tobacco, and the poison in it is called *nicotine*. Nicotine is a habit-forming drug. It can cause lung cancer, heart disease, and other illnesses. Because it is poisonous, nicotine is also used as a natural insecticide (insect killer).

Poisoning by most plants can be an accident in which you have no choice, but you do have a choice with tobacco. You can choose not to be poisoned. God's Word says in 1 Corinthians 6:19, 20: "What? know ye not that your body is the temple of the Holy Ghost which is in you, which ye have of God, and ye are not your own? For ye are bought with a price: therefore glorify God in your body, and in your spirit, which are God's."

Determine today to keep the temple God has given you free of nicotine poisoning. It will be a choice you will never regret!

Comprehension Check 3.8   Answer each statement *true* or *false*.
1. Some plants that produce food for us have parts that are poisonous.
2. Never chew on any part of any plant unless you know it is harmless.
3. Every part of the tomato plant is poisonous.
4. If someone you know has eaten part of a poisonous plant, you should throw away the rest of the plant immediately.
5. The best way to recognize poison ivy or poison oak is to look for leaflets in groups of three.
6. If you have touched poison ivy, wash your skin immediately with warm water and a clean washcloth.
7. The poison found in tobacco is used in products that kill insects.

3.9 Plants: Helpful and Beautiful

Plants for good health

Many medicines that we use today either come directly from plants or are the results of discoveries that scientists made while working with plants. The Indians used to make a brew from willow bark for people with arthritis. Years later, when scientists examined willow bark, they discovered a chemical that became the main ingredient for aspirin.

In 1928, Sir Alexander Fleming, a British scientist, discovered **penicillin**, a life-saving antibiotic that is produced by a green mold. Although the mold from which penicillin is made is called a green mold, it does not contain chlorophyll and is not a true green plant. It is a type of fungus. (Fungus is a singular word; the plural of fungus is fungi [fun´ji].) **Fungi** are plants that do not contain chlorophyll and cannot make their own food. Mushrooms are one kind of fungus with which you are familiar. Many kinds of fungi are valuable to man. The mold that produces penicillin is only one of them.

The best way you can use plants for good health is to eat a balanced diet. Vitamins C, D, B_1, E, and K all come from either green plants or fungi. When you eat the right foods, including plenty of plant products, you prevent such deficiency diseases as scurvy, beriberi, and rickets. You are also building a healthy body that can fight off other diseases.

Other important uses

Many shelters are made of plant material. Wooden houses, canvas tents, and grass huts are all made from plants. Much of the clothing we wear is made of plant fibers. Cotton and linen fibers come from plants. Wool comes from sheep that depend on plants to live. Silk is made from the cocoons of a certain moth that feeds on mulberry leaves. Although many man-made fibers are also used in clothing today, quite often these are blended with natural fibers.

The rubber in your eraser and in the tires of your parents' car comes from a tree. The hevea tree produces a milky substance called latex which is used to make rubber. A similar substance from another kind of tree produces chicle, from which chewing gum is made.

The paper on which this book is printed was once a plant. Very fine paper is made from cotton and linen rags. Less expensive paper is made from wood pulp.

Plants for beauty

God's first gift to Adam and Eve, the first people, was a beautiful garden filled with plants and animals. Although sin soon entered into the world and spoiled much of its loveliness, some of that beauty remains for us to enjoy. Think of the marvelous variety of colors we enjoy in plants—golden yellow daffodils, deep red roses, waxy white lilies, soft blue forget-me-nots, cool green fir trees. Some flowers have even given their names to shades of color, such as rose, violet, and lilac.

Think of the wonderful variety of floral fragrances. An apple blossom does not smell like a pine tree, but each has its own refreshing and lovely scent. We can enjoy the variety of designs in the plant world. In the same forest, growing side by side, we can find massive oaks and tiny velvety mosses. The Creator designed each plant to live in a certain place and to do a special job.

Of course, not all plants are beneficial to man today. When Adam sinned, God cursed the ground, or withheld His full protection from it. Without God's blessing, thorns, weeds, and poisonous plants began to grow. A few plants are poisonous to eat or even to touch. Others keep beneficial plants from growing well. You are probably not very grateful for those weeds you had to pull out of the vegetable garden last summer, but the birds that eat the weed seeds are! If you have hay fever, you do not enjoy the clouds of pollen that plants produce in the spring. Without that pollen, however, flowering plants could not make seeds, and without seeds, no new flowering plants could grow.

Purple Finch

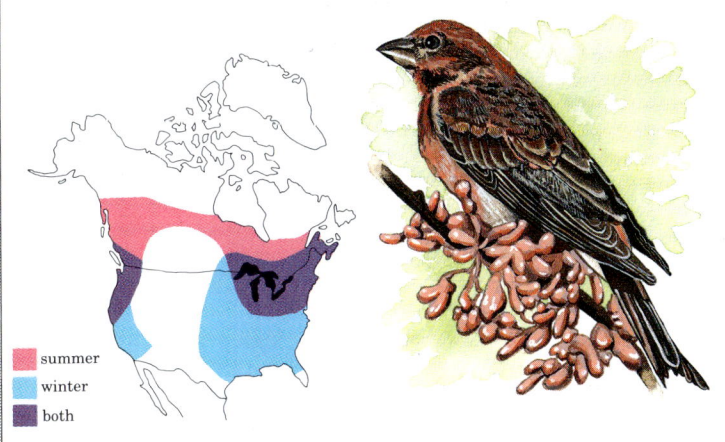

summer
winter
both

The purple finch is a shy little bird, about six inches long. It is often confused with other birds of similar size and color. It is not easily identified because most purple finches have little or no purple in their plumage. Famous bird watcher Roger Tory Peterson says that the male looks "like a sparrow dipped in raspberry juice,"* with a head and rump of deeper rose red. The female and immature birds look very much like sparrows with their brown striped plumage.

Found in most of North America, the purple finch lives throughout most of the eastern half of the United States, across southern Canada, and into the Pacific states. Like other members of the finch family, the purple finch is a seed eater. It also eats wild fruits and a few insects.

*Roger Tory Peterson, *A Field Guide to the Birds* (Boston: Houghton Mifflin, 1980), p. 270.

Comprehension Check 3.9
1. What life-saving antibiotic is produced by a green mold?
2. Why are molds and other fungi not able to make their own food?
3. How can you best use plants to stay healthy?
4. Name two other uses for plants.
5. Write a sentence describing a plant that you think is especially beautiful.

3.10 George Washington Carver: The Plant Doctor

From the time he was a very young boy, George Washington Carver loved plants. He also wanted to know all he could about them. What made some plants thrive while others withered and died? Why were some flowers pink and others blue? George was filled with curiosity and a thirst for knowledge. Whenever he had free time, he roamed the woods. He learned to use his eyes and ears. Because he was a careful observer, George became familiar with all living things; however, the study of plants was his special love. He recorded his observations accurately in the beautiful pictures he drew. George also had a talent for helping sick plants to become healthy again. He used this God-given ability to help any neighbor with an ailing plant. Even though he was only a boy, he earned the nickname "the Plant Doctor."

It sounds as though George had a wonderful childhood, doesn't it? But George was an orphan who had been born a slave. When he was young, he was small and not very strong. It would have been easy for him to feel sorry for himself, but George was too busy learning. There was no school nearby for him to attend, so when he was almost nine years old he left home to go to school in another town. For many years George worked hard and did without things so that he could go to grade school, high school, and then college. George never stopped learning. Many years later, to honor him for his outstanding work, his college presented him with a Doctor of Science degree. One of his professors said that George was a brilliant student, the best scientific observer he had ever seen. How do you think George developed those qualities? He looked carefully, thought about what he saw, and asked God to help him see and understand even more.

Understanding God's World

Dr. Carver was a superb artist and an excellent musician; probably he could have had a career in either of those fields. But he was determined to use his talents to help his people—the poor farmers of the South. For many years, most southern farmers had grown only cotton or tobacco. These crops had removed important minerals from the soil. Now the soil was poor—and so were the farmers! The soil would not produce enough for them to make a living. Dr. Carver knew he could help the farmers by teaching them better methods of **agriculture,** the science of farming. He saw his chance when, in 1896, he was asked to teach at Tuskegee Institute, a college in Alabama.

Dr. Carver got right to work setting up a model farm at Tuskegee. This helped not only the students but also anyone who wanted to come, watch, and ask questions. To help those who could not come, Dr. Carver began a "movable school." He traveled and taught people better ways to farm. He taught them to rotate crops. Instead of always growing cotton, farmers learned to grow peanuts, vegetables, or soybeans. These crops enriched the soil. But what would farmers do with bushels and bushels of peanuts?

So Dr. Carver got to work again. He set up a laboratory with whatever odds and ends he could find for equipment. His most valuable piece of equipment, however, was his Bible. He kept a copy in his laboratory at all times. Before he began working with a plant, Dr. Carver would ask God to show him His plan for that plant. Dr. Carver often said that he leaned on Genesis 1:29.

And God said, Behold, I have given you every herb bearing seed, which is upon the face of all the earth, and every tree, in the which is the fruit of a tree yielding seed; to you it shall be for meat.

Dr. Carver's laboratory became known as "God's Little Workshop."

Dr. Carver began his investigation of plants. He formed hypotheses, experimented, and then recorded his observations. He did not discover everything at once, but over the years he found 75 uses for pecans, 115 uses for tomatoes, 118 uses for sweet potatoes, and over 300 uses for peanuts! He also made a marblelike product from wood shavings, concrete from cotton stalks, dyes from clay, and rubber from goldenrod milk. Many times people offered him large sums of money to leave Tuskegee and work for them instead. One of these men was his good friend Henry Ford. Dr. Carver always refused, however. He chose to use his marvelous talents to help others, not to enrich himself. By his life and teaching, Dr. George Washington Carver showed that science is a wonderful tool to unlock and use the wonders of God's creation.

Chapter Check-up

A *Make sure you know the name of each plant pictured in this chapter and at least one thing about the plant. You should also know the Canadian floral emblems from chapter 1.*

B *Write the letter of the phrase that identifies each term.*

___ 1. acorn
___ 2. chlorophyll
___ 3. conifer
___ 4. deciduous
___ 5. embryo
___ 6. fungi
___ 7. germinate
___ 8. key
___ 9. nicotine
___ 10. penicillin
___ 11. photosynthesis
___ 12. pollinate
___ 13. seed coat

A. a tree which produces cones instead of flowers
B. the poison found in the tobacco plant
C. the seed of a maple tree
D. to move pollen from the stamens to the pistil
E. an antibiotic made from green mold
F. the covering which protects the seed
G. plants without chlorophyll
H. to sprout
I. a poisonous plant
J. green coloring matter in plants
K. the process by which green plants make food
L. "falling down"
M. the seed of an oak tree
N. the part of the seed which is the new plant

C *Follow the directions.*

1. Label the three parts of this seed.

2. Label the parts of this flower and tell what each part does.

D Write true or false in the space before each statement.

_____ 1. There are some living things on earth which do not need green plants in order to live.
_____ 2. All weeds are useless and harmful plants.
_____ 3. Insects, birds, and bats are pollinators of plants.
_____ 4. Every seed contains a new plant.
_____ 5. Most seeds ripen in the fall.
_____ 6. It is important for seeds to stay close to the parent plant.
_____ 7. Some seeds are able to germinate without water.
_____ 8. Evergreen trees lose a few of their needles at a time.
_____ 9. Most tree flowers are large and brilliantly colored.
_____ 10. If it is safe to eat one part of a certain plant, then it is safe to eat every part of the plant.

E What parts of the following plants are poisonous?

a. potato _____

b. rhubarb _____

c. apple _____

d. tomato _____

e. asparagus _____

F Answer the questions about this picture.

1. How many flowers are in the picture? _____

2. The plant is probably a member of what family?
   _____

3. How is the leaf-cutting bee helping the plant? _____
   _____

4. How is the plant helping the bee? _____
   _____

Plants ■ 95

G Write the letter of the correct answer.

_____ 1. Which seed would most likely be spread by the wind?

_____ 2. Which seed would be most likely to hitch a ride on an animal's fur?

A

C

B

D

H Answer the questions about the pictures.

A

1. Which flower is an aster? _____

2. How can you tell? _____
   _____

3. What is the other flower? _____

B

96 ■ *Understanding God's World*

American goldfinch

4. BIRDS: Winged Wonders

4.1 Birds in Your Back Yard

A sharp whistle and a flash of red in a nearby pine tree alert you to the presence of a cardinal. Across the damp lawn runs a robin with a vivid red vest, searching for his earthworm breakfast. The screeching of the blue jay may be a warning that danger is at hand—or it may only mean that he is claiming the bird bath for himself! In the scarlet trumpet vine you think you see a large moth, but looking more closely, you are delighted to discover a tiny hummingbird.

These are a few of the birds that commonly visit our back yards. Each one is a unique part of the creation of God. Some are very useful; others are known for their beauty. Still others will amuse you with their clever antics. How many can you recognize by sight or by their song?

The friendly robin

Perhaps the first bird you learned to recognize was the robin, a friendly bird with an enormous appetite. It feasts on wild fruit and earthworms, its two favorite foods. Robins also eat insects and some seeds. You may see one running across your lawn in search of its next meal. Then it stops, standing absolutely still with its head cocked to one side. It is not listening for anything; it is using its eyes to hunt earthworms. Because the eyes of most birds are on the sides of their heads, they have to cock their heads and look at an object with just one eye. The other eye keeps busy looking at things in the opposite direction.

A robin often returns to the same spot each year to build its nest. It may choose a crotch of a tree or a spot among some branches. Some build on a ledge or windowsill. The female robin is responsible for most of the nest building. She uses grass, twine, and twigs held together solidly with mud and then lines the nest with dry grass. There are three to six blue eggs in each clutch, and robins often have two or three broods each year. When the young birds hatch, both parents help feed them.

The robin is about ten inches long from the tip of its bill to the tip of its tail. You should keep the robin's size well in mind, because it is often used to compare with the size of other birds.

The brilliant cardinal

Is the cardinal singing about himself when he sings "purty, purty, purty, purty"? He is a gorgeous fellow a little smaller than a robin, with brilliant red feathers and an impressive feathered crest ("cap") on his head. Would you know the female cardinal if you saw her? She does not share the bright plumage of the male, but is a soft brown color. Look for a few touches of red among her feathers, and notice her crest. She and her mate both have bright red or orange bills. Both male and female cardinals are enthusiastic singers. In the wild, they frequent thickets, woodlands, and swamps. Weed seeds, wild fruit, and insect pests make up the main part of their diet, but they will come to your bird feeder, especially if you supply them with sunflower seeds, their favorite food.

The talented mockingbird

As you sit in your favorite outdoor spot, you think you hear a choir of birds. There must be fifteen different kinds in that tree taking turns singing. You look closely and discover that the choir is made up of one bird. You have been listening to a mockingbird. This cheerful songster is about the size of a robin but more slender and with a longer tail. It is not especially colorful in its gray suit with a few white patches, but its song is amazing. It sings day and night and at almost any time of the year. Although its own song is very lovely, the mockingbird also enjoys mimicking the songs of other birds and the noises made by cats, dogs, cars, and people. Since it eats many harmful insects, the mockingbird is helpful as well as entertaining. You will find this bird throughout most of the United States except in the Northwest and in a few parts of southern Canada.

Understanding God's World

blue jay

Steller's jay

The sassy blue jay

The noisy, bossy blue jay thinks he rules the back yard. He takes first place at the bird feeder and goes to the head of the line at the bird bath. His song is loud but not very musical. His large size, his bright blue plumage marked with black and white, and his blue crest catch your eye. He is about twelve inches long, or two inches longer than a robin. Both male and female are beautifully colored.

The blue jay is found only in the East, but the Steller's jay lives in the West. This widespread western jay is bluish gray with a crested black head and no white in his plumage.

Jays are members of the crow family, and many people who have studied birds believe that jays and other members of the crow family are the most intelligent of all the birds. Like mockingbirds, blue jays are able to mimic the songs of other birds. They are also very alert and warn the other birds if they see a predator come near. Perhaps the smaller songbirds put up with the blue jay's bossy ways because they appreciate his alarm system. The blue jay eats just about anything—nuts, seeds, fruit, insects, small fish, and small amphibians (such as frogs and toads). Acorns are probably his favorite food. Jays have a habit of storing acorns by planting them in the ground. Sometimes the jay fails to return for his acorns, and they grow into beautiful oak trees. Prince Edward Island, Canada's smallest province, has chosen the blue jay as its provincial bird.

Birds 101

Comprehension Check 4.1

Name the bird or birds that fit the following descriptions. *Choose from this list:*

a. robin   b. mockingbird   c. cardinal   d. blue jay

1. probably the most intelligent of the birds in the list
2. a dull-colored bird that is a superb singer and clever mimic
3. runs as it searches for food
4. very helpful because it eats many insect pests
5. both male and female like to sing
6. two birds with crests
7. about ten inches long
8. the smallest bird in the list
9. larger than a robin
10. planter of oak trees

Key to birds

1. mockingbird
2. starling
3. bluejay
4. chipping sparrow
5. robin
6. house sparrow
7. English sparrow
8. tree sparrow
9. house wren
10. cardinal
11. Eurasian tree sparrow

102 ◼ *Understanding God's World*

4.2 More Backyard Birds

You have already learned about some of our most familiar backyard birds—the friendly robin, the melodious mockingbird, the colorful cardinal, and the jeering jay. They are just a few of the birds that seem to feel at home around people.

The squawking starling

Loud, squawking starlings are as bossy as blue jays. Starlings are not native American birds; in 1890 a flock of them was brought from Europe and turned loose in New York City. Starlings are now found in every part of the United States and Canada. From a distance, they look like any other black birds, but if you look closely, you will

Birds 103

see that their coats are spangled with purple, blue, and green. Starlings are a little smaller than robins. They are chunky birds with short tails and long, sharp bills. They travel in large flocks, even in nesting season, and seem always to be in a hurry. When you see a flock walking through a field in a jerky, zig-zag fashion, you wonder how they can possibly find any food that way. They do; starlings are greedy eaters. Some people dislike them because they are noisy and dirty, they will take over the nesting places of other birds, and they have been known to ruin crops. On the other hand, they eat many insect pests including grubs (insect larvae) and cutworms. Cutworms are pests because they feed on young plants, often cutting the shoots off just above the ground. Starlings are one of the very few birds that will eat the Japanese beetle, another very destructive insect.

The chubby wren

Chubby and brown, with a long bill and a turned-up tail, tiny jenny wren is about half the size of a robin (five inches long). There are many kinds of wrens found throughout our continent. Some kinds live in the deep woods, others in the desert. The house wren likes to live near people. You might spy one in a thicket or a garden, but wrens are known for choosing unusual places to nest. The pocket of a pair of overalls on the clothesline, an old hat, or a mailbox—all these are considered suitable nests by this cheery, sociable bird. House wrens will readily accept a birdhouse if you put one up, and they may return to nest in that same spot for several seasons. If you have neglected to clean out the old nest, the wren may take it apart piece by piece and then build a new nest using the old material. Should an earlier arrival take over her nesting place, the wren may show her disdain by dumping nesting material into the other bird's nest. If you are not sure whether a bird you spot is a wren, look at its tail. Wrens often tip their tails up in the air rather than holding them straight out as most birds do.

104 ■ *Understanding God's World*

The musical sparrow

A large flock of small brown birds has arrived at your bird feeder on a cold winter day. As they munch on millet seeds and cracked corn, you observe them. Some have streaked breasts, others plain white. Some are wearing little rust-colored caps. Still others have black bibs tucked under their chins. They are all sparrows. Sparrows are found throughout North America, and there are many different kinds. There are sparrows of the desert, forest, marsh, and prairie. The song sparrow is one of the most common. It is from five to seven inches long, making it quite a bit smaller than a robin and a little larger than a house wren. You will find it throughout the United States and Canada in bushy areas, thickets, and gardens. Its white breast is streaked with brown. Its most noticeable mark is the triangle formed by three large spots in the center of its breast. As it flies, it pumps its tail up and down. The song sparrow has a pleasant, melodious song.

The tiny hummingbird

The ruby-throated hummingbird is only 3 1/2 inches long and weighs about as much as a penny. The hum you hear comes from the vibration of its wings, which beat at the furious rate of about 60 times per second. This bird, which might be mistaken for a large moth, is found throughout the East. In fact, it is the only eastern hummingbird. There are many kinds of hummingbirds found in the West, among them the broad-tailed and the rufous. Hummingbirds are attracted to water and to flowers, especially red flowers. Their long, needlelike bills are perfectly designed for sipping nectar, and

ruby-throated hummingbird

Birds 105

they are the chief pollinators of plants whose flowers are too long and narrow for insects to reach into. Hummingbirds also snatch tiny insects from flowers or in mid-air and will plunder a spider's web for a tasty morsel. You might walk by a hummingbird's nest and not know it, because it is about the size of a golf ball, and the tiny eggs are pea-sized. A newly hatched hummingbird is no larger than a bee. The nest is made of plant down and spider webs and is camouflaged by bits of moss and lichen that the hummingbird has stuck to the outside. The hummingbird is in constant motion, and it is the only bird that can fly backward.

Anna's hummingbird

long-billed marsh wren

SCIENCE CONCEPTS   *How do birds sing?*

Almost every kind of bird in the world has a voice that it uses to communicate with other birds. Most kinds of birds can call. A call is a single note. A baby bird calls to let its parents know when it is hungry, injured, or frightened. An adult bird calls so that its mate will recognize it. Each individual bird has its own distinctive voice, just as each person does. Birds also call to warn each other of danger and to let each other know that food is available.

Some kinds of birds sing as well as call. A bird's song is a special pattern of notes. In most cases, only the male bird sings. He uses his song to establish his territory and to attract a mate. A very few kinds of birds such as vultures and ostriches can neither call nor sing.

Birds are able to call or sing because of a special structure in the windpipe that is called the **syrinx.** The syrinx is the bird's voice box. It is much closer to the bird's lungs than your larynx, or voice box, is to your lungs. The bird's syrinx is located at the lower end of the windpipe, just before the windpipe branches and enters the lungs. Air coming out of the lungs passes over membranes inside the syrinx. The membranes vibrate, and sound is produced. The pitch and volume of the sound are determined by muscles that control these membranes.

106   Understanding God's World

8 Wren

summer
winter
both

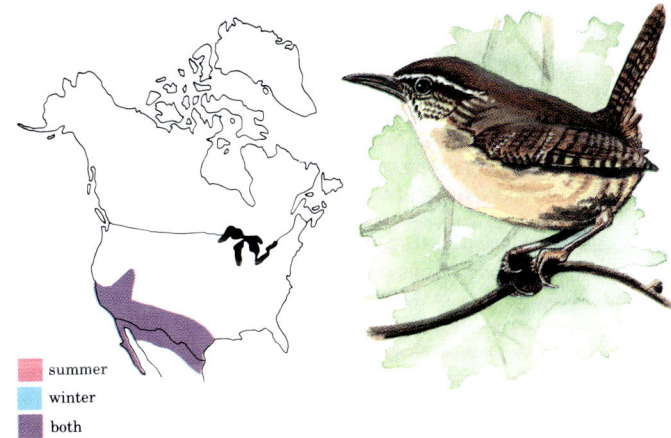

You will know that you have spotted a wren when you see a small, stocky, brown bird holding its tail straight up in the air. Wrens seem to be perpetually on the move. Their slender, curved bills are ideally suited to hunting for insects and spiders.

The cactus wren lives in the deserts of the Southwest. It doesn't mind the yucca plant's sharp leaves, and it is right at home on a prickly cactus, where it builds an oval-shaped straw nest. The nest is covered; the cactus wren gets in through a side entrance.

The Carolina wren lives throughout the eastern United States and eastern Mexico. It prefers thickets or any area with good ground cover. Its nest, made of sticks and lined with feathers, might be built in a hollow tree stump or in a stone wall.

Comprehension Check 4.2

A Making Comparisons
Put the following birds in order from largest to smallest.
a. robin, mockingbird
b. cardinal, starling
c. blue jay
d. wren
e. song sparrow
f. hummingbird

B Library Research
The starling is a helpful bird because it feeds on the Japanese beetle. Read about this destructive insect in an encyclopedia or a nature study book. Try to find the answers to these questions:
1. Where did the beetle come from?
2. How did it get here?
3. Where does it live?
4. What does it look like?
5. Why is it harmful?
6. What methods are used to control it?

C Best Choice
Name the bird or birds that fit the following descriptions.
Choose from this list:
a. hummingbird
b. starling
c. wren
d. song sparrow

1. likes to nest near people
2. camouflages its nest
3. will eat Japanese beetles
4. can fly backward
5. are the best singers in the list
6. is not a native American bird
7. is attracted to red flowers
8. pumps its tail up and down when it flies
9. holds its tail straight up in the air

Birds 107

4.3 Recognizing Birds

As she was weeding the garden early one morning, Karen saw a bird she had never noticed before. Karen quietly watched the bird for as long as she could and looked for special characteristics that would help her recognize the bird if she saw it again. If you learn to look for these characteristics, you will be able to identify new birds, also.

Things to look for

Size. Is the bird small like a sparrow (5–7 inches long), large like a crow (almost 20 inches), or medium-sized like a robin (10 inches)? Becoming familiar with the sizes of these three common birds will help you to recognize others. (1)

Shape. Would you describe the bird as plump or slender? (2) Also notice the size and shape of the bird's tail and wings. Is the tail rounded, squared, pointed, or forked? (3) Look at the bird's bill. Is it thick and heavy or narrow and long? (4)

108 *Understanding God's World*

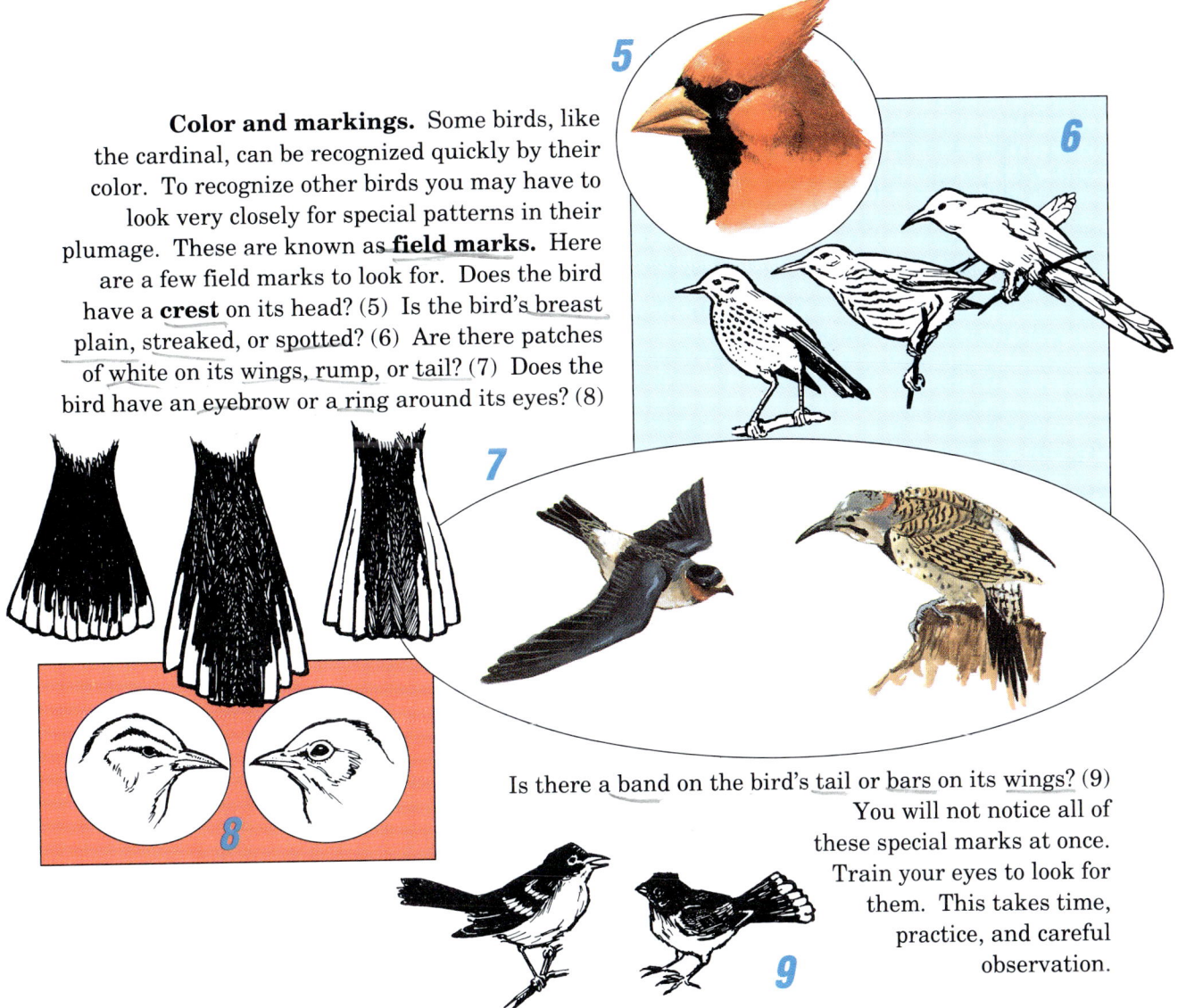

Color and markings. Some birds, like the cardinal, can be recognized quickly by their color. To recognize other birds you may have to look very closely for special patterns in their plumage. These are known as **field marks.** Here are a few field marks to look for. Does the bird have a **crest** on its head? (5) Is the bird's breast plain, streaked, or spotted? (6) Are there patches of white on its wings, rump, or tail? (7) Does the bird have an eyebrow or a ring around its eyes? (8) Is there a band on the bird's tail or bars on its wings? (9) You will not notice all of these special marks at once. Train your eyes to look for them. This takes time, practice, and careful observation.

Behavior. Many birds have unusual ways of flying, walking, or perching. For example, nuthatches climb down the trunk of a tree head first. Some birds, such as goldfinches and sparrows, travel mostly in flocks. Other birds, such as kingfishers and flycatchers, are more solitary. Some birds move in peculiar ways. Mockingbirds flash their wings as they walk; doves bob their heads. Notice also if the bird strolls, hops, or runs as it walks. How does it fly? Some birds fly in straight lines; others dip like a roller coaster. Do you remember what is unusual about the way a wren holds its tail?

Habitat. An animal's **habitat** is the particular kind of area where it lives, such as a forest, fields or meadows, or wetlands. Two different kinds of birds may live in the same range but never be seen together because each one lives in a different habitat. For example, hairy woodpeckers and mallard ducks share the same range, but you would not find them living side-by-side, because each requires a different habitat. Hairy woodpeckers live in the woods; mallard ducks live near marshes or ponds. Notice the habitat in which you find your new bird. Did you see it in an open field? Was it perched on a tree in the woods? Or was it hiding in the reeds by a pond? Birds can and do travel around, but each species has a favorite place to live, the place God designed for it. Noticing the kind of surroundings where you found the bird will help you to identify it.

Birds 109

Birding

The best place to begin watching birds is in your own neighborhood. Early morning is the best time. Most birds are very active beginning at sunrise and continuing for the next two hours. If you take along a small pad of paper and a pencil you can jot down characteristics of the birds you observe.

When a bird appears, keep your eyes right on it until it leaves. Remain very quiet so you do not scare it away. Concentrate on the whole appearance of the bird, and notice what makes it special. Use your eyes to get a good picture of the bird in your mind. After the bird is gone, write down a few words about its appearance. Then you can look it up in a field guide.

Once you have trained yourself to be quiet and observant, you may enjoy birding in other places. It helps to go with someone who knows more about birds than you do. Never go by yourself without your parents' permission, and be sure to dress suitably for the area you will be exploring. Here are some things to take with you: notebook, pencil, field guide, insect repellent, and binoculars (if you have them and know how to use them). Remember to move quietly as you look for birds. Making a soft, squeaking noise with your mouth on the back of your hand often brings birds closer to you. They think the sound is made by a baby bird in distress. Try to keep the sun to your back; you will be able to see the birds much better if you do. Use your eyes and ears well. They are your most valuable pieces of equipment for learning to know the birds.

> **Comprehension Check 4.3**
> 1. To judge the size of an unfamiliar bird, you should become familiar with the sizes of three common birds. What three birds are these?
> 2. On what part of a bird's body might there be a crest?
> 3. What bird can be identified by its ability to walk down a tree trunk head first?
> 4. What is a habitat?
> 5. At what time of day are most birds very active?
> 6. What are your two most valuable pieces of equipment for successful birding?

4.4 Feeding the Birds

There are several things that you can do to attract birds to your back yard. If you do some or all of these things, you will be able to observe many kinds of birds at close range, and you will also be helping the birds by providing things that they need.

One of the most enjoyable and helpful activities is feeding birds, especially during the winter months when it is hard for many birds to find food on their own. If you supply a variety of foods, you will be rewarded with your own backyard bird show.

Your family may already have a bird feeder. If so, you may want to take the responsibility of checking regularly to see that there is a good supply of food in the feeder. If you do not have a bird feeder in your back yard, you may enjoy making one of your own.

Simple feeders

Many birds feed at table-top level. A wicker tray filled with bird seed and placed on a platform such as a picnic table, bench, or window sill will attract cardinals, chickadees, wrens, and grosbeaks. Sunflower seeds are favorites with these birds. If you do not have a wicker tray, another shallow container will work, but be sure to make holes in the bottom of the container. This allows moisture to drain off, keeping the food from becoming soaked and spoiling.

Some birds prefer to feed on the ground. Sparrows, mourning doves, juncos, and bobwhites will come to a cleared spot protected by a few trees. They relish sunflower seeds, millet, and cracked corn. (Millet, like corn, is a member of the grass family.)

Another simple feeder can be made from half a grapefruit rind. Fill it with small chunks of citrus fruit, apples, and berries. Then place it on your platform, and you may be rewarded with the appearance of orioles, thrushes, thrashers, and warblers.

Insect-eating birds love beef suet, a hard animal fat. You can find suet in the meat department at the grocery store. A suet feeder can be made from a mesh bag, the kind that onions come in. Hang this on a tree trunk, and you will delight the woodpeckers, chickadees, wrens, and nuthatches in your neighborhood. These birds also enjoy peanut butter. You can fill half of a coconut shell with a mixture of peanut butter and seeds or cornmeal and place it on the platform.

Several types of feeders can be purchased. Although many people prefer hanging feeders, most birds do not. This is because most birds cannot hold on to the feeder and eat at the same time.

If you place your feeder near a window, you will be able to enjoy seeing at close range many birds that you have only seen from a distance before. Chickadees, nuthatches, cardinals, and woodpeckers will feed quite close to humans. Just be careful not to startle them by any sudden moves or loud noises.

Birds 111

The birds' Christmas tree

Instead of throwing out your family's Christmas tree when you are finished with it, you can decorate it for the birds to enjoy. Actually, you could use any tree growing in your yard for a birds' Christmas tree. This is a very old custom that dates back to the 1500s. Use your imagination to create a tree with a variety of unusual foods. Birds enjoy such things as stale bread, strings of popcorn and cranberries, doughnuts, chunks of fruit, and nuts.

What else is on the menu?

After your feeder has become the attraction for birds in your area, you can also try giving the birds some other kinds of food. Birds seem to enjoy crumbled dog biscuit, dried fruit, leftover eggs, lettuce, potato, coconut, corn, and oatmeal. They also appreciate a supply of coarse salt and some gritty material like eggshells or sand. They need grit to digest their food, and in the winter they sometimes cannot find it on their own.

When to feed the birds

You should begin feeding early in the fall, before the birds really need it. Once you have begun feeding birds for the winter, it is most important that you continue to do it faithfully. Late winter is a dangerous time for birds that have become dependent on you for food. There may not be enough wild food in the area to feed the number of birds that stayed around because you began to feed them. Once birds discover that you are putting out food for them, they usually stop searching for other food in the area. Whenever there is a heavy snowstorm or a crust of ice forms, it is very important that you check the food on the feeder so that the birds do not go hungry or even starve. You may continue limited feeding through the spring and summer. This may give you the chance to get very near to your visitors and observe their habits at close range.

Understanding God's World

> **Comprehension Check 4.4**
> 1. Cardinals, chickadees, and grosbeaks prefer _?_ seeds.
> 2. Birds that eat insects will eat _?_ or _?_ in the winter.
> 3. Tell one thing you could put on your bird feeder that is not food.
> 4. List three things you could put on a birds' Christmas tree.
> 5. Write a short paragraph explaining why you need to continue to feed birds throughout the winter once you have begun.

4.5 Birdbaths and Birdhouses

Make a birdbath

A supply of water attracts birds just as much as food does. Birds need water to drink and to keep their feathers in good condition. Their feathers will not work correctly in flight or serve as insulation if they are not in proper condition.

If you already have a birdbath, you could take on the job of keeping it full of clean water. Change the water often so mosquitoes cannot complete their life cycles there. If you do not have a birdbath, you can make a simple one from the lid of a plastic garbage can. Never use a metal lid; it will become too hot for the birds. Choose a spot that is fairly open with some trees nearby. Birds do not feel secure when their feathers are wet. They want to bathe in areas that are out in the open so that predators cannot sneak up on them. Birds also want some cover nearby to escape to if they feel threatened. After you choose the spot, turn the lid upside down, surrounding it with stones to keep it in place. An even simpler birdbath can be made by filling an old baking dish (not a metal one) with one to two inches of water and setting it out on a platform.

Birds love moving water. You may see some birds flying through the sprays of water shot out by your lawn sprinkler. You may want to try hanging a dripping bucket over your birdbath. An ordinary wooden or plastic bucket with a very tiny nail hole in it can be filled with water and hung from a limb. The sound of dripping water will attract birds to your birdbath.

Build a birdhouse

An excellent way to bring birds close to you is to provide places for them to build their nests and lay their eggs. Birdhouses can be purchased or made.

Key to Birds

1. chickadee
2. phoebes
3. bluejay
4. bluebird
5. cardinal
6. purple martins
7. house wren
8. goldfinch
9. song sparrow
10. purple finch
11. nuthatch
12. downy woodpecker

At your local library you could probably find complete instructions. Hollowed-out gourds can also be used for birdhouses. Here are a few guidelines to follow:

1. Wood is the best material; never use metal.
2. Birds prefer rough surfaces on the inside.
3. Do not put a perch on your birdhouse. Most birds do not need them, and the perch could make it easier for a predator to rob the nest.
4. Follow the directions very carefully about the size of the entrance hole. If you make it too large, bigger birds such as starlings and jays will crowd out the smaller songbirds.
5. Each fall, clean out your birdhouse, take it down, and store it with the entrance hole plugged up.

When should you have your birdhouse ready? In the South, mid-February is the best time. In the North, you should wait until mid-March. Because most birds choose a territory and defend it against other birds of the same species, you will not want to put up several birdhouses for the same kind of bird in one area. Purple martins, however, like to nest together in colonies; so you could put up an apartment house for them.

You will be able to get a real "bird's-eye view" by watching the birds that are using your birdhouse.

Understanding God's World

Record your observations. Do both parents incubate the eggs, or is this the job of just the female? Does the male bring food to his mate? How often does the female leave the nest? How long is it before the eggs hatch? Do both parents care for the babies? Listen to the noises the babies make. How long will it be before they leave the nest? The answers to these questions will depend upon the kind of bird you are observing.

Even if you cannot set out a birdhouse, you can help birds by providing nest-building materials for them. Short pieces of yarn or string, short strips of cloth, cotton, hair, loose wool, straw—all of these are acceptable to birds. Do not put out plastic materials. Be sure that pieces of yarn, string, or cloth are short, about 6 to 8 inches. Long pieces may entangle the birds. You can hang the materials in a mesh bag or from a clothesline, or you can place them in the crotch of a tree.

Sometime you may find a baby bird that appears to be an orphan. The best thing you can do for it is to leave it alone. Probably its parents are nearby but afraid to show themselves to you. Even if the baby bird is alone, it has a better chance to survive if it is left as it is.

If you are successful in attracting birds to your yard, you will receive many hours of pleasure and enjoyment as you learn about a special part of God's creation.

Birds 115

SCIENCE CONCEPTS   *Why should a birdbath not be made of metal?*

When you build a birdhouse or a birdbath, you want to be sure to use a material that is safe for the birds. Why is metal an unsafe material?

To understand this, we must know something about heat and how it travels. Heat can travel from one object to another. It always travels from something that is hot to something that is cooler. The speed with which heat travels depends upon the kind of material it is traveling through. Some materials are especially good at passing heat on to other objects. We say such materials are good **conductors** of heat. *Any kind of metal is a good conductor of heat.* Wood and plastic are poor conductors of heat. You can observe how heat travels quickly and easily through a good conductor as your teacher performs the following demonstration.

You will need a large candle, a small candle (like those used on birthday cakes), *a match, a large nail, a wooden clothespin, and something to hold the large candle upright securely.* (A lump of clay will work if you do not have a secure candlestick.) Light the large candle with the match, and then use the large candle to light the small one. Use dripping wax from the small candle to make a row of wax drops on the nail. Using the clothespin as a holder, stick the tip of the nail into the flame of the larger candle.

Observe the row of wax dots on the nail. Do they all melt? If so, which one melts first, or do they all melt at once?

You should have noticed that the drop of wax closest to the flame melted first. As heat traveled up the nail, the next drop and then the next melted in turn. Because the nail is made of metal, it conducts heat quickly and easily.

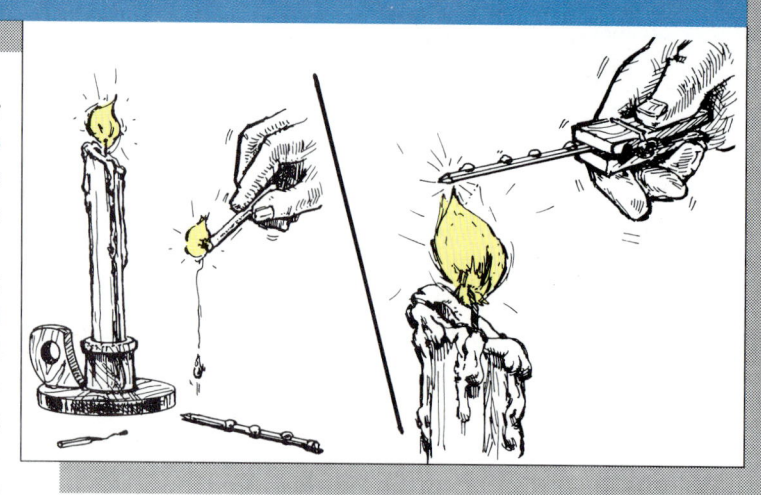

Why wasn't heat from the candle conducted to your teacher's fingers? The clothespin that your teacher used to hold the nail is made of wood, a poor conductor of heat. Heat does not travel as quickly and easily through a poor conductor as it does through a good conductor. Can you explain why your mother often uses wooden or plastic spoons to stir hot things that she is cooking?

Let's see how this information about heat affects the birdhouse or birdbath that you are building. Since metal is a good conductor, a metal birdhouse will quickly absorb heat from the sun. Heat from the metal passes to the air inside the birdhouse, making the air too hot for the birds. Why is wood, a poor conductor of heat, a safe material to use?

Metal birdbaths are unsafe for the same reason. The sun quickly heats the metal birdbath to a high temperature. The water in the birdbath also becomes very hot as heat from the metal is transferred to the water. On a very warm day, the water would soon become so hot that no bird would want to drink it or bathe in it. Birdbaths made of plastic or ceramic are safe, because those materials are poor conductors of heat.

Understanding God's World

9 Bluebird

Comprehension Check 4.5
1. What material should you never use for a birdhouse or a birdbath? Why?
2. How can you help the birds in your neighborhood build their nests?

Thought Question
You have put five wren houses in a tree in your back yard. Only one family of wrens has moved in. Why?

summer
winter
both

Bluebirds are members of the thrush family, and like most other thrushes, they eat insects and fruit. Beetles, grasshoppers, weevils, and caterpillars are among their favorite foods.

Three kinds of bluebirds live in North America. All three kinds have blue backs and white bellies. Eastern and western bluebirds have rusty red patches on their breasts, but mountain bluebirds are peacock blue all over.

Eastern bluebirds live east of the Rocky Mountains, from southern Canada to the Gulf of Mexico. Mountain bluebirds are found in Alaska, western Canada, and the southwestern United States. Both the eastern and the mountain bluebirds are known for their lovely songs. Western bluebirds live west of the Rockies, from British Columbia to Mexico.

Because there were fewer natural nesting places for bluebirds after the early 1900s, the number of eastern bluebirds began to decrease. In recent years, people in several areas of the United States and Canada have put up special bluebird houses, and today a larger number of bluebirds are again being seen.

4.6 Birds of the Forest

An early morning walk through the woods is the perfect opportunity to see some birds in their own homes. You will recognize many of them as winter visitors to your feeder. Other forest birds **migrate,** or travel to distant places, because they cannot survive the winter in cold climates. They must move to an area that has warmer weather and a supply of the right kind of food for them. The forest provides homes for birds in the branches or the cavities of dead or living trees. Trees also protect birds from their enemies by giving birds a good place to hide. Food is abundant in the forest. There birds find insects, seeds, berries, and nuts. Many birds that live in the forest are brightly colored. As you observe the different species of birds, notice how their Creator designed them to live in the habitat, or special place, for which they were created.

Birds 117

The cheerful chickadee

On a cold winter day, a flock of friendly chickadees will probably be the first birds to appear at your feeder. If you are still and patient, you might be able to get one to eat from your hand. There are seven species of chickadees in North America, each living in different parts of the continent. Others live in Europe and Asia. All of them are small, gray birds with touches of black, white, and buff. They are sparrow-sized, but their tails are long for their bodies. They are easy to identify, because they sing their name: "chickadee-dee-dee."

In the summer, pairs of chickadees head for the woods, where they nest in tree cavities and raise their young. Throughout the summer they eat large numbers of insect pests. Because chickadees can **hang upside down on the undersides of twigs,** they can find insects and their larvae that other birds have not seen. The chickadee may not be as visible in the woods as he is at your bird feeder, but when you hear "dee-dee-dee" you will know he is near.

least flycatcher

The skillful flycatcher

Darting out from a treetop or a telephone wire, a flycatcher snatches an insect in mid-air and returns to his perch to devour his prey. If he is teaching his babies to hunt insects, he will disable the insect he has caught, turn it loose, and allow the young birds to recapture it. The flycatchers that inhabit our forests are very difficult to tell apart; their song is the only sure way to distinguish them. Most are sparrow-sized grayish birds with eye rings and wing bars. One of the most common is the *least flycatcher*. You will recognize it by its call of "che-bec." It is a very

118 ■ *Understanding God's World*

friendly bird that sometimes will allow people to touch it as it sits on its nest. The *phoebe* is another very trusting flycatcher. It will nest near homes. Because it calls its own name and has a habit of bobbing its tail, it is easy to recognize. Another common flycatcher is the *kingbird*. You will find this bird in the open country. If you see a small grayish bird attacking a crow or a hawk, you are watching a kingbird protecting its nest. The handsome *scissor-tailed flycatcher* is the state bird of Oklahoma.

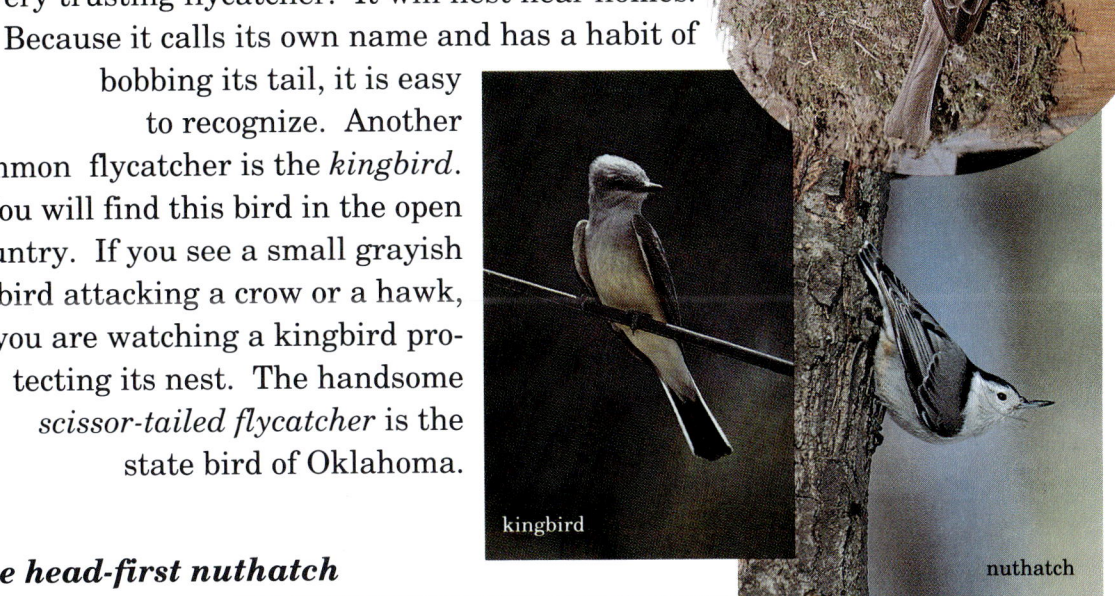

The head-first nuthatch

As you walk quietly through the woods on a chilly winter day, you are astonished to find two chubby, bluish-gray birds walking down a tree trunk, head first. The nuthatch is the only bird that does this successfully. Nuthatches are sparrow-sized birds with short tails, stubby wings, beady black eyes, and long, slender bills. Although they are famous for coming head first down the tree trunk, they can move in any direction. You may spot them crawling among the branches searching for insects. They are so agile that they can catch a falling nut in mid-air or race down the tree trunk to snatch the nut before it hits ground. They like to hoard nuts and seeds under the loose bark of trees. *Red-breasted and white-breasted nuthatches are the two most common kinds.* The red-breasted nuthatch is a small, busy, chattering bird. The slightly larger white-breasted nuthatch is more likely to visit your bird feeder. Watch him select a sunflower seed, take it to a nearby tree, wedge it into the bark, chop it to pieces, and eat it. Like the chickadee, the nuthatch can be trained to eat from your hand if you are quiet and patient.

Comprehension Check 4.6
1. List three reasons why the forest is a good habitat for birds.
2. How does a flycatcher get its food?
3. Name two birds that search among tree branches for insects and insect larvae.

Birds

4.7 Designer Birds

The woodpecker: designed to be a living hammer

"Rat-tat-tat, rat-tat-tat"—a woodpecker hammers away at his favorite tree. He may be sending a signal to any other woodpecker close by that this is his territory. He may be carving out a hole for his nest. Or he may be busily working for his dinner. Woodpeckers are uniquely designed to live on trees. They can be as small as the six-inch downy woodpecker or as large as the nineteen-inch pileated woodpecker. The state bird of Alabama, the yellowhammer, or yellow-shafted flicker, is a member of the woodpecker family. All woodpeckers have sharp, pointed bills to bore holes in trees, strong claws to hang on to the bark, and stiff tails to prop themselves up as they climb.

Head and neck. The woodpecker's head is especially designed for his job as a living hammer. Because his skull is extra thick and almost as hard as concrete, it can withstand the pounding that would injure the skull of another bird. Extremely strong neck muscles also help support the woodpecker's head.

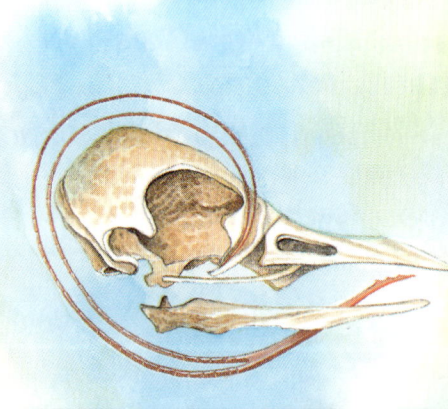

Tongue. The woodpecker's tongue is three to five times longer than the tongue of any other bird. How does such a long tongue fit inside his head? It begins at the right nostril, splits, wraps around the skull beneath the skin, rejoins, and comes up through the lower jaw. The tongue is also stretchy, like elastic. This special design makes it possible for the woodpecker to extend his tongue as he probes holes in the tree for insects. Different species of woodpeckers have more special features that help them get the kind of food they eat. Some have tongues with sharp, horny tips to spear insects. Others have barbs on the tip of the tongue and a sticky saliva to help them slurp up insects. Still others, those that feed mostly on tree sap, have brushlike tongue tips to lap up sap.

pileated woodpecker

Understanding God's World

Two woodpeckers that are found in almost any wooded area of Canada or the United States are the downy woodpecker and the hairy woodpecker.

downy woodpecker

10 Chickadee

summer
winter
both

The cheerful little chickadee is a welcome sight at northern bird feeders. His saucy behavior and acrobatic antics make him a favorite with many bird watchers. He is small and plump, about five inches long. He wears a black cap on his head and a black bib under his chin. His cheeks and breast are white and his back is pale gray with slightly darker tail and wings.

The black-capped chickadee lives in Alaska, Canada, and the northern half of the United States. The Carolina chickadee lives in the South.

In the winter, chickadees travel in little bands that usually include downy woodpeckers and white-breasted nuthatches. Suet, peanuts, or sunflower seeds will attract them to your back yard. In the summer, chickadees eat insect pests and weed seeds, and thus the friendly chickadee is a helpful bird.

They are almost identical in their black-and-white checked suits. The males have red head patches. The hairy woodpecker is about two inches bigger than the downy woodpecker and has a much longer bill. He stays mostly in the woods, ridding the trees of insect pests. The downy woodpecker is more friendly. He will visit your bird feeder with a troop of chickadees and nuthatches. If you approach his tree, he will hitch over to the other side and peek around to get a good look at you.

hairy woodpecker

Birds 121

Designer beaks

Different birds were designed to eat different kinds of food. God wisely gave each bird the kind of beak it would need to eat its particular food. When you are birding, notice the different styles of bird beaks. By looking at the beak, you can often tell what kind of food a bird eats.

Birds with short, hard, cone-shaped beaks usually eat seeds (1). Seed eaters use their sharp beaks and powerful muscles to crush their food. The largest family of birds, the finches, are seed eaters. Observe some of the members of this family while they are eating. Many of them will come to bird feeders. Goldfinches, grosbeaks, cardinals, and sparrows are a few of the common finches. One finch, the crossbill, has a beak especially designed to pick the seeds from pine cones.

Insect-eating birds usually have long, slender beaks (2). Some insect eaters, such as the flycatchers and the warblers, capture insects in mid-air. Others, such as the nuthatches and the creepers, use their delicate, pointed beaks to pluck insects from cracks in the bark of trees. Swifts, swallows, and whip-poor-wills are insect eaters that have wide-gaping mouths. These rapid-flying birds sweep through the air with their mouths wide open, trapping small insects.

Some birds live on nectar. Honey-creepers, sunbirds, and hummingbirds have very slender, needlelike bills which reach deep into flowers to sip their nectar (3).

Meat-eating birds, such as eagles (4) and hawks (5), have sharp, hooked beaks designed to hold their prey and to tear flesh. Herons and bitterns have long, daggerlike beaks to spear fish (6). The pelican uses its oversized bill

122 ■ Understanding God's World

Flicker

The flicker is a large, showy woodpecker. It got its official name from its cry of "flicka-flicka-flicka." You may know it by one of its many other names—yellowhammer, high-hole, yaffle, golden-winged woodpecker, or wicky-up. Can you guess why Alabamians call it the "yellowhammer"? The flicker has a sharp, chisel-like bill, a very long tongue, and a stiff tail which it uses as a prop in tree climbing.

The flicker is found all over North America, from coast to coast and from Alaska to Mexico. The yellow-shafted flicker lives east of the Rockies, the red-shafted flicker west of the Rockies, and the gilded flicker in the desert Southwest.

You will recognize the flicker by its cry and its habit of hopping across the ground. It is the only North American woodpecker that commonly searches the ground for insects.

and huge pouch to scoop up his catch (7). Other water birds, such as ducks (8) and flamingos (9), which eat small plants and animals, have special strainers in their bills to filter out water and mud.

Birds 123

Designer feet

Can you imagine a duck trying to perch like a chickadee, or a woodpecker trying to swim like a swan? Each kind of bird has the type of feet it needs in order to live the life God planned for it.

Birds that scratch the ground to find food, such as chickens and pheasants, have powerful claws with strong, blunt nails (1). Perching birds, such as robins and orioles, have toes designed to hang on to branches (2). Did you ever wonder why birds do not fall off their perch when they fall asleep? Their legs are designed to lock in place to keep the birds from falling off.

Birds designed to live in flat, open country are often better runners than fliers. God gave the roadrunner strong feet with long, flat toes to help it move quickly. The ostrich is another swift runner. Its powerful, two-toed feet are also designed for kicking its enemies (3). But birds such as swallows and hummingbirds, which are designed to spend most of their time in flight, have small, weak feet (4). How do you think large feet would affect the flight of these birds?

Swimming birds, such as ducks and geese, always have their paddles with them. Their webbed feet are perfectly designed to propel them swiftly through the water (5).

124 ■ *Understanding God's World*

⁶ Eagles, hawks, and other birds of prey have feet that are exactly right for grasping their prey (6).

Woodpeckers' feet have two toes facing forward and two toes facing back. This unique design enables the woodpecker to hold on to the bark of trees (7).

Comprehension Check 4.7

1. How are the following parts of the woodpecker's body designed to make the woodpecker a living hammer?
   a. skull   b. tongue   c. bill
2. Describe the bills of the following birds and tell what each bird eats.
   a. grosbeak   b. creeper
   c. sunbird   d. hawk
3. Why does the pheasant need powerful claws with strong nails?
4. Why does the hummingbird have small feet?
5. In two or three complete sentences, explain how the duck's bill and feet are designed for life in the water.

7

4.8 Designed for Flight

A bird's body is designed so that all parts work together to make it possible for the bird to fly. The bird's body is streamlined so that the bird can move easily through the air. Especially notice the shape of the bird's wing. It is designed so that air moves quickly over the curved upper part. The rapid movement of the air creates low air pressure above the wing. Air rushes upward to fill the low pressure area. The air rushing upward against the lower side of the wing causes the wing to lift. Airplanes work on this same principle. Men studied the design of God's creation, the bird, to understand how the principle of lift works.

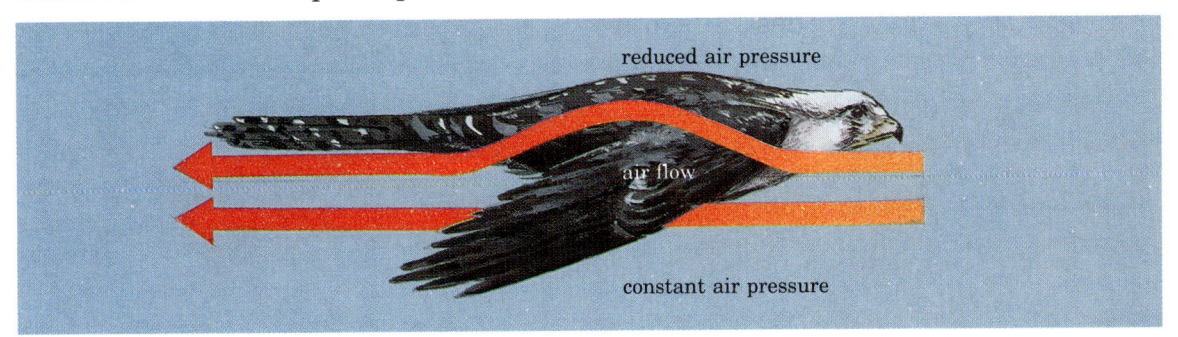

reduced air pressure

air flow

constant air pressure

Birds 125

SOMETHING TO DO   *Observing lift*

Cut a sheet of tablet paper in half lengthwise. With one hand, hold an end of the paper just below your lower lip. The other end of the paper should hang down over your hand. Blow as if you were whistling. What happens to the paper?

The stream of air flowing rapidly over the top of the paper created an area of low air pressure above the paper. The air below the paper rushed up to fill in the low pressure area. Lift, the special force of the moving air, caused the paper to rise. Lift also causes airplanes and birds to rise.

Bird bones

Most birds have hollow bones strengthened by tiny cross ribs inside. This makes the bird's body much lighter than it would be if the bones were solid and yet keeps the bones strong. Some of the hollow bones are connected by air sacs to the bird's lungs. This allows the bird to carry an extra-large air supply. The air which is stored in the bones and air sacs also helps to control the body temperature of the bird. God designed the arrangement of the bones and the air sacs in such a way that the bird's body is perfectly balanced for flight.

Our skeletons are very flexible. We have joints so that we can bend in many places. The bones of a bird, especially the spinal column and the ribs, are joined together firmly. This provides a solid foundation for the bird's wings and legs. The bones in the bird's neck, however, are very flexible. This allows the bird to move its neck freely.

Feathers

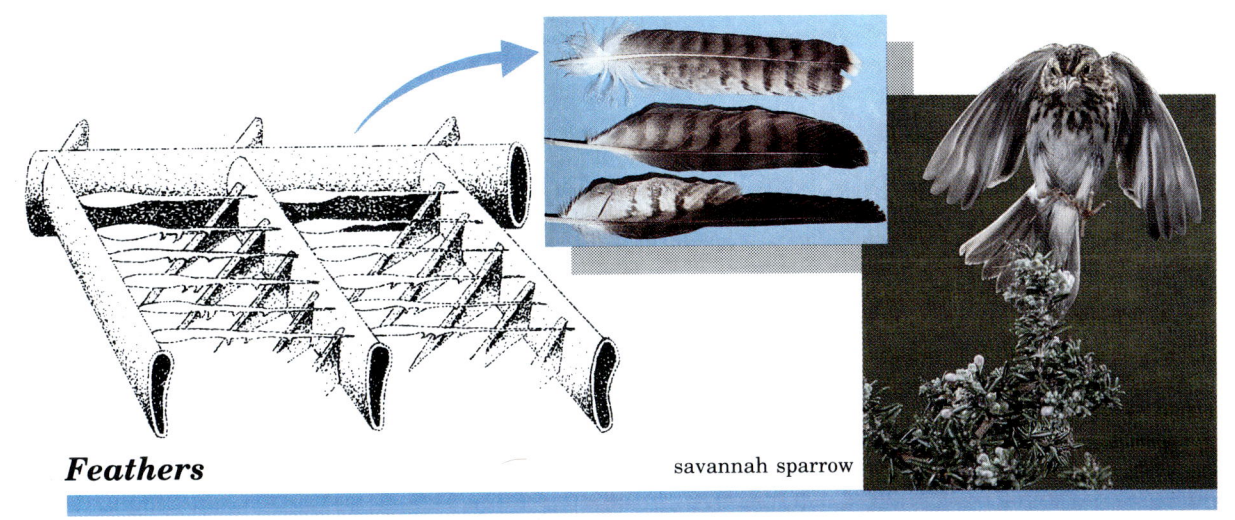

savannah sparrow

The next time you find a feather that a bird has lost, pick it up and examine it closely. You will notice that it has a stiff, hollow **quill.** Attached to the quill are soft, hairlike **barbs.** The barbs are held in place by **barbules,** which are even smaller segments that have tiny hooks to keep the barbs in place. You can "unzip" the barbs by running the feather through your fingers. Start at the tip of the feather and work toward the big end of the quill. Then smooth the barbs back in place by running the feather through your fingers in the other direction. (Be sure to wash your hands after handling feathers, because parasites that can cause diseases are often found on feathers.) A bird "zips" its ruffled feathers back together when it **preens,** or cleans its feathers.

As the bird flies, it often needs to change the position of its feathers to take advantage of air currents. It can adjust its feathers perfectly and automatically in flight because there are nerve endings in the bird's skin near the quill of every flight feather. These nerves carry messages to the bird's brain to let the bird know which feather needs to be moved. Then the brain sends a message to one of the thousands of tiny muscles on the wing, telling it which feather to move. A bird is able to move each individual feather into just the right position.

Birds are the only feathered animals. Feathers are very important, even to those birds that do not fly. The feathers work together to trap a layer of air close to the bird's skin. This layer of air **insulates** the bird, or keeps it warm even in freezing temperatures. Some birds have a layer of small, fluffy feathers called **down** underneath their body feathers for extra warmth.

You have probably heard the expression "as light as a feather." Individual feathers are very light, but if you weighed all of a bird's feathers you might be surprised by how heavy they are. A nine-pound eagle has over 1 1/4 pounds of feathers. All of the eagle's bones put together weigh less than half as much as its feathers. Maybe we should say "as light as a bird's bone!"

Birds

Why don't birds get tired?

Parts of a bird's body that you cannot see also help the bird to fly. The power for flight comes from the bird's two large breast muscles. The bird's digestive system is also designed to make flight possible. A bird is able to turn its food into energy very quickly. It takes only thirty minutes for a thrush to digest its dinner of berries. How can a bird do this so quickly? A bird does not have teeth, powerful jaws, or large intestines. It depends on its stomach to do the work. The first part of the stomach softens the food with digestive juices. The second part, or **gizzard,** has hard, ridged walls that grind up the softened food. Sometimes a bird will eat gritty material like sand to make its gizzard work more quickly. How does this help the bird to fly? Since the bird has no teeth, jaws, or large intestine, the bird's body is light. Since food does not remain in the body long, the bird does not have the extra weight of undigested food to slow it down.

Another reason birds can fly long distances without getting tired is that the same muscles that help birds fly also work to make the bird breathe. As the bird beats its wings, it is also filling and emptying its lungs. When you breathe in, you take in air; you do not take air in as you breathe out. But the bird's body is uniquely designed so that it takes in air at *both* times, breathing in and breathing out.

Seeing and hearing

Most birds do not have sharp senses of taste and smell, but the bird's senses of sight and hearing are very sensitive. In fact, a bird's sense of hearing is much sharper than that of a man. Have you ever seen a bird's ears? You can't; they are inside the bird's head. Why do you think God put them there instead of on the outside?

No other animal has a sense of sight that is as sharp as a bird's. A bird is able to focus its sight on two things at once. Birds are also able to see small objects clearly from far away. Some birds are even able to see markings on flowers that humans cannot see. These markings guide them to where the nectar is. Many birds have a transparent third eyelid. The bird is able to close this eyelid to protect its eyes from dust and wind as it flies.

Comprehension Check 4.8
1. List two reasons why birds need hollow bones.
2. Why does a bird preen its feathers?
3. Why are feathers important even to birds that cannot fly?
4. Are the muscles that give the bird power to fly located in its breast or its wings?
5. Tell two things that are unique about the bird's eyes.

SCIENCE CONCEPTS — How do a bird's feathers keep it warm?

When it is cold outside, you reach for your favorite coat or sweater to help you keep warm. Birds do not wear coats, and yet you may have seen them cheerfully hopping about on very cold days. Birds are warm-blooded, just as mammals and people are. How can they endure the cold weather?

God has provided each bird with a coat of feathers. Feathers help the bird to fly, and they also work in a marvelous way to keep the bird warm. You will remember that some materials are good conductors of heat while other materials are poor conductors of heat. Usually heat travels from warm objects to cooler ones. If much of the heat produced by the bird's body traveled into the cold, outside air, the bird would become very cold indeed. But the bird's feathers act like a blanket. The feathers trap a layer of air next to the bird's body. Since air is a poor conductor of heat, the trapped layer of air insulates the bird's body. This means that the air keeps heat from getting in or out. The heat from the bird's body is trapped by the air under the feathers, and the bird stays warm. For more warmth, the birds fluff up their feathers so they can trap more air. Some birds, especially those that live in the water, have an extra layer of small, fluffy feathers, known as **down,** underneath their outer feathers. Down provides extra insulation.

Now that you know how a bird's feathers keep it warm, can you explain why a coat or sweater keeps you warm on a cold day? How does the fur of your cat or dog protect it from the cold?

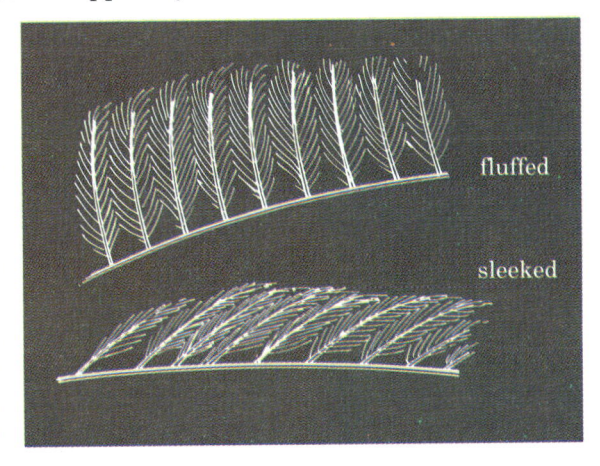

4.9 The Jack Miner Bird Sanctuary

Around the year 1900, a Canadian farmer, hunter, and trapper named Jack Miner became interested in protecting birds, especially waterfowl such as ducks and Canada geese. He decided to turn his farm into a bird sanctuary.

A bird sanctuary is an area of land which is set apart as a place where birds can live undisturbed. Birds in a sanctuary are fed, protected, and cared for. When birds are provided with a special place to live, people are able to study them in their natural surroundings. This is the best way to learn about birds and their habits. Mr. Miner began learning about birds by observing them and studying their ways. Large numbers of ducks came to his sanctuary on the northern shore of Lake Erie. Later, he made artificial ponds on his land to attract migrating Canada geese.

In 1909, Mr. Miner began banding birds. He trapped a wild black duck and placed a strip of aluminum which had his name and address stamped on it around the duck's leg. The next year, a hunter in North Carolina returned the band to him. Mr. Miner enjoyed banding birds because it enabled him to learn about the travels of migrating birds. Because he trapped and banded hundreds of ducks and geese, he was able to gather a large amount of information about their habits.

In 1914, Mr. Miner began stamping Bible verses on the blank side of the birdband, making the birds "winged missionaries." He said, "From the very first time I stamped such a verse on a band, I felt the help of God, and knew I now had my tagging system complete."

People all over the United States and Canada were helped and encouraged by Mr. Miner's use of Scripture. As the years went by, many hunters wrote to Mr. Miner, telling how their lives had been changed because of the Bible verses on his birdbands. A missionary living in the remote regions of northern Canada once came to visit Mr. Miner. He brought news of a revival that was taking place among the Indians and Eskimos in his territory because of the Bible verses on the birdbands. Mr. Miner gave the credit to the Lord: "My bird sanctuary would never have been what it is, nor gained world recognition, had I not taken God into the partnership and given Him first place."

In 1943, one year before his death, King George VI gave Jack Miner a very special honor, the Order of the British Empire.

JACK MINER'S TESTIMONY

The Lord is my Guide and Teacher, I will not get lost;

He makes my heart a receiving station for His wireless [radio];

He sits down beside me in the pathless woods and opens up His book of knowledge;

He turns the leaves very slowly that my dimmed eyes may read His meaning.

He makes the trees I plant to grow, and flowers to arch my path with their fragrant beauty; gives me dominion over the fowls of the air and they honk and sing their way to and from my home.

Yea, He has brought me up from a barefooted underprivileged boy to a man respected by millions of people, and I give Him all the credit and praise whenever, wherever and forever.

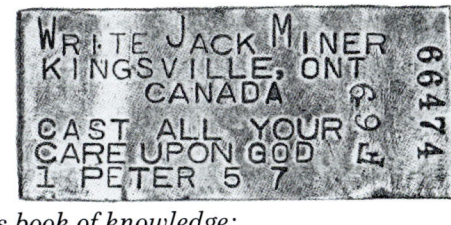

Jack Miner

Chapter Check-up

A *Match the correct definition with each term by writing the letter in the blank space.*

_____ 1. field marks

_____ 2. crest

_____ 3. quill

_____ 4. migrate

_____ 5. preen

_____ 6. down

_____ 7. gizzard

_____ 8. habitat

_____ 9. syrinx

A. to clean the feathers with the beak
B. the part of the bird's stomach that grinds up food
C. a tuft of feathers on a bird's head
D. the particular kind of area in which an animal makes its home
E. the bird's voice box
F. to spend the winter in sleep
G. to move from one place to another with the change of seasons
H. small, fluffy feathers
I. identifying marks found on birds
J. the stiff, hollow portion of the feather

B *Name one bird which:*

1. catches insects in mid-air
2. walks down the tree trunk head first
3. uses its stiff tail as a prop when it climbs
4. hangs upside down on the underside of twigs
5. mimics other birds
6. eats acorns and "plants" trees
7. eats Japanese beetles
8. holds its tail straight up
9. flies backward
10. eats fruit and earthworms

Birds 131

C Label these birds.

1.
2.
3.
4.
5.
6.
7.
8.

D Write the kind of *food* each bird would eat.

1.
2.
3.
4.
5.
6.

132 ■ *Understanding God's World*

E *What do these **feet** tell you about the habits of the birds to which they belong? Write one or two sentences describing each bird.*

1. _____

2. _____

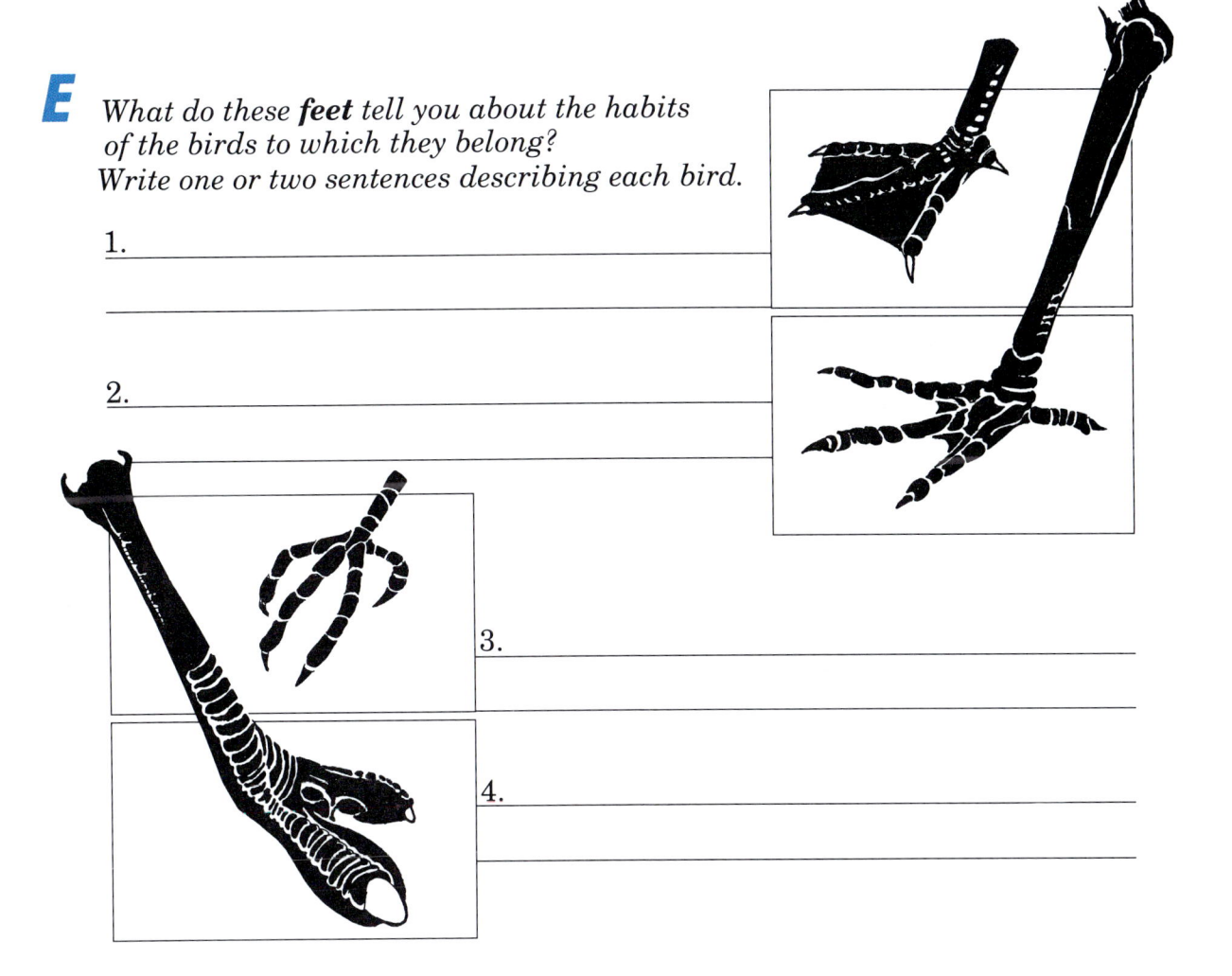

3. _____

4. _____

F *Write **true** or **false** for each statement.*

_____ 1. All the birds within a range share the same habitat.

_____ 2. Noon is the best time to look for birds.

_____ 3. Most birds cannot use hanging feeders.

_____ 4. All birds feed high off the ground.

_____ 5. Insect-eating birds will eat suet or peanut butter.

_____ 6. Metal is the best material for birdbaths.

_____ 7. All birds are able to sing.

_____ 8. A bird is able to adjust the position of each feather individually.

_____ 9. Some feathered animals are not birds.

_____ 10. Birds have better hearing and eyesight than men.

Birds 133

5 MATTER: Water, Air, and Weather

5.1 God's Gift of Water

*I would seek unto God . . .
who giveth rain upon the earth,
and sendeth waters upon the fields.* – Job 5:8a, 10

What is the oldest thing in your house? Is it books? Is it pictures? Is it furniture? No. There is something older than any of these. It is water. Water is as old as anything in the world. The second verse in the Bible, Genesis 1:2, says, *"And the earth was without form, and void; and darkness was upon the face of the deep. And the Spirit of God moved upon the face of the **waters**."*

Water everywhere

How much water is there in the world? A look at a globe or a world map will show you that **three fourths of the earth is covered by oceans, lakes, and rivers.** If all the ice in the world melted, there would be enough water to raise the level of the oceans about 300 feet.

What would happen if all the land in all the continents were pushed

134 ■ Understanding God's World

into the oceans? The land would disappear! There is enough water in the oceans to cover all land on earth more than a mile deep, if the land were all the same level and the valleys of the ocean were filled.

Water is found not only in oceans, lakes, and rivers, but also in the soil. Have you ever felt the water in the moist soil of a garden? Water also flows in underground rivers and lakes. You could dig a hole anywhere on earth, and sooner or later you would find water if you dug deep enough.

Large amounts of water are also found in the air. Scientists say that on a pleasant summer day there are about 50,000 tons of water vapor in the air above a square mile of land. Some of this water is given off by plants, which release it into the air through the thousands of pores in each of their leaves. Plants with broad leaves give off the most water. From the time it is planted until it is harvested, a crop of corn can give off enough water to cover its field eleven inches deep.

People and animals also release water into the air. Every day, each man, woman, and child throws out from the skin (as perspiration) and from the lungs (as moisture in air breathed out) an average of nearly one quart of water.

The Bible tells us that when God created the world, He divided the waters with a firmament, which is the layer of air surrounding the earth. God gathered the waters below the firmament together to make the seas. The rest of the water was above the firmament. The Bible says that during the Flood, "the windows of heaven were opened" (Genesis 7:11). At this time of great turmoil, the waters above the firmament were poured out upon the earth.

Matter 135

Clouds

When you look up into the sky, perhaps the first thing you notice is whether or not there are clouds. Clouds are made of water and air. Although most clouds look fluffy and light, a single cloud may contain from 100 to 1,000 tons of water.

How high up are the clouds? Each kind of cloud has its own range of height. The height of the clouds also depends upon the condition of the atmosphere (the layer of air surrounding the earth). The more humid the air is, the lower the clouds will be. When a cloud is so low that it is at ground level, we call it fog.

Clouds which are high in the sky are made of tiny ice crystals. Clouds which are low are made up of very tiny droplets of water. Each of these droplets is so small that it would take about one million of them to make a raindrop.

Clouds are always changing shape, because whenever warm air touches a cloud, some of the cloud evaporates. Clouds have been divided into three main groups, depending upon their shape. You should learn to recognize these shapes. Later, you will learn how they are combined to form other kinds of clouds.

Cirrus. The word *cirrus* means "curly." Cirrus clouds (1) are thin and featherlike. Because they are very high in the sky, they are *made entirely of ice crystals and air.* Cirrus clouds look hazy and delicate. Usually they appear in *dry weather,* but they often mean that *a storm is on its way*.

Cumulus. Cumulus clouds (2) are the large, puffy clouds that you often see on hot summer afternoons. They have flat bottoms and high, domed tops like heads of cauliflower. Usually cumulus clouds are bright white and appear during *fair weather,* but sometimes they become thick, heavy, and dark. Then they are called **thunderheads** because of the heavy *rain, thunder,* and *lightning* that they bring.

Stratus. Stratus clouds (3) are thick layers of clouds that look like a blanket. They are flat and often gray, and they frequently bring *drizzling rain* or *fine snow*. They are fairly low clouds. **Fog** (4) is a stratus cloud that is very close to the earth's surface.

Comprehension Check 5.1

1. How much of the earth's surface is covered with water?
2. Of what are clouds made?
3. Which kind of cloud . . .
    a. is large and puffy?
    b. is light and feathery?
    c. looks like a blanket?
    d. sometimes forms thunderheads?
    e. is called fog when it is very close to earth?
    f. is made of air and ice crystals?
    g. is often a sign of an approaching storm?
    h. usually brings light rain or snow?
    i. usually appears during fair weather?

12 Common Loon

summer
winter
both

The common loon is a large, heavy bird. It is rarely seen out of water unless it is in flight. Its feet are set so far back on its body that moving about on land is very difficult. In the water, however, the common loon is right at home. Because its bones are almost solid, it rides low in the water, sometimes almost submerged except for its head. It is able to use its wings as well as its feet when it swims after its prey. Common loons feed mostly on fish, but they also eat shellfish, frogs, and insects.

In the winter the common loon lives along the Pacific, Atlantic, and Gulf coasts. In summer it lives in lakes and rivers throughout northern North America. Its weird, yodeling wail is a familiar sound in these areas.

5.2 Water for Life

Necessary for life processes

Without water, nothing could live, because all living things must contain some amount of water in their body tissues. The kangaroo rat, which lives in the desert, is about 65% water, but the jellyfish, which lives in the sea, is about 95% water. All living things need to take in water so that their bodies can perform the processes that keep them alive.

Did you know that you are about 65% water? Your body needs to take in about 2 1/2 quarts of water each day. You get this from the water and other beverages that you drink and from the food that you eat. The driest food, baked pumpkin seeds, contains about 5% water. The food that contains the most water has a very appropriate name—watermelon! Watermelon is about 97% water.

If you do not take in enough water each day, your body cannot function as it should. Your blood uses water to help it flow throughout your body carrying nutrients and waste products. As the body loses water through the day, the blood tends to become thicker

Matter 137

and more difficult to pump. The heart must work harder to pump blood that does not have enough water. You can live for over a month without eating food, but if you went without water you would die in about a week.

Different plants and animals need different amounts of water in order to live. Some kinds of animals, such as the jellyfish, must spend their entire lives in water. Others can go for long periods of time without drinking water. The camel can live for months without taking a drink. God designed its body so that the camel can get the water it needs when it uses the fat it has stored in its body. Some animals never drink, but they still need water. The kangaroo rat gets all the water it needs from the dry seeds it eats. Scientists have found that the kangaroo rat gets two ounces of water every five weeks from its food.

Although they require different amounts of water, all animals would eventually die if they were forced to do without the water that they need. When you consider all the animals, plants, and people that there are in the world, is it any wonder that God created so much water?

Water is matter

Although water is a very common substance, it is an unusual substance. In order to understand just how unique water is, we must first understand what all of the things around us are made of.

All of the things you can see are **matter.** Matter is anything that takes up space and has weight. Your desk and your books are matter. Since your body has weight and takes up space, it is matter, also. There are some things which are real but which are not matter. God is not matter; the Bible tells us He is a Spirit (John 4:24). Love, wisdom, and truth are also real things which are not matter. None of these real things take up space or have weight. Your brain is matter, but your mind is not. Is water matter? How do you know? Tell why each of these things is or is not matter: a thought, a brick, an acorn, peace, hope.

Matter is made of molecules

All matter is made up of tiny particles called **molecules.** A molecule is the smallest piece of a substance that still has all the qualities of that substance. The smallest particle of water is a water molecule. Water molecules are very tiny. If you could line up 60 million molecules of water side by side, they would reach across the face of a penny. Do you think you could see a molecule of water?

2 hydrogen atoms
1 hydrogen molecule

2 oxygen atoms
1 oxygen molecule

2 hydrogen molecules + 1 oxygen molecule =

2 water molecules

Molecules are made of atoms

If a molecule of water is broken down into smaller particles, the particles are no longer water. The particles which make up molecules are called **atoms**. Atoms are so small that there are a million billion trillion atoms in every teaspoonful of water. A water molecule is made of hydrogen and oxygen atoms.

Every water molecule is made of two atoms of hydrogen and one atom of oxygen. **Hydrogen** and **oxygen** are gases found in the air. God has so designed the world that **when two atoms of hydrogen and one atom of oxygen join together, they make a molecule of water.** During the process of photosynthesis, a leaf uses the energy of sunlight to split water molecules into atoms of hydrogen and atoms of oxygen. The leaf uses the hydrogen to make simple sugars by combining it with carbon dioxide from the air. Sugar is made of carbon, oxygen, and hydrogen. The plant releases extra oxygen into the air, where it can be breathed by people and animals. This is all part of God's wonderful balance of nature, and there is more to it than this. Did you know that the cells of your body produce water every day? Your cells and the cells of animals have been designed to use the oxygen taken in by breathing to help you release energy from food. In the process, hydrogen atoms from food combine with oxygen from breathing to form water. Carbon and oxygen from the food are released as carbon dioxide. Both carbon dioxide and water molecules are released into the air when people and animals breathe out. Then what becomes of them?

Comprehension Check 5.2
1. What percent of your body is water?
2. How much water does your body need to take in each day?
3. What happens to your blood if you do not replace the water your body loses each day? How does this affect your heart?
4. What is matter?
5. What is a molecule?
6. What are the particles that make up a molecule called?
7. What happens to molecules of water during photosynthesis?
8. What happens to atoms of hydrogen and oxygen when your body uses food?

Matter

5.3 Water, Steam, and Ice

Karen put some ice cubes into a glass. Before she could fill the glass with water, the phone rang. Her favorite aunt was calling to wish her a happy birthday. They talked for some time, and then Karen returned to the kitchen, where she found water instead of ice in her glass.

What happened to Karen's ice cubes? When she put them in her glass, the ice cubes were solid, but by the time she came back, they were liquid. The substance in her glass did not change; it was still water, but the water had had a **change of state.** What caused the water to change from a solid to a liquid?

You will remember that water is matter, and that all matter is made up of molecules. When the ice melted, or changed from a solid to a liquid, something happened to the molecules.

solids

liquids

gases

water vapor

Water has three states

Matter can exist in three states, or forms. Matter can be a **solid,** a **liquid,** or a **gas.** Water is the only substance which exists naturally in all three states. When water is a solid, it is called *ice.* Water in its liquid state is usually just called *water.* Water is a gas when it is *water vapor.* (Hot water vapor is often called *steam.*) **Whether water is ice, liquid water, or water vapor, it is still water.** The substance of the water has not changed. Water is always made of the same kind of molecules, two hydrogen atoms and one oxygen atom. Only the state that the water is in has changed.

Solids. Many kinds of matter are found naturally as solids. Rocks are solids. What is water called when it is a solid? Solids have a definite shape and take up a certain amount of space. **Solids do not**

140 ■ *Understanding God's World*

change shape easily. Solids are very **dense.** This means that the molecules in solids are packed very close together. Molecules in solids do not move quickly, but they do **vibrate** (move back and forth). It may surprise you to learn this. When you look at a piece of ice, your desk, or some other solid, you do not see it vibrate. The molecules are so small and vibrate so rapidly that you cannot see or feel any movement.

Liquids. When matter has no shape of its own and yet it takes up a certain amount of space, the matter is a liquid. Vegetable oil, orange juice, and milk are examples of liquids. When you think of water, you probably picture it in its liquid state. Liquids change shape easily. You have probably noticed that **a liquid takes the shape of any container it is put into.** Unlike ice, water changes its shape to fit its container. Liquids are not as dense as solids are. The molecules of liquids are spread farther apart than the molecules of solids. Molecules in liquids vibrate far more rapidly than molecules of solids do. Molecules of liquids vibrate *and* travel around within the liquid.

Gases. Matter that **has no shape** and does not fill up a certain amount of space is a gas. Many gases are colorless. Air is a mixture of gases. Water in its gaseous form is found in the air. Do you remember what water is called when it is a gas? Water vapor is invisible. You have probably seen clouds of very hot water vapor, or steam, above a boiling kettle. You did not actually see the water vapor. You saw extremely tiny drops of liquid water carried along in the steam.

Gas has the lowest density of the three states of matter. **Molecules in gases are far apart and are the fastest moving molecules.** They whiz around and bump into each other all of the time.

Amazing water

Because of the way molecules of water fit together, water is able to do some amazing things.

The molecules in liquid water stick together far more readily than the molecules of many other liquids do. This quality is called **surface tension.** Because water has such a high degree of surface tension, objects which are heavier than water will float on the surface unless the surface film of the water is broken.

Water is able to dissolve many substances. When a solid substance is dissolved, its molecules become part of the liquid which is dissolving it. Water is able to dissolve large amounts of substances. God gave water this special ability so that water can carry the nutrients which plants, animals, and people need.

Matter 141

SOMETHING TO DO
Observing surface tension and dissolving substances

Surface tension. *You will need a bowl of water, a small piece of window screen, an eyedropper, and some liquid detergent.* Carefully place the screen flat on the surface of the water. Surface tension will keep the screen afloat, even though the screen is heavier than the water. Try placing a cork on top of the screen. Both the screen and the cork will float if you do this demonstration carefully and do not break the surface of the water. Now, with the eyedropper, add a drop of the liquid detergent near your "raft." What happens? Why?

Dissolving substances. *You will need two large glasses, a measuring cup, a spoon, and twelve sugar cubes.* Fill both glasses with equal amounts of water. (Use the measuring cup to make sure.) Add the sugar cubes, one at a time, to only one of the glasses of water. Stir the water after adding each cube. When all of the cubes have been dissolved, notice the levels of water in both glasses. The levels will be almost the same, even though you added several cubes of sugar to one glass, because the water dissolved the sugar completely. How does this work? There are empty spaces too small for you to see between the molecules of water. When the water dissolved the sugar, or broke it down into molecules, the molecules of sugar fit into the empty spaces between the molecules of water.

Comprehension Check 5.3
1. In what three states does matter exist? Give an example of each.
2. Are ice, water, and steam different substances? Why or why not?
3. Which state of matter . . .
   a. has no shape and does not fill up a fixed amount of space?
   b. has a definite shape and fills up a fixed amount of space?
   c. has no shape of its own but fills up a fixed amount of space?
4. List the states of matter according to the speeds of their molecules, from fastest to slowest.

5.4 Water Changes State

Water's melting point

Molecules of solids are packed tightly together and vibrate very slowly. In most solids, the molecules have a strong attraction for each other. This means that they will stay close to each other and hold together.

Understanding God's World

When solids are heated, the molecules begin to vibrate more rapidly. If they vibrate fast enough, the attraction between molecules is not enough to hold them together as a solid. The solid can melt and become a liquid. The molecules have not changed, but their motion has overcome the attraction that holds them together.

Not all solids melt, and solids that do melt do not all melt at the same temperature. The ice cubes in Karen's glass melted at room temperature, but the glass itself did not melt. The temperature at which a solid changes to a liquid is its **melting point.** The melting point of water is **32°F.**

Water's boiling point

Just as heat can cause a solid to turn into a liquid, so heat can cause a liquid to change into a gas. Increased heat causes the molecules to move faster, and finally the attraction between the molecules is not enough to hold them together as a liquid. The molecules break apart, and the liquid becomes a gas. The temperature at which a liquid changes to a gas is its **boiling point.** The boiling point of water is **212°F.**

Liquids also become gases through the process of evaporation. We will discuss evaporation later in this chapter.

Unique water

Because of the way its molecules are made, water does not behave as other liquids do when it changes state.

Most substances **expand,** or get bigger, when they are heated and **contract,** or get smaller, when they become colder. This is true of solids, liquids, and gases. It is true of water at most temperatures.

The temperature at which liquid water changes to a solid is 32°F. This is called the **freezing point** of water. Did you notice that water's freezing point and melting point are the same? When water is at 32°F, some of its molecules are solid and some are liquid.

Just before water gets cold enough to freeze, a strange thing happens. At 39°F, water begins to expand and become less dense as it gets colder. Water that is colder than 32°F has completely changed to a solid, ice. Ice is larger and less dense than the same amount of liquid water. This is what causes ice to float. If water behaved as other liquids do, ice would be smaller and denser than an equal amount of liquid water, and it would sink.

Matter 143

Why does this happen? Scientists have not discovered exactly why, but if you think for a minute, you can see that it is a good plan.

Think of a very cold winter day. The water on top of a pond will freeze. If water acted like other liquids, the ice would contract, become denser, and sink to the bottom of the pond.

More and more ice would form and sink. Soon the pond would be solid ice. What would become of the fish and plants in the pond? What if the same thing happened in lakes, rivers, and oceans?

Instead of contracting and sinking, ice expands and floats. Ice on top of a pond or lake helps protect water plants and fish during very cold weather. They live securely beneath the ice until it melts in warmer weather.

Because water expands when it reaches the freezing point, water life continues. You can see that this is a good plan. Who do you suppose thought of that plan? Could it have happened by accident?

> **Comprehension Check 5.4**
> 1. Describe the action of molecules in a solid.
> 2. What causes molecules to move more rapidly?
> 3. What happens when the motion of the molecules in a solid or a liquid becomes stronger than the attraction of the molecules to each other?
> 4. What is water's melting point? Boiling point?
> 5. What happens to most liquids when they become colder? What happens to water?
> 6. Why is this unusual characteristic of water important?

5.5 Water's Energy

One day when Ben and his father were fishing, they came to a spot in the stream where the water rushed quickly along. Ben could feel the force of the stream as he waded in. Farther downstream was a dam. Here the water stopped flowing and formed a deep pool. Would it surprise you to discover that both the swiftly flowing stream and the still, quiet pool contain energy?

What is energy?

If something has energy, it is able to do work. Thus **energy is the ability to do work.** Scientists say that **work is done when an object is moved.** Are you doing any work right now? If you are sitting at your desk, holding your book, and reading silently, you are not doing any work in the way scientists use the term. Your mind is very busy, but it is not moving. If you hold your book up long enough, your arms might get tired, but you are not

144 ■ *Understanding God's World*

doing any work unless you move the book or turn the page. If you close your book and put it away, then you have done work.

What is force?

Have you ever tried to lift a very heavy box? As you pushed and pulled and struggled, you probably thought that you were working very hard. But if you were unable to move the box, you did not do any work. You did not exert (put forth) enough force to move the box. **Force** is a push or a pull on an object.

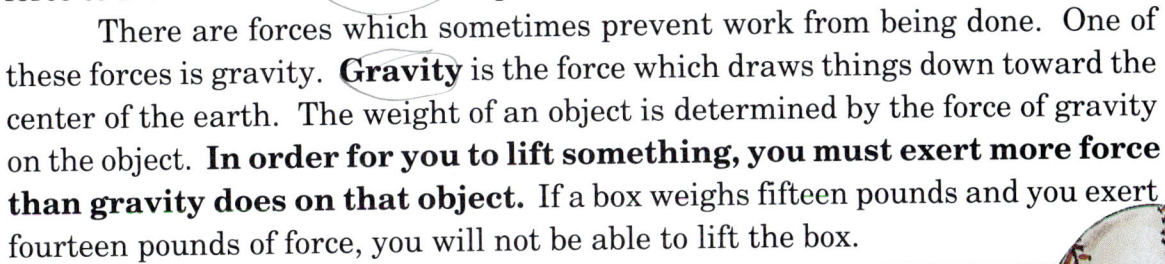

There are forces which sometimes prevent work from being done. One of these forces is gravity. **Gravity** is the force which draws things down toward the center of the earth. The weight of an object is determined by the force of gravity on the object. **In order for you to lift something, you must exert more force than gravity does on that object.** If a box weighs fifteen pounds and you exert fourteen pounds of force, you will not be able to lift the box.

Two kinds of energy

The water in the stream that rushed by Ben was moving, and all moving things have energy. A baseball zooming out to center field is full of energy, because it is moving.

Some objects which are not moving have the potential of moving. They have energy stored in them. The energy in these objects is ready to be used. This kind of energy is called **potential energy.** If you stretch a rubber band, it is full of stored energy, or potential energy. However, as soon as you let the rubber band go, its stored energy becomes **moving energy.**

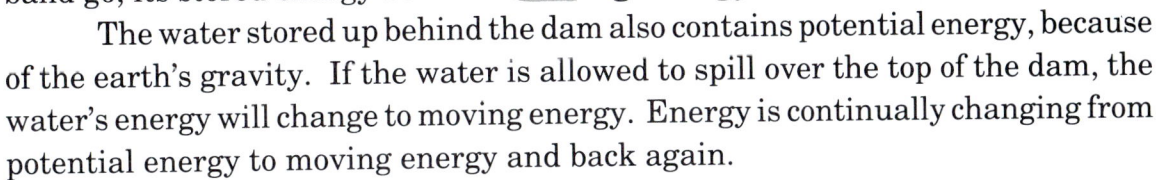

The water stored up behind the dam also contains potential energy, because of the earth's gravity. If the water is allowed to spill over the top of the dam, the water's energy will change to moving energy. Energy is continually changing from potential energy to moving energy and back again.

Matter 145

Using the energy of water

Long ago, people found that they could use water's energy to get things done. Water wheels have been used to run machinery since the time of the ancient Egyptians. The energy of moving water turns a wheel. Energy is passed along from the water to the wheel, to the axle, and finally to a machine. The water's energy causes the machine to do work. Water wheels were once used to run a machine which ground grain into flour. Today, water wheels are sometimes used in small power plants to generate electricity.

Steam is also full of energy. You will remember that when water is heated, its molecules increase in speed and spread farther apart. Heat supplies energy to the water. Steam expands to take up more space than the water it came from. One quart of water can produce 1,700 quarts of steam! If the steam is not given room in which to expand, it presses against the sides of its container with a great deal of force. When steam energy is used to do work, the steam is allowed to escape through a very small opening. As the steam escapes from its container, its energy turns a wheel which transfers the energy to a machine. Steam power was once used to run railroad locomotives, steamships, and machines for weaving cloth. Today steam power is widely used to run generators which produce electricity.

SOMETHING TO DO

To observe how a water wheel works, try the following demonstration. *You will need an old foil pie plate, scissors, and a six-sided pencil.*

Cut the rim off the pie plate. Then cut one-inch long slits around the edge of the pie plate. Be sure to space the slits evenly. Fold each of the sections to make the blades of the water wheel. (See the picture.) Make a hole in the center of the pie plate and insert the pencil. Holding each end of the pencil, place your water wheel under a stream of water running from a faucet. Notice how the falling water hits the ends of the blades and turns the wheel.

Comprehension Check 5.5
1. The ability to do work is ___?___.
2. Work is done when an object has been ___?___.
3. The force which draws things down toward the center of the earth is ___?___.
4. Potential energy is ___?___ energy.
5. The energy in steam comes from ___?___.
6. The energy in water flowing over a dam comes from ___?___.

146 ■ Understanding God's World

5.6 The Atmosphere: An Ocean of Air

13 California Gull

summer
winter
both

The California gull is most famous for saving the lives of the early settlers of Utah. In 1848, swarms of grasshoppers were destroying the crops, causing famine. Flocks of California gulls suddenly appeared and devoured the grasshoppers, saving the crop and the settlers.

Gulls are large birds with long wings and heavy bills. They are known for their shrill voices. The California gull is about 22 inches long. The adult is white with a mantle, or back and upper wings, of medium gray. The tips of its wings are black, spotted with white.

The California gull is found from the northern prairie provinces of Canada, south to northwestern Wyoming and Utah, and west to northeastern California. It winters on the coast and migrates inland during the spring, where it nests in large colonies on islets in fresh or salt lakes.

One of the most important substances on earth is the invisible blanket of air which completely surrounds us. Air is a mixture of colorless, odorless, tasteless gases. You cannot see, smell, taste, or pick up a piece of air, but air is there. You can feel air when it moves. You can see and hear some of the effects of moving air, such as leaves rustling in the trees or seeds being scattered by the wind. There is no place on the surface of the earth that is without air.

The air surrounding the earth is called the **atmosphere.** No other planet has an atmosphere which can support life the way the earth's atmosphere can. People, plants, and animals depend on air in order to live. There are only a very few living things which do not need air. You can live for weeks without food and for days without water, but you cannot live for more than a few minutes without air.

The gases in air

nitrogen
oxygen
other gases

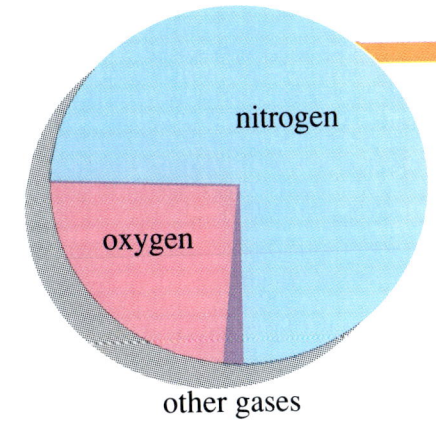

Air is made up of several different gases. The atoms of these gases do not combine to form a molecule of air in the same way that atoms of hydrogen and oxygen combine to form a molecule of water. Instead, they remain separate substances.

About 21% of air is **oxygen.** People and animals need oxygen to breathe and to create energy. Plants need oxygen in order to use the food they have stored.

Matter 147

Another gas, **nitrogen,** makes up most of the air. Air is about 78% nitrogen. Nitrogen from the air also goes into the soil, where the bacteria on the roots of certain kinds of plants turns it into nitrates. Plants need nitrates in the soil in order to produce food.

Very small amounts of other gases make up the remaining 1% of the air. One of those gases is **carbon dioxide,** which is needed by plants. Do you remember what the process is called in which plants use carbon dioxide, sunlight, water, and minerals to make sugars?

Dust, water vapor, and ice particles are also found in the air, but scientists do not consider these things to be a part of the air.

Besides the gases which we need in order to live, air also provides protection. The atmosphere shields us from the sun's tremendous heat and from certain rays of the sun which are deadly. The atmosphere also prevents the earth from becoming too cold at night. Air stores up heat during the day and releases this trapped heat slowly at night. This helps to keep the earth's temperature about the same at all times.

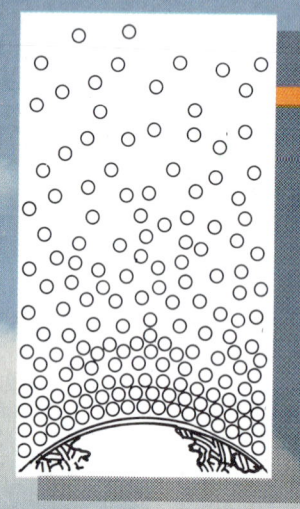

Layers of air

The air surrounding the earth (the atmosphere) goes up to about 1,000 miles above the earth. Earth's gravity holds the atmosphere in its place and keeps air from floating off into outer space. Because of the force of gravity, the air closest to the earth is the densest air. This means that the molecules of air close to the earth's surface are packed together more closely than the molecules of air high above the earth. The higher up into the atmosphere you go, the thinner the air becomes, because the molecules are spread farther and farther apart.

It is part of God's wise plan that the densest air is closest to earth. If you traveled up even six miles above sea level, you would suffocate in a few minutes, because the air up there is less dense. The molecules of oxygen are too far apart, and you would not get enough oxygen to breathe.

Air in other places

Although most of the earth's air is in the atmosphere, some air is mixed in the earth's soil. If you have ever tended a garden, you know that if there is not enough air in the soil, the soil becomes packed together too closely, and the plants will not grow properly. Earthworms are a gardener's friends because they plow through the soil, leaving holes for the air.

Air is also dissolved in water. Plants and animals which must live in water all the time are especially designed to take air from the water. If you allow a glass of water to stand at room temperature overnight, you will be able to see little bubbles of air in the water the next morning.

> **Comprehension Check 5.6**
> 1. What is the layer of air surrounding the earth called?
> 2. In which of the three states of matter does air exist naturally?
> 3. Which of the gases in air is the most plentiful?
> 4. Why is oxygen important for people, animals, and plants?
> 5. Which gas do plants take from the air in order to make food?
> 6. What keeps the blanket of air around the earth?
> 7. Besides the atmosphere, where would you find air?

SCIENCE CONCEPTS
Why is the sky blue?

If air is made up of colorless gases, how is it that the sky looks blue? The sky appears to be blue because of the way light behaves when it passes through the molecules of gases in the air.

Sunlight appears to us to be white, but it is actually made up of waves of different colors of light. If you have ever seen a rainbow, then you have seen sunlight broken down into its different colors. Light travels through the atmosphere in waves. Each color of light travels in a wave of a different length. Blue and violet have the shortest wavelengths. The molecules of gas in the air bend the shorter wavelengths more than the longer wavelengths. Waves of blue light are scattered throughout the air. The sky appears to be blue because we see waves of blue light in all parts of the sky.

5.7 Air's Weight and Pressure

For He looketh to the ends of the earth, and seeth under the whole heaven; to make the weight for the winds; and He weigheth the waters by measure.
— Job 28:24–25

Air has weight

You have probably heard the expression "as light as air." You may have thought that air does not weigh anything; after all, air does not feel heavy. But air does have weight. A cubic foot of air weighs just about one ounce. It would be impossible for you to measure air by itself, but you and a friend can try the demonstration on page 150, which shows that air does have weight. The Bible talked about "the weight of the winds" long before scientists learned that air has weight (Job 28:25). Since air has weight and takes up space, air is matter.

Matter

SOMETHING TO DO *The weight of air*

You will need two balloons, a wire clothes hanger, a pin, and two pieces of string which are the same length. Blow up the balloons. What are you filling the balloons with? When both balloons are the same size, you will have filled them with equal amounts of air. Tie the balloons so that the air cannot escape. Tie a string to each balloon, and then tie the other end of each string to opposite corners of the hanger. Hook the hanger over one finger and extend your arm out straight. Wait for the balloons to balance each other. Now have your friend pop one of the balloons with the pin. What happens?

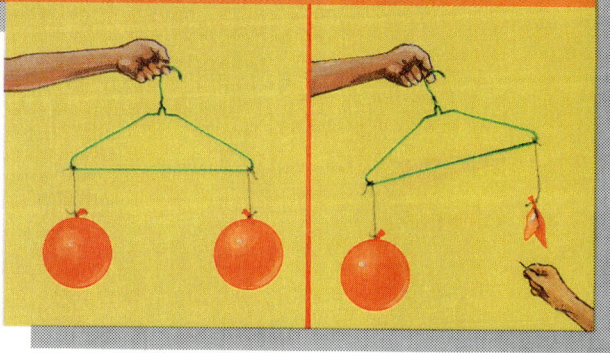

When the balloon popped, it lost all of its air. Now you have one balloon full of air and one empty balloon tied to the hanger. Is the hanger still balanced? The end of the hanger with the full balloon is lower than the end with the empty balloon because the air inside the balloon has weight. This amount of air is far lighter than the same amount of a liquid or a solid, but it does have some weight.

Air has pressure

Because air has weight, it creates pressure. Pressure is the measurement of the force that matter exerts over a certain amount of area. Solids exert pressure. If you have ever pressed flowers, you have used the pressure of solid books to flatten out the flowers. Liquids exert pressure, too. You can feel the force of water pressure if you put your hand over the end of a garden hose when it is turned on. Gases also exert pressure. You may want to try the demonstration at the left in order to observe air pressure.

SOMETHING TO DO *Observing air pressure*

You will need a glass, a flat piece of cardboard, and some water. (You should do this demonstration outside or over a sink or a bucket in case anything goes wrong.) Fill the glass with water. Run water over the cardboard so that it is wet, and put the cardboard on top of the glass. Hold the cardboard in place as you turn the glass upside down very carefully. Remove your hand from the cardboard. The cardboard will remain over the end of the glass, keeping the water in, because air pressure holds the cardboard in place.

150 Understanding God's World

Air pressure changes

Do you remember how far up the atmosphere extends? Every bit of that air, which goes up for about 1,000 miles, has weight. The weight of all the air in the atmosphere creates pressure as it presses down. Air pressure is greatest close to the surface of the earth. As you go up higher into the atmosphere, air pressure gradually decreases (becomes less). This happens because there is less air above to press down. Air pressure on earth varies. If you are on top of a high mountain, air pressure is less than if you are at sea level. Air pressure at sea level is about 15 pounds per square inch.

Right now, about one ton of air is pressing down on you. How is it that you do not feel that ton of air? Since air is exerting upon you the same amount of pressure on all sides, you do not feel that pressure. If you have ever flown in an airplane, you may have experienced what it feels like when air pressure becomes unequal. When the airplane gets to a certain height, you can feel the air inside you pressing against your eardrums. When your ears "pop," the pressure has suddenly become equal on both sides of the eardrum.

You can observe how a change of air pressure affects liquids by watching what happens when you drink through a straw. The straw that you put into a glass of liquid looks empty, but it is full of air until some other substance fills it. When you put the straw into the glass of liquid, the liquid forces out some of the air and fills the straw to the same level as the liquid fills the glass. When you suck on the straw, you remove the rest of the air that is inside the straw. Air pressure inside the straw becomes less than the air pressure outside the straw. The straw works because the air outside the straw presses down on the liquid and forces it up the straw. If you put a straw in a container which was completely airtight except for the opening made by the straw, the straw would not work, because the air pressure on the liquid would not be changed.

Comprehension Check 5.7
Answer each statement *true* or *false*.
1. Air is matter.
2. Air weighs less than an equal amount of a solid or a liquid.
3. Although solids exert pressure, liquids and gases do not.
4. Air pressure at the top of a high mountain is equal to air pressure at sea level.
5. You do not feel air pressing down on you because pressure on all sides of you is equal.

5.8 Wind: Moving Air

The wind goeth toward the south, and turneth about unto the north; it whirleth about continually, and the wind returneth again according to his circuits.
—Ecclesiastes 1:6

Air has temperature

Have you ever noticed that the earth and water become warmer during the day than the air surrounding us? Since the atmosphere is closer to the sun, it seems as though air should receive heat from the sun first. However, this does not happen. The sun heats the earth and water directly, but it warms the air very little. Why is this so?

Air is clear, or **transparent.** Things that are transparent allow light to pass straight through to the other side. Very little of the light's energy is absorbed by the transparent object. Heat and light from the sun pass straight through the air to the earth and the water. The earth and water absorb the sun's energy and are heated.

But we know that the air has warmth. How is air heated? You will remember that the molecules of matter are always moving. Molecules of gases move faster than molecules of solids or liquids. Molecules in the air move very rapidly. They bump into the earth, and some of the heat passes from the molecules of the earth to the molecules in the air.

Temperature and pressure cause wind

Because the earth is tilted, the surface of the earth is not heated evenly by the sun. The part of the earth closest to the sun receives the most heat. The air above this part of the earth becomes warmer than the air in other places.

When air is heated, its molecules spread out. As warm air expands, it becomes less dense than cool air. **Warm air rises** because it is less dense. When warm air rises, it leaves an area of low pressure near the earth's surface. Cooler, denser air flows into the low pressure spot to replace the warm air

152 ■ *Understanding God's World*

that rose. As air continually heats and rises, cooler air continually flows in to take the place left by warmed air. This constant motion of the air is what causes wind.

The importance of wind

There are many things that we enjoy doing which would be impossible without the wind. Can you imagine trying to fly a kite or sail a boat without the wind?

If the wind stopped blowing, the effects would be far more serious than not being able to fly a kite. If the air did not circulate (move around), the hot parts of the earth would become hotter and hotter until no one could bear to live there. The cold places of the earth would become colder and colder. Because air does circulate, winds flow around the earth and help even out the earth's temperature.

The wind performs many useful jobs. Some plants depend on the wind to pollinate them. The wind lets us know of changing weather. In some parts of the world, warm, dry winds form over mountain ranges. These winds are sometimes called "snow eaters," because they evaporate snow. These winds help to prevent the flooding which would occur if all of the snow melted in the usual way and ran down the mountainsides.

Although wind is beneficial in many ways, it can also do damage. Winds spread forest fires and cause sandstorms. Wind causes soil erosion. (Erosion is the wearing away of soil by wind or water.) Since air is not as dense as water, the wind cannot carry away large pieces of earth as quickly as water can, but over a period of time erosion by the wind can cause great damage to the soil.

The wind's energy

The wind's energy can be used to do work for man. If you have ever hung out wet clothes on a windy day, you have used the wind to help dry the clothes. Long ago, men used the wind's energy to sail large ships across the ocean. Today people still enjoy sailing for pleasure.

Several hundred years ago, people discovered that windmills could use the wind's energy to provide power for machines. A windmill works when a wheel driven by the wind turns a shaft. The shaft is connected to a machine that does the work. Since

Matter 153

the wind does not always blow at a constant speed, windmills cannot be used if a steady supply of power is needed. Windmills are used today in some places to grind grain, to pump water into storage tanks, and to generate electrical power which will be stored until needed.

SOMETHING TO DO — *The power of moving air*

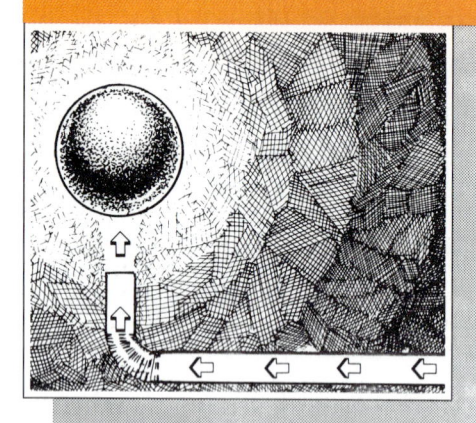

To observe the energy of moving air, try the following demonstration. *You will need a jointed plastic straw and a ping pong ball.*

Bend the straw into an L-shape with the short end straight up. Place the long end in your mouth. Begin blowing a steady stream of air and gently place the ping pong ball just above the short end. What happens to the ball? The moving air beneath the ball has raised the ball up in the air. The ball will remain in place as long as you continue to blow steadily, because the molecules of air around it are moving quickly.

Comprehension Check 5.8
1. How is the air warmed?
2. Why is it that not every place on earth receives the same amount of heat?
3. How does uneven heating of the earth cause wind?
4. List three helpful things the wind does.
5. List three harmful effects of the wind.
6. Why would you not want to depend on wind power for all of the electricity you need?

5.9 Water in the Air

All the rivers run into the sea; yet the sea is not full; unto the place from whence the rivers come, thither they return again.

Ecclesiastes 1:7

The water cycle

There is always water in the air. You will remember that although scientists do not consider water vapor to be a part of air itself, there is no air which does not contain some water vapor.

The earth and its atmosphere are constantly exchanging water. As water moves from the earth to the air and back again, it changes from a liquid to a solid or a gas. This process is called the **water cycle.** The water cycle is part of God's plan for keeping the earth supplied with water.

154 ■ Understanding God's World

14 Lark Bunting

Because of the water cycle, we are able to use over and over again the water that God made when He created the world. The raindrops that fell on you the last time it rained may be made up of water that has existed for thousands of years. That same water has probably fallen as raindrops many times before. The rain falls into the rivers, and the rivers flow into the sea, and yet the sea never overflows because of the way the water cycle works.

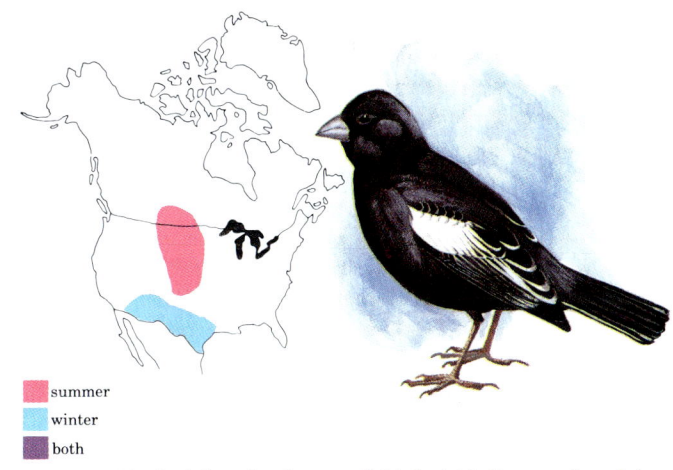

■ summer
■ winter
■ both

The lark bunting is a small bird which lives on dry plains and prairies. It is about six inches long, slightly larger than the house sparrow. Lark buntings are seedeaters with sharp, pointed bills. Their strong cone-shaped bills enable them to crush seeds easily. The lark bunting is a sociable bird, preferring to live in flocks.

The spring plumage of the male lark bunting is very striking. He is all black with white wing patches. Females, immature birds, and males in the winter all look alike. They are light brown streaked with darker brown above and white below.

The summer home of the lark bunting is on the western plains, from southern Canada through the west-central United States. In the winter, the lark bunting migrates southward, where it makes its home in the American Southwest and in Mexico.

Humidity

Water can be in the air as a solid, a liquid, or a gas. We can see solid water (ice or snow) or liquid water (rain or fog) when it is present in the air around us. But water in the gaseous form, or water vapor, is invisible.

The amount of water vapor, or **humidity,** in the air is changeable. If the air has high humidity, there is a lot of water vapor in the air. The temperature of the air affects humidity. ***Warm air is able to hold more water vapor than cool air.*** When we talk about the water in the air, we use the term **relative humidity** to describe the amount of water vapor in the air in relation to the temperature. If the air has a relative humidity of 100%, then the air is holding all of the water vapor that it can at that temperature.

Matter 155

Evaporation

How does water vapor get into the air? Molecules of water are always moving. When water is heated, its molecules move faster. The molecules bump into each other and bounce. Sometimes when molecules at the surface of the water are bumped by other molecules below, they are thrown out of the water. These molecules escape into the air. We say they *evaporate,* or become vapor. They are no longer a part of the liquid. The escaped molecules of water move into the spaces between the molecules of gases in the air. The water has turned into a gas, water vapor. The process by which liquid water becomes water vapor is called **evaporation.**

Energy from the sun provides the heat which causes evaporation. Water evaporates more quickly on hot days than on cool days. When we talk about the air being hot or cool, you must remember that is like saying a book is old or new. It depends upon the other book that you are comparing it with. Your school book from last year is an old book compared to the one you are using this year. But if we compared last year's school book to a book used by children in colonial times, we would say that last year's book was a new book. When we say that something is hot or cold, we are comparing that thing to something else.

SOMETHING TO DO *Evaporation and heat*

You may try the following demonstration to see that water evaporates more quickly when the air around it is warm. *You will need two saucers that are the same size.* Put a spoonful of water into each saucer. Put one saucer in a warm place and the other in a cool place. Notice how long it takes the water in each saucer to evaporate.

Comprehension Check 5.9
Answer each statement with **true** or **false.**
1. Some of the air that we breathe does not contain water vapor.
2. Water changes state as it travels from the earth to the air, over and over again.
3. Water can be in the air as a gas or a liquid but not as a solid.
4. There is always the same amount of water vapor in the air.
5. Cool air can hold more water vapor than warm air.
6. The process by which water becomes water vapor is called evaporation.
7. Heat from the sun causes evaporation.
8. Water evaporates more quickly on cool days than on hot days.

5.10 Condensation and Precipitation

Thou visitest the earth, and waterest it: thou greatly enrichest it with the river of God, which is full of water: thou preparest them corn, when thou hast so provided for it.
—Psalm 65:9

Since there is water vapor in the air at all times, what causes water vapor to change back into liquid water and fall to the earth as rain?

You will remember that warm air is able to hold more water vapor than cool air. Because water vapor is less dense than the other gases in air, warm air which is moist is also very light. The warm, moist air rises, because it is less dense than either warm, dry air or cool air. As it moves farther away from the earth's surface, the warm, moist air begins to cool. Can you explain why this happens? Since air is warmed by the earth, and not directly by the sun, the air moves away from its source of heat as it moves away from the earth.

As the air cools, something happens to the water vapor it is carrying. Because cool air cannot hold as much water vapor as warm air can, the water vapor begins to turn back into very tiny droplets of liquid water. This process is called **condensation.** The temperature at which water condenses is called the **dew point.** The dew point is not a constant temperature. It varies, depending on the relative humidity of the air.

Water does not condense easily unless it has something on which to condense. Tiny droplets of water condense on the particles of dust that are in the air. This is how clouds are formed.

As the clouds become colder, more and more water condenses. The droplets of water bump into each other and stick together to form larger drops. When the drops of water become too large and heavy to stay in the cloud, they fall to the earth as *rain.* If the temperature of the air near the earth's surface is lower than the freezing point of water, *sleet* or *snow* is formed. Under certain conditions, the water droplets become *hailstones.* Any form of water which falls from the clouds to the earth is called **precipitation.** What four forms of precipitation have been mentioned? Precipitation falls back to earth, and the water cycle continues.

Dew and frost

Have you ever gone outside early in the morning and found that the grass was wet, and yet you knew that it had not rained the night before? The moisture you found on the grass was **dew.**

Since dew does not fall from clouds in the sky, dew is not a form of precipitation.

When the sun sets, the earth and everything on the earth become cooler. The air close to the earth also begins to cool, but it does not become quite as cool as the earth, because it is absorbing the earth's heat. The air touches the slightly cooler surfaces of things on the earth, such as the grass and the leaves. Dew forms when water vapor from the air condenses and forms droplets on these cool surfaces.

Sometimes the temperature drops below 32°F, the freezing point of water. If the air comes in contact with a freezing cold surface, the water vapor in the air does not condense into dew. It changes directly from a gas to a solid. The tiny crystals of ice which are formed by frozen water vapor are known as **frost.** Have you ever seen beautiful frost pictures on your windowpane after a cold night? Even if you live in a place where it is not cold enough for frost to form outside, you may have seen frost in your refrigerator freezer.

SOMETHING TO DO
Observing condensation

To observe condensation, you will need a glass, some ice cubes, and some water. Fill the glass with the ice cubes and water. Make sure that the outside of the glass is dry. Let the glass of ice water stand in a warm room for a while. Notice what forms on the outside of the glass. Where did the droplets of water come from? Because the surface of the glass is colder than the air around it, water vapor from the air condensed and formed dew on the outside of the glass.

Comprehension Check 5.10
1. There is always water ___?___ in the air.
2. Warm, moist air is ___?___ than cool air.
3. As it rises away from the earth's surface, warm air begins to ___?___.
4. Cool air cannot hold as much ___?___ ___?___ as warm air can.
5. When water vapor in the air cools and turns into tiny droplets of liquid water, ___?___ takes place.
6. Water in the air condenses on tiny pieces of ___?___.
7. Four kinds of precipitation are ___?___, ___?___, ___?___, and ___?___.
8. Water vapor that condenses on the grass at night is called ___?___.
9. Tiny crystals of ice that are made of frozen water vapor are ___?___.

5.11 Kinds of Precipitation and Clouds

> *Hast thou entered into the treasures of the snow? or hast thou seen the treasures of the hail?*
> — Job 38:22

Precipitation

Rain is only one of the forms of precipitation. Other forms are sleet, snow, and hail.

Sleet. When falling rain or melted snow passes through a layer of very cold air, it freezes into little, hard, solid balls of ice called sleet. Sleet sometimes looks white because air has been included in the frozen pellet. Often when sleet hits the ground, it bounces. However, if it is very cold, sleet freezes to the surface of everything it touches, coating everything with ice. It sleets only during the winter.

Snow. You may have thought that snow was rain that had frozen, but snow is actually formed in a different way. Snow can form in clouds that are colder than 32°F. Water droplets in these very cold clouds sometimes remain liquid even though the temperature is below freezing. The water droplets evaporate, and the vapor freezes into tiny crystals of ice. As more vapor continues to freeze, the ice crystals join together. This forms a snowflake.

Snowflakes may be of different sizes and shapes, but they always have six sides or six points. Large flakes may be one inch in diameter and be made up of one hundred ice crystals. Much air is trapped in snowflakes as they form. This is why you must melt about ten inches of snow in order to get one inch of water.

Snow is part of God's wise provision for living things. The winter snowfall forms a blanket over the colder parts of the earth. It protects plants and animals by insulating them from the winter air. With the return of warmer temperatures in the spring, the blanket of snow melts to provide the water needed by germinating seeds.

Hail. Hail is particles of ice which fall from the sky during some thunderstorms. Most hailstorms occur during the spring. Hail begins as raindrops that pass through a very cold layer of air and freeze. Instead of falling to the ground, the ice drops are tossed back up into the clouds by a blast of air. Another layer of water covers the ice drop. It falls again through the layer of cold air, and the new layer of water freezes. This happens over and over again until finally the hailstone is too heavy to be blown back up to the cloud, and it falls to the earth.

Most hailstones are about the

size of grapes, but a hailstone can be as small as a pea or as large as a baseball. If you have the opportunity to see a hailstorm, try collecting hailstones after the storm has passed. Cut the stones in half and count the layers of ice to see how many trips up and down the hailstone took before it landed.

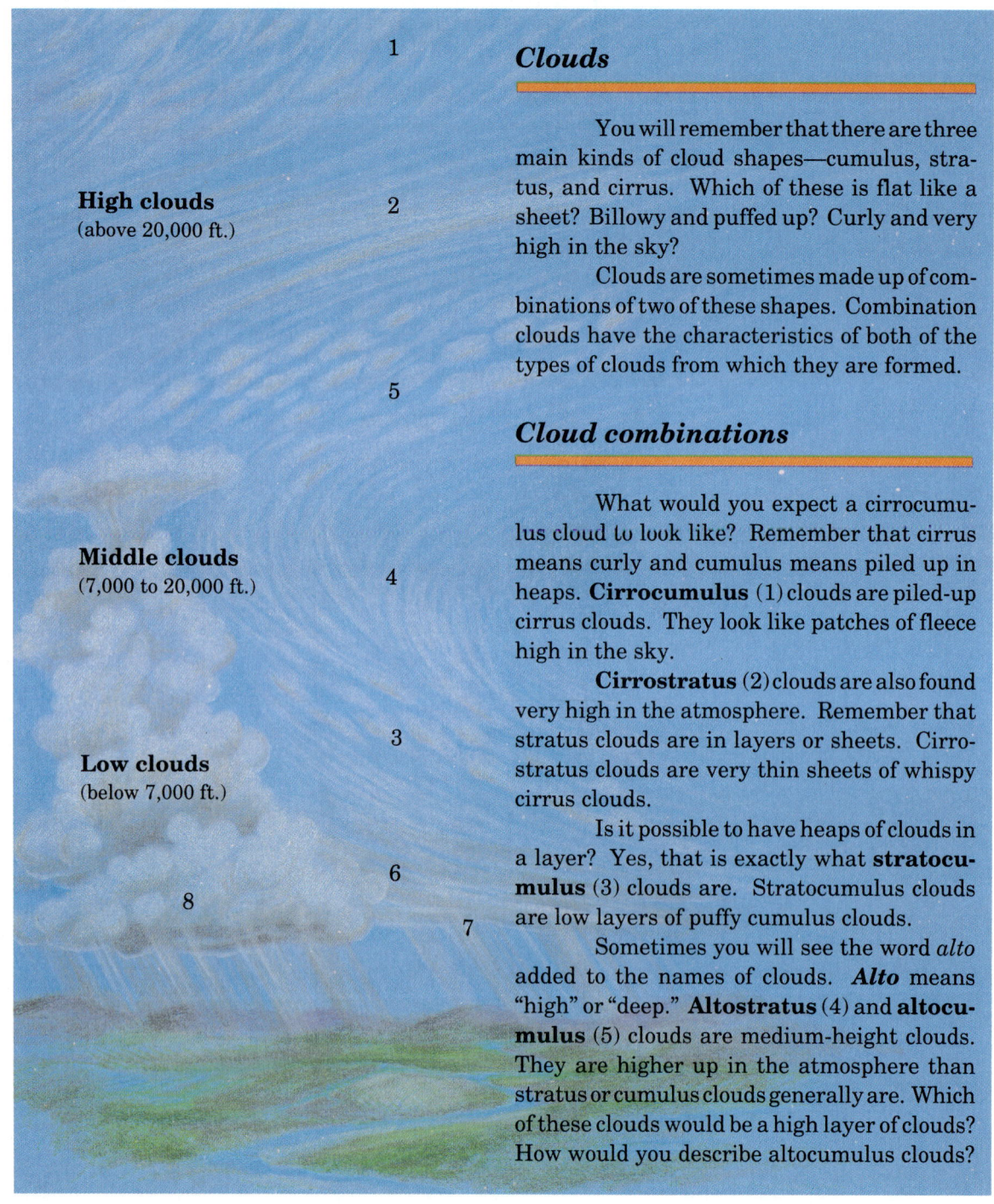

High clouds
(above 20,000 ft.)

Middle clouds
(7,000 to 20,000 ft.)

Low clouds
(below 7,000 ft.)

Clouds

You will remember that there are three main kinds of cloud shapes—cumulus, stratus, and cirrus. Which of these is flat like a sheet? Billowy and puffed up? Curly and very high in the sky?

Clouds are sometimes made up of combinations of two of these shapes. Combination clouds have the characteristics of both of the types of clouds from which they are formed.

Cloud combinations

What would you expect a cirrocumulus cloud to look like? Remember that cirrus means curly and cumulus means piled up in heaps. **Cirrocumulus** (1) clouds are piled-up cirrus clouds. They look like patches of fleece high in the sky.

Cirrostratus (2) clouds are also found very high in the atmosphere. Remember that stratus clouds are in layers or sheets. Cirrostratus clouds are very thin sheets of whispy cirrus clouds.

Is it possible to have heaps of clouds in a layer? Yes, that is exactly what **stratocumulus** (3) clouds are. Stratocumulus clouds are low layers of puffy cumulus clouds.

Sometimes you will see the word *alto* added to the names of clouds. **Alto** means "high" or "deep." **Altostratus** (4) and **altocumulus** (5) clouds are medium-height clouds. They are higher up in the atmosphere than stratus or cumulus clouds generally are. Which of these clouds would be a high layer of clouds? How would you describe altocumulus clouds?

160 ■ Understanding God's World

Storm clouds

You will also see the word *nimbus* added to the names of clouds. **Nimbus** means "rain" or "storm." **Nimbus** (6) clouds are dark clouds which bring rain. **Nimbostratus** (7) clouds are dark, gray sheets of rain clouds. They are fairly low in the sky, and they provide steady rain or snow.

Cumulonimbus (8) clouds are very tall cumulus clouds with dark undersides and towering tops. They bring quick, heavy downpours of rain. Some cumulonimbus clouds are so large that they are eight miles high from top to bottom. These very tall cumulonimbus clouds often have anvil-shaped tops made of ice crystals.

Comprehension Check 5.11

1. What do we call rain that freezes into small, hard balls of ice?
2. What are snowflakes made of?
3. How many sides or points do snowflakes have?
4. Why must you melt ten inches of snow to get one inch of water?
5. Explain how hail is formed.
6. Describe the appearance of the following clouds:
   a. cirrostratus
   b. stratocumulus
   c. cirrocumulus
7. What does *nimbus* mean?
8. Compare the rain from nimbostratus clouds to the rain from cumulonimbus clouds.

5.12 Weather Forecasting

Today's weather began in some other part of the world several days ago. By tracking the weather and observing the changes which occur as it travels, **meteorologists,** scientists who study the weather, are able to forecast, or predict, weather a few days ahead. Weather forecasting is a matter of knowing and understanding God's laws of nature about weather. Because weather is changing all the time, we cannot always forecast weather accurately even when all the facts are available, but when the proper information is available, weather can be forecast with some degree of accuracy. Meteorologists are careful to base their predictions on facts, but no one except God can know exactly how and when the weather will change. How is weather forecasting done?

Gathering information

First, information must be gathered from weather observation stations over a widespread area. Meteorologists carefully observe and measure the weather conditions of air masses. An **air mass** is a large body of air which has the same temperature and humidity. ***Most air masses in the United States and in southern Canada move from west to east.***

Matter 161

There are weather observation stations all over the world recording weather information all the time. Each hour, meteorologists measure these conditions: (1) temperature, (2) air pressure, (3) humidity, (4) precipitation, (5) wind speed.

Some weather stations send balloons into the upper atmosphere twice a day to measure weather conditions. After the information is automatically radioed back to the observation station, the balloon rises higher into the atmosphere and pops. The equipment on board the balloon parachutes back to earth. Airplane pilots also report weather by radio, and ships at sea send weather reports regularly. Weather satellites orbiting from 100 to 800 miles above the earth have television cameras which take pictures of cloud patterns and weather fronts. These pictures are especially helpful in tracking severe storms which begin over the sea. All of these methods—balloons, ships, planes, and satellites—are used by meteorologists to make accurate observations of the condition of the air.

A vast amount of weather information is collected each day. Countries around the world exchange the information they have collected.

Predicting the weather

After weather observations are gathered from many places, the meteorologists think carefully about the information. They use computers to process the information. Using computers saves time in putting all the information together. The information is used to make weather maps which forecast the results of the many observations. Weather forecasts are made by comparing the information which has been gathered that day with information on past weather. For example, if it rained six out of ten days with similar weather conditions, the meteorologist will predict that there is a 60% chance of rain. This prediction is a sensible guess. Computers which keep records of the weather for many years are a great help to meteorologists. When meteorologists have all the information about past weather, they are able to make more accurate forecasts.

There are several kinds of forecasts, depending on the information available. *Short-range forecasts* predict the weather only 18 to 36 hours in advance. Short-range forecasts are usually quite reliable because they are based on current information. Meteorologists continually update short-range forecasts. *Long-range* or *extended forecasts* predict the weather five days to a month ahead. Information given in the forecast is based on current weather observations and averages based on normal patterns of weather. Extended forecasts are not as detailed nor as accurate as short-range forecasts.

One of the most important things done by the National Weather Service is to track severe storms such as hurricanes. The meteorologists check with other stations, ships at sea, satellite readings, and radar. They try to pinpoint a storm and determine where it is heading. If a hurricane approaches an area, the people living there may be given warning to fasten down things easily moved by strong winds or to leave their homes and seek shelter in a safe place. Advance warnings of severe storms have saved many lives.

> **Comprehension Check 5.12**
> 1. What are meteorologists?
> 2. What is an air mass?
> 3. What conditions of an air mass are measured by a meteorologist?
> 4. What are two different ways meteorologists measure conditions in the upper atmosphere?
> 5. Why is a short-range forecast more reliable than an extended forecast?

5.13 Robert Boyle: Father of Chemistry

Robert Boyle was born in Ireland in 1627, the fourteenth child of the wealthy and powerful Earl of Cork. When Robert was eight, he was sent to school at Eton in England. During his four years at Eton, Robert developed a love of reading that lasted throughout his life.

When Robert was twelve, he and his tutor set off for Europe. Robert was an eager scholar; he studied Latin, French, Italian, and mathematics with his tutor, and science on his own. While he was in Switzerland, thirteen-year-old Robert accepted Christ as his Savior and decided that God was calling him to be a scientist.

Robert did not return to England until 1644. He settled on a beautiful estate which his father had given him and spent much of the next ten years reading, studying, observing nature, and writing.

While visiting his sister Katherine in London, Robert Boyle met a number of brilliant scholars who encouraged Boyle to make the study of science his life work. Although he was so wealthy that he did not need to work, Boyle chose to work as a scientist because he believed that the proper study of creation demonstrates the power and wisdom of God to the world.

Matter 163

In 1654 Boyle went to live at Oxford, England. There he met Robert Hooke, a scientist and inventor who became his assistant and friend. Together they built an air pump, a machine that can create a vacuum. Boyle and Hooke began a series of experiments that dealt with the nature and characteristics of air.

Unlike many scientists of his day, Robert Boyle believed that a scientist should do more than think of hypotheses; a scientist must conduct experiments to show whether his ideas are correct or not. During his experiments, Boyle discovered air pressure. He also found that the space which a certain amount of gas takes up is directly opposite to the amount of pressure placed upon the gas as long as the temperature stays the same. For example, if the pressure upon a gas is doubled, the gas will take up half its original space. This is known as Boyle's law.

Boyle was also the first scientist to understand that there is an element in the air which people and animals must breathe in order to live, and that the same element is necessary for burning. Today we know that he was right and that the special element is oxygen.

Boyle experimented with many substances other than air. In one experiment he proved that water expands when it freezes.

As a result of his many experiments, Robert Boyle concluded that matter consists of particles too small to be seen. Boyle called the particles *corpuscles;* today we call them *atoms.*

Boyle published his observations and conclusions in a number of books. His experiments and writings brought him great honor and fame. Today he is considered the "father of chemistry."

In 1668, Boyle returned to London, where he spent the rest of his life. Although his health was poor, he continued to supervise experiments. However, most of his time was taken up with his concern to spread the gospel to other lands. Boyle believed that God is glorified by the study of His creation, but he also knew that people must have the Scriptures to rightly know God. He spent large sums of money to have the Bible translated into a number of languages. Boyle was the chief supporter of John Eliot, missionary to the American Indians. Boyle also set money aside to pay for a series of lectures to be given in his own country to combat atheism.

It is a tribute to Robert Boyle that all who knew him considered him to be an honest, upright man whose chief goal in life was to influence as many people as he could to accept the truth of Christianity. When he died in 1691, he was mourned all over Europe.

Chapter Check-up

A *Write the letter of the phrase that identifies each term.*

_____ 1. matter
_____ 2. molecule
_____ 3. atoms
_____ 4. gravity
_____ 5. atmosphere
_____ 6. humidity
_____ 7. precipitation
_____ 8. nimbus
_____ 9. meteorologist
_____ 10. dew point
_____ 11. energy
_____ 12. force

a. the layer of air that surrounds the earth
b. anything that takes up space and has weight
c. the temperature at which water condenses
d. any form of water that falls from the clouds to the earth
e. the force which draws things down toward the center of the earth
f. a push or a pull
g. the amount of water vapor in the air
h. the smallest particle of a substance which has all the qualities of that substance
i. the temperature at which a solid changes to a liquid
j. rain or storm cloud
k. a scientist who studies the weather
l. the particles which make up molecules
m. the ability to do work

B *Write* **true** *or* **false** *in the space before each statement.*

_____ 1. Less than half of the earth's surface is covered with water.
_____ 2. Your body is about 65% water.
_____ 3. Water molecules contain two atoms of hydrogen and two atoms of oxygen.
_____ 4. Water contracts and becomes more dense when it freezes.
_____ 5. Air is made of oxygen, nitrogen, and small amounts of other gases.
_____ 6. Air has weight.
_____ 7. Warm air is denser than cool air.
_____ 8. Dew and frost are types of precipitation.
_____ 9. Long-range weather forecasts are more reliable than short-range forecasts.
_____ 10. Satellites are important tools used in weather observation.

C *Answer the questions about the pictures.*

1. Which type of cloud is illustrated in each of the pictures below?

A _____   B _____   C _____

Matter 165

2. Which state of matter is represented in each of the pictures below?

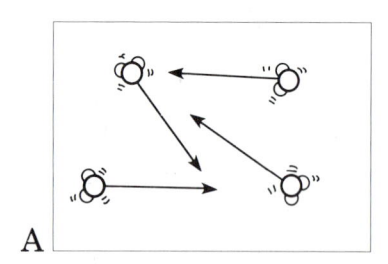

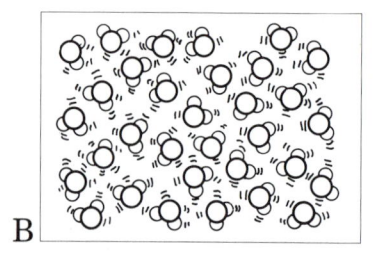

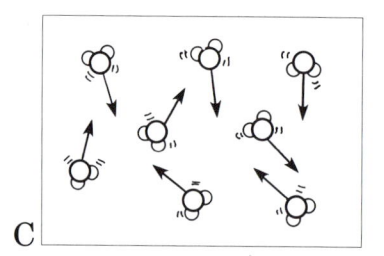

A _____   B _____   C _____

3. Which picture shows the more reliable form of energy? Why?

A   B

_____

_____

_____

4. Pictures **A** and **B** represent the same water.
   What happened to make the molecules behave differently?

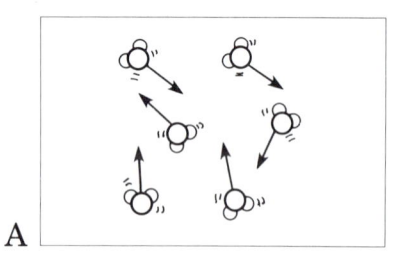

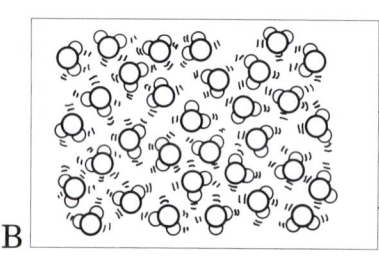

A   B

_____

_____

5. Which picture best represents the density of the air surrounding the earth? Why?

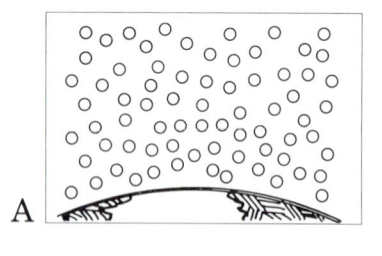

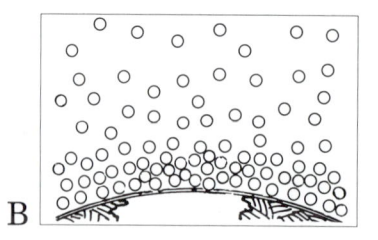

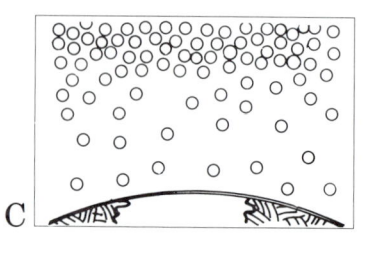

A   B   C

_____

_____

166 ■ *Understanding God's World*

6. On which day can the air contain more water vapor? Why?

_____

_____

_____

_____

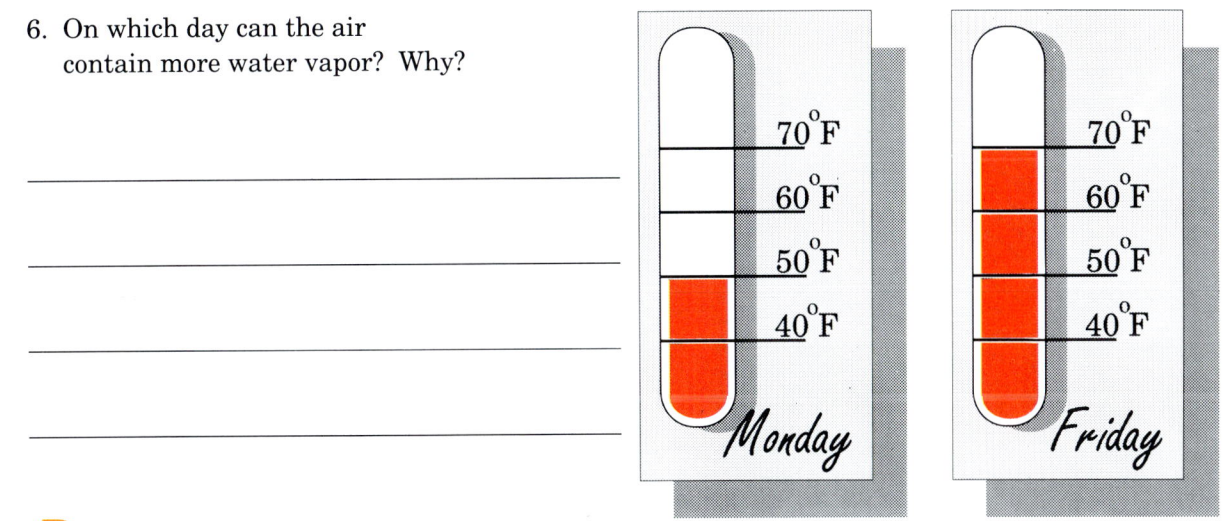

D *Fill in the word that best completes each statement.*

1. A cloud at ground level is called _____.

2. Clouds are made of _____ and _____.

3. The only substance that exists naturally in all three states is _____.

4. Energy that is stored is called _____ energy.

5. Large, puffy clouds are called _____ clouds.

6. Layers of clouds are _____ clouds.

7. Featherlike clouds are _____ clouds.

8. The melting point of water is _____.

9. The boiling point of water is _____.

10. A large body of air which has the same temperature and humidity is called an _____.

E *Write a short paragraph to answer each of the following.*
1. Explain what takes place during the water cycle.
2. Describe how the following are formed: snow, hail, frost.

Matter 167

6 ENERGY: Sound and Hearing

6.1 Sounds All around Us

Singing birds, chirping crickets, rustling leaves—many things can be recognized by the sounds they make. How is sound produced? How does it travel to your ears?

Vibrations make sounds

Sound is produced when an object **vibrates,** or moves rapidly back and forth. Sound is a form of energy that is released when an object vibrates. To see how vibrations produce sounds, loop a rubber band around a doorknob and pull it as far as you can without breaking it. Now pluck it with your finger. What happens? The rubber band vibrates and produces a hum. What happens to the hum when the rubber band stops vibrating?

When the rubber band vibrated, it made the air around it move. As you know, air is matter, and matter is made up of very small particles called molecules. The moving energy of the rubber band was changed into sound energy when it caused the molecules of air to collide, or bump into one another.

168 Understanding God's World

Since air is invisible, you cannot observe its movements, but you can observe the similar movements of water. Throw a stone into a lake, or drop a stone into a puddle or a tub of water. The stone causes a disturbance in the water. Watch the ripples spread out in all directions from where the stone entered the water. What causes the ripples?

The weight of the stone pushes down on the water, creating a hollow, or a depression. The water that was in that spot has to go somewhere, and so it goes to the side, pushing up the water that is there, before it returns to its original position. Now we have a depression surrounded by a ring of raised water.

When the ring of raised water falls back, its weight acts like the weight of the stone. It pushes the water that is underneath it downward and forces up a wider ring of water slightly farther away from the point where the stone was dropped. As rings of water continue to rise and fall, you will see a series of ripples spreading out from the center like a bull's eye.

Keep in mind that the water is moving up and down only. It looks as though the stone has caused the water to move outward, but this is not what happens. Only the disturbance caused by the stone is moving outward. If you put a cork on the rippling water, the cork will rise and fall with the rise and fall of the water it rests on, but the moving rings will not move the cork outward.

Energy ■ 169

Sound waves

Sound travels through the air in the same way that a disturbance travels through the water. At the point where a sound is made, sound energy compresses, or pushes together, the molecules of air. The molecules bump against each other and then return to their original position. They form waves that we call **sound waves.** Sound waves spread out in all directions. The air itself does not move away from the source of the sound, just as the water itself did not move away from the source of the disturbance. Only the disturbance moves outward. Sound waves become weaker as they travel away from the source of the sound until finally they cannot be heard at all.

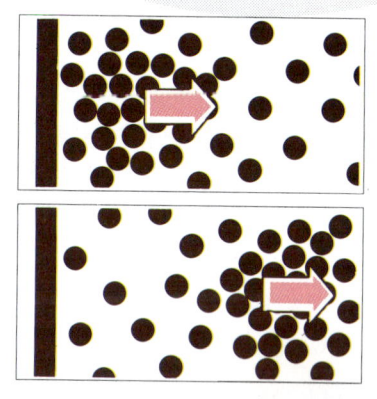

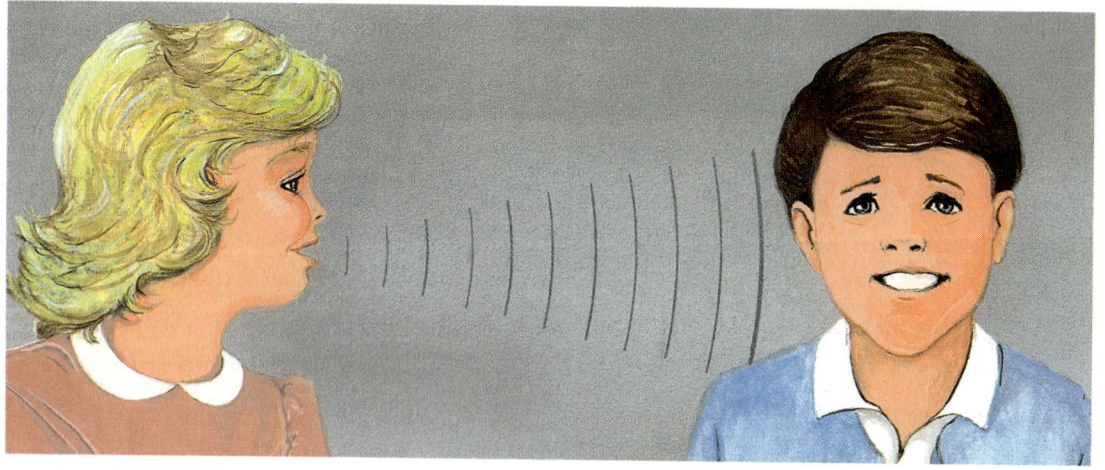

170 Understanding God's World

Sound travels

Sound waves travel through all three states of matter. Sound waves can travel through liquids, such as water, and solids, such as metal, as well as through the air. Water is a better carrier of sound than air is. Metal carries sound more efficiently than water or air does. If you strike a metal pipe with a hammer, you will hear the sound through the metal before you hear it through the air. Sound waves travel rather slowly through gases, faster through liquids, and fastest through solids.

Would sound waves travel more quickly through the earth or through the air? Why?

Sound waves can travel only when there are molecules of matter to transmit the vibrations. Sound waves cannot travel through empty space.

In 1660, the great English scientist Robert Boyle proved that this was true. He placed a clock with a dependable alarm inside a sealed glass jar. Using a pump, he removed the air that was inside the jar. When it was time for the alarm to ring, Boyle heard nothing. He allowed air back into the jar; he was then able to hear the alarm ringing. Boyle repeated his experiment many times, sometimes using a bell instead of the clock. When air was removed from the jar, Boyle could see the bell vibrating, but could hear nothing. Only when molecules of air were present to transmit the sound waves could sound be heard.

The speed of sound

Sound waves are traveling through the air all of the time. The speed at which sound waves travel depends upon several conditions. Sound usually travels through air at the speed of about 1,100 feet per second. This seems very fast to us, but it is not nearly as fast as the speed of light. Light travels at the speed of 186,000 *miles* per second. Because there is a difference between the speed of sound and the speed of light, you will see the flash of lightning from a distant storm before you hear the roar of thunder.

Energy 171

SOMETHING TO DO   *Observing sound travel*

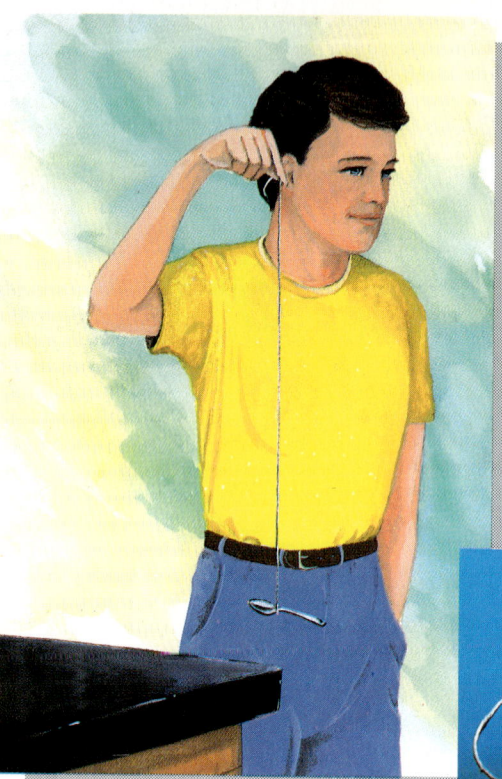

To see how sound travels, take a three-foot piece of string and tie a spoon to the middle of it. Hold the ends of the string up to your ears. Swing the spoon back and forth a few times, and then let the spoon hit a table or chair. You will hear the sound of a bell. Try it again with a larger spoon and then with a fork. What differences do you notice? How does the sound travel to your ears?

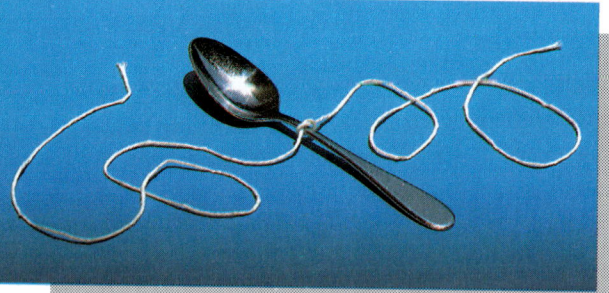

Comprehension Check 6.1
True or *False*

1. When an object vibrates, sound is produced.
2. Sound is a form of energy.
3. To vibrate means to move very slowly.
4. Molecules are large particles of matter.
5. As sound waves travel away from their source, they become stronger and stronger.
6. Sound waves are able to travel through solids and liquids as well as through the air.
7. Solids, such as metal, are the best carriers of sound waves.
8. Sound waves travel most quickly through empty space.
9. Sound usually travels through the air at the speed of 1,100 feet per hour.

Understanding God's World

6.2 Making Sound

Many animals are able to make sound in order to communicate with each other, but only man has the special ability to speak a language. God's gift of language makes it possible for us to express ourselves to each other and to Him in ways that no animal can.

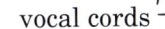

How people speak

In your throat is a passageway for air. A section of this passageway is a boxlike chamber called the **larynx.** Inside the larynx are two stretchy bands of tissue which are called the **vocal cords.** There is one vocal cord on each side of the windpipe opening. The vocal cords are attached to the sides of the larynx by small muscles. When you speak, the muscles tighten the vocal cords, making the opening smaller. Air from your lungs passes over the vocal cords and causes them to vibrate. The vibrations produce the sound of your voice. The tighter the vocal cords are pulled, the higher your voice will be.

People who cannot speak

Some people cannot speak because of birth defects or illnesses. They express their needs by using sign language. They may learn to spell; then they are able to communicate by pointing to letters on a board or by using a special typewriter or computer.

Since people learn to speak by listening to the speech of others, hearing-impaired people often cannot speak because they cannot hear the sounds made by themselves or others.

The first school for the hearing impaired was opened in Paris in 1760. The students were taught not only to read and write but also to speak by using finger spelling and sign language. To do this, the hearing-impaired person learns twenty-six different hand positions, one for each letter of the alphabet, and as many as 1,500 special signs for particular words. Hearing-impaired people communicate in this way to other people who have learned sign

Energy 173

The American Manual Alphabet

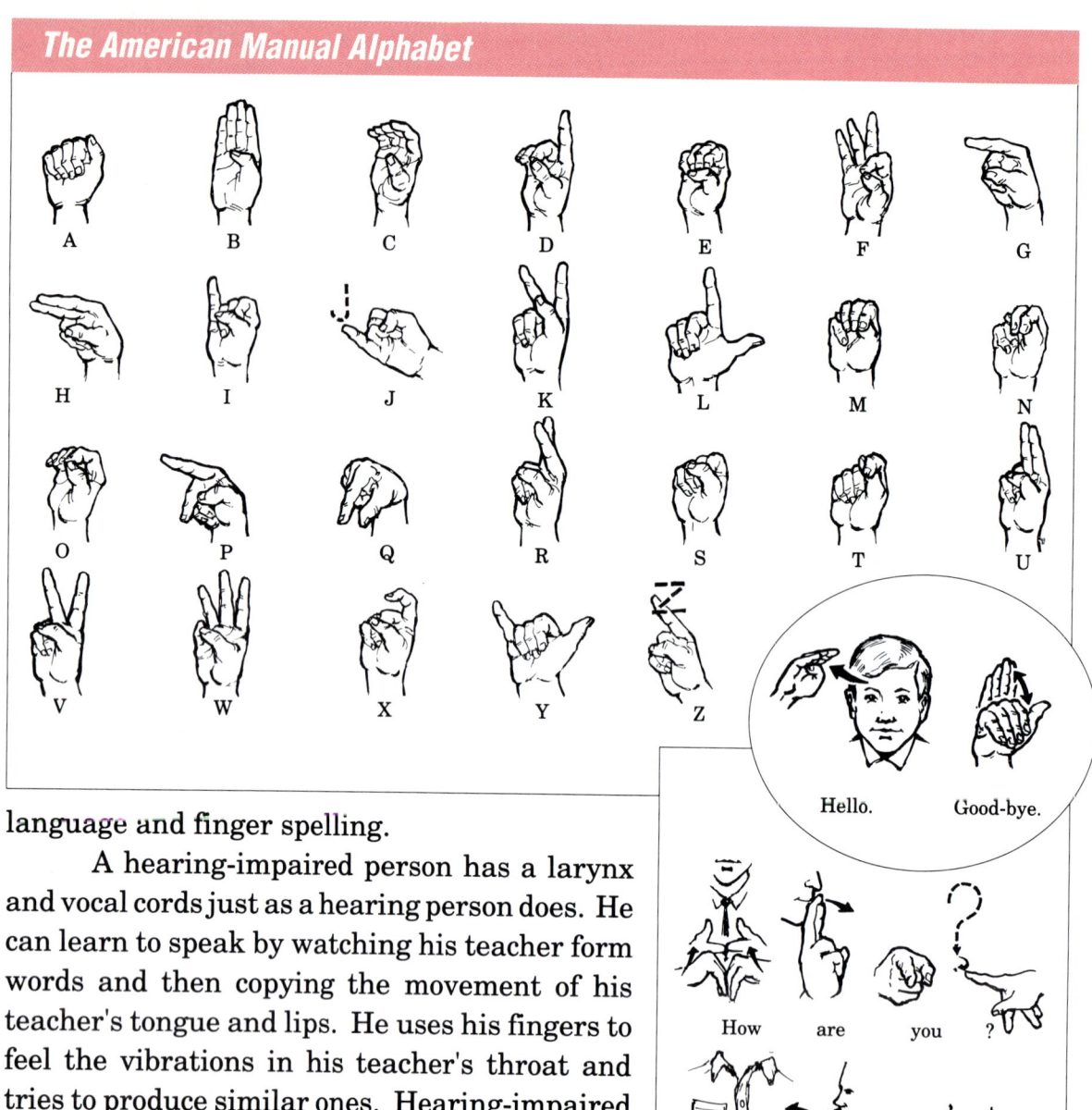

language and finger spelling.

    A hearing-impaired person has a larynx and vocal cords just as a hearing person does. He can learn to speak by watching his teacher form words and then copying the movement of his teacher's tongue and lips. He uses his fingers to feel the vibrations in his teacher's throat and tries to produce similar ones. Hearing-impaired people can learn to speak in this way, although they usually cannot speak as clearly as people who can hear.

    Alexander Graham Bell became a teacher of the hearing impaired in Boston, Massachusetts, when he was a young man. He realized that if his students could feel vibrations of sound, it would be easier for them to learn how to speak. In trying to find a way to transmit several telegraph messages over one wire at the same time, Bell discovered how to transmit voices over a wire. Bell is famous not only as the inventor of the telephone but also as a leading authority on the education of the hearing impaired.

174 ■ *Understanding God's World*

Other sounds

We make sounds not only with our mouths and vocal cords but also with other parts of our bodies. Our feet make sounds when we walk, run, or jump. Our hands make sounds when we clap them, hit an object, or catch a ball. Each time, sound is produced by vibrations.

Animal sounds

Animals also make sounds. The roar of a lion tells you not to get too close. A bear growls. A wolf howls. Cattle bawl, and sheep bleat. Elk bugle, elephants trumpet, dogs bark, birds sing and call. A kitten purrs when happy and mews when hungry or distressed. A hen cackles when she has laid an egg and clucks to her chicks to announce dinner. The alligator's bellow to attract a mate sounds like thunder.

Crickets rub the rough surfaces of their wings together to make chirps. Beavers warn other beavers of danger by slapping the water with their tails. Insects make buzzing sounds with their wings. Fish and other aquatic animals grunt, squeal, or hiss. Frogs croak by filling their mouths with air, then letting it out quickly.

All of these sounds are made because sound waves are created when something moves very fast, or vibrates.

15 Thrush

summer
winter
both
hermit thrush's range

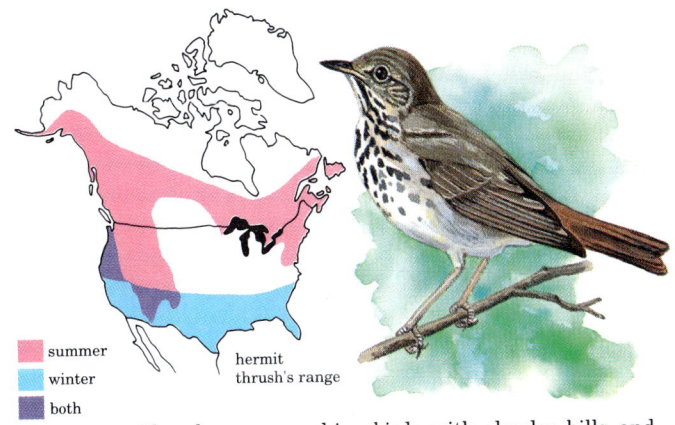

Thrushes are perching birds with slender bills and large eyes. Many adult thrushes and all young thrushes have spotted breasts. Most thrushes have strong legs and sturdy feet. They usually prefer to live in wooded areas and often spend much time on the ground in search of insects to eat.

The wood thrush, which is probably the most common thrush in the East, is a plump bird about eight inches long. It lives in woodlands east of the Mississippi, from southern Canada to the southern United States. It is not as shy as many other thrushes, and sometimes nests near houses.

The hermit thrush is a slightly smaller bird. It lives in southern Alaska, southern Canada, and most of the United States. Many people think that the hermit thrush has the most beautiful song of any bird in North America.

Comprehension Check 6.2
1. Describe the larynx and the vocal cords.
2. Explain how speech is produced.
3. Why do hearing-impaired people often find it difficult to learn to speak?

Energy 175

6.3 Receiving Sound

Your ears

The human ear is a marvel of creation. The parts of the ear work together to receive sound waves from the air and to make hearing possible. Your ear is divided into three main parts: the outer ear, the middle ear, and the inner ear.

The outer ear. The outer ear is made up of two parts. The **auricle** is the fleshy part of the outer ear that is clearly visible. There are no bones in the auricle. It is made mostly of a strong, flexible tissue covered with skin. The job of the auricle is to collect sound waves.

The other part of the outer ear is the **auditory canal.** You can see the opening of this canal when you look into someone's ear. The auditory canal guides sound waves to the middle ear.

Separating the outer ear from the middle ear is a thin membrane called the **eardrum.** Sound waves travel down the auditory canal, strike the eardrum, and cause it to vibrate.

The middle ear. A chamber behind the eardrum contains three small bones that are joined together. These bones are the **hammer,** the **anvil,** and the **stirrup.** The stirrup, the smallest bone in your body, is about half the size of a grain of rice. The vibration of the eardrum causes the hammer, anvil, and stirrup to vibrate also.

The inner ear. Within the inner ear is the **cochlea** [kŏk'lē-é], a snail-shaped organ filled with liquid. The stirrup is attached to a small membrane on the outside wall of the cochlea. Inside the cochlea is the actual organ of hearing. Special little hairs in the organ of hearing are attached to fibers of the **auditory nerve,** the nerve that carries the message of sound to the brain.

When the stirrup vibrates against the membrane on the outside wall of the cochlea, it causes the liquid inside the cochlea to vibrate. The vibrating liquid causes the little hairs to bend, stimulating the nerve fibers. The auditory nerve carries signals to the brain. The brain receives the message and interprets it as sounds. This entire process takes much less time than one second!

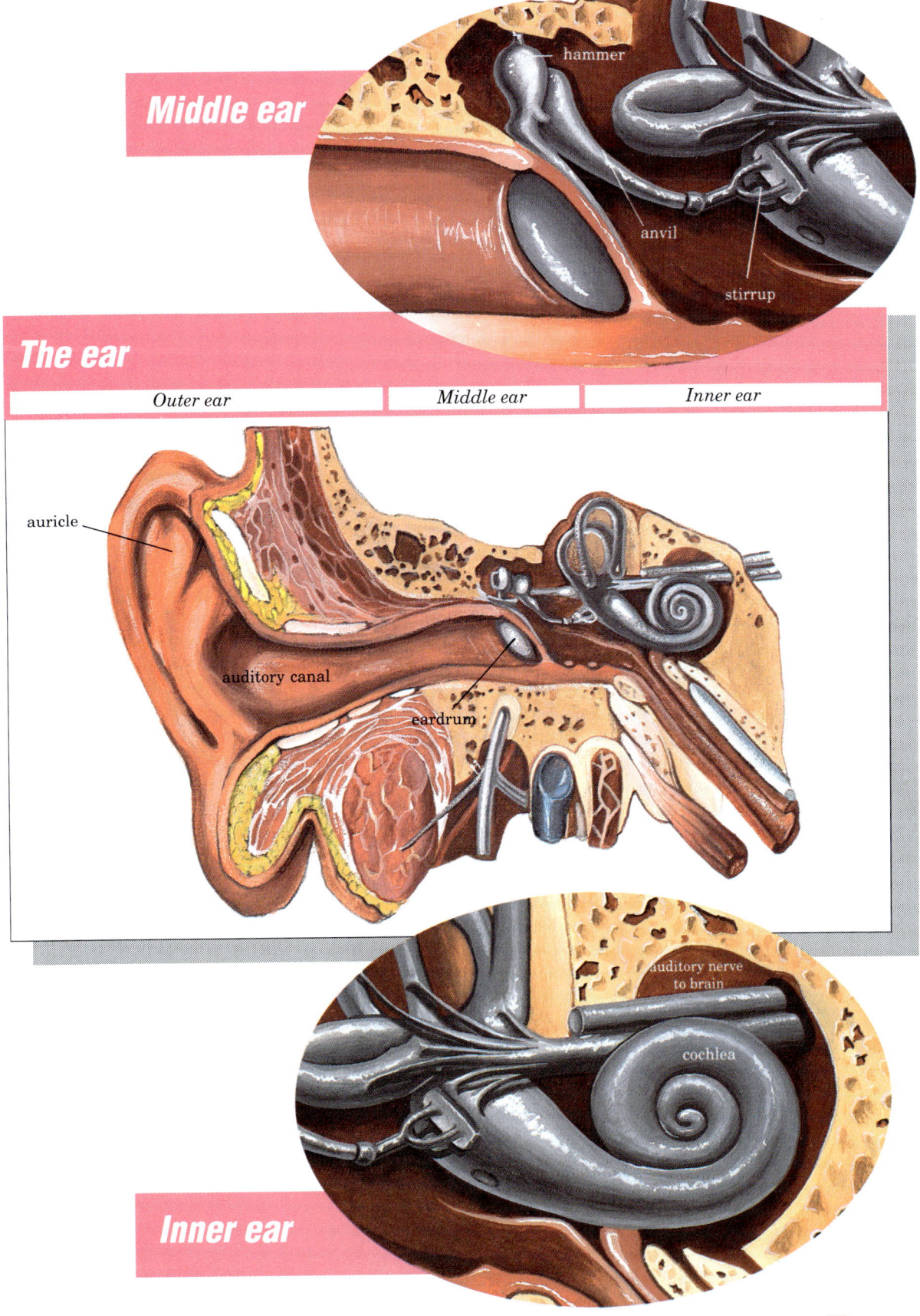

Middle ear

The ear

| Outer ear | Middle ear | Inner ear |

Inner ear

Energy ■ 177

Hearing aids

The sense of hearing can be partially lost because of illness or injury. Most people lose some of their ability to hear as they grow older. Hearing aids help many people who have a partial hearing loss.

A hearing aid is a device like a little telephone that makes sounds louder. Electronic hearing aids change sound vibrations into electrical signals. A tiny loudspeaker in the hearing aid changes the electrical signal back into sound vibrations.

Some kinds of hearing aids are put into the outer ear. They send increased sound vibrations to the middle ear. Another type of hearing aid is clamped against the bone behind the ear. This type of hearing aid sends vibrations through the bones. The bones indirectly transmit the sound.

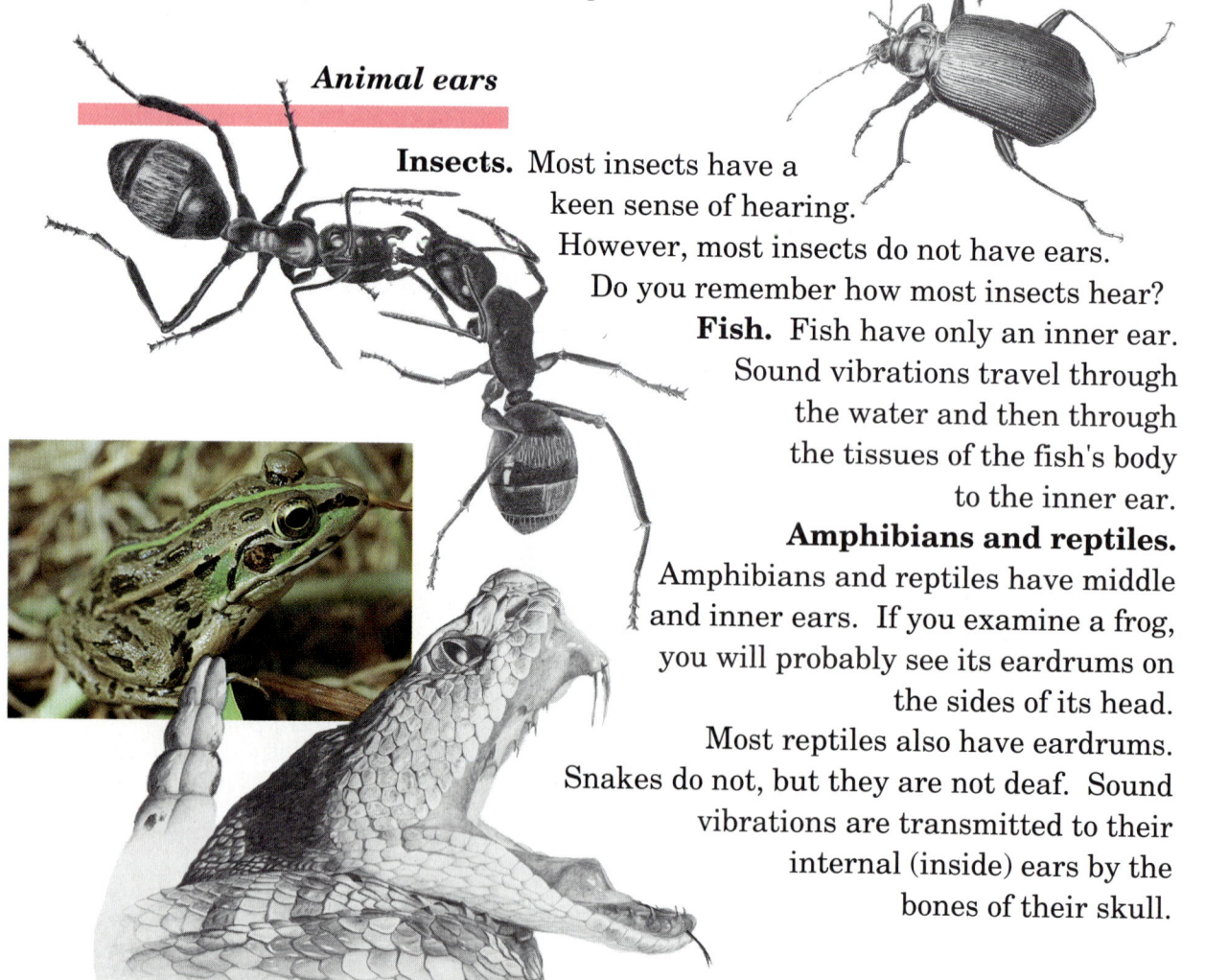

Animal ears

Insects. Most insects have a keen sense of hearing. However, most insects do not have ears. Do you remember how most insects hear?

Fish. Fish have only an inner ear. Sound vibrations travel through the water and then through the tissues of the fish's body to the inner ear.

Amphibians and reptiles. Amphibians and reptiles have middle and inner ears. If you examine a frog, you will probably see its eardrums on the sides of its head.

Most reptiles also have eardrums. Snakes do not, but they are not deaf. Sound vibrations are transmitted to their internal (inside) ears by the bones of their skull.

Birds. Most birds have a good sense of hearing. Birds have eardrums, middle ears, and inner ears, but no outer ears. Do you remember why this is a wise design?

Mammals. Although not all mammals have auricles, mammals are the only animals that have auricles. Many mammals have muscles on the sides of their heads with which to adjust the position of their auricles. Moving the auricles in the direction of the sound helps the animal to hear sound more distinctly.

Comprehension Check 6.3

1. What are the three main parts of the human ear?
2. Define: *auricle, eardrum, cochlea, auditory nerve.*
3. Snakes do not have eardrums. How do sound waves get to their inner ears?
4. What is the only class of animals which has auricles?
5. Tell the name for each part of the ear labeled on the picture. Use the terms listed below.

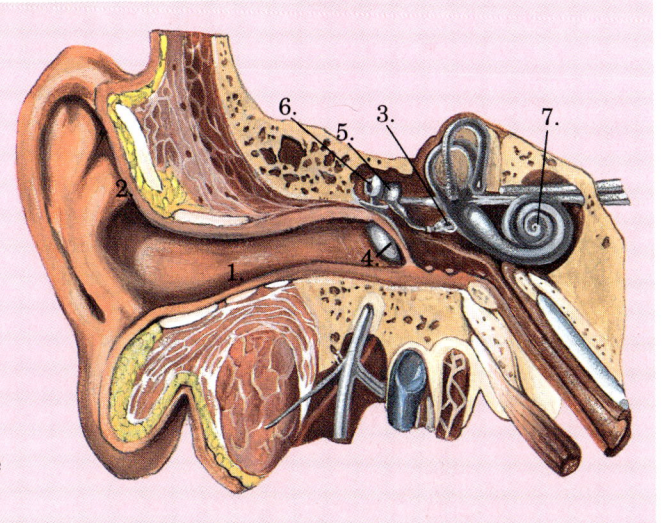

A. *eardrum*   B. *stirrup*   C. *cochlea*   D. *anvil*   E. *hammer*   F. *auditory canal*   G. *auricle*

Energy ■ 179

SOMETHING TO DO *Observing sound vibrations*

You cannot usually see sound vibrations, but in this activity you will be able to observe the vibrations that are made when you speak.

You will need a metal can with both ends removed, a balloon, a piece of foil, a rubber band, scissors, and glue.

Cut the balloon so that it can be stretched tightly over one end of the can. Fasten the balloon in place with the rubber band. Cut a small piece of foil and glue it to the balloon, slightly off center.

Hold the can up to your mouth with the open end toward you. Stand so that a spot of sunlight is reflected from the foil onto a surface such as a wall or a chalkboard.

As you talk into the can, notice the spot of light. What do you see? Talk louder. What happens to the spot of light?

SOMETHING TO DO *Tin can telephone*

Find two tin cans and poke a hole just large enough to pass a string through in the bottom of each can. Find a long string. Put it through the hole in one can and tie a knot on the end so it will stay. Put the other end through the hole in the bottom of the other can and knot the string. Talk to your friend through this "telephone." Your voice will make vibrations, and the string will carry these vibrations to the other can. Your friend's ear will pick up the vibrations, and he will hear your voice.

Ships in the navy use "sound-powered phones" that work on this principle and do not require electricity. By using these phones, men are able to keep in contact with all parts of the ship.

6.4 High and Low Sounds

16 Baltimore Oriole

In the 1790s, an Italian scientist named Lazarro Spallanzani discovered that bats are able to fly with ease in a totally darkened room. But if their ears or mouths were covered, the bats blundered around the room, crashing into walls and furniture. Spallanzani concluded that bats use their ears to "see." Few people would listen to such an idea. People said that if bats were guided by their sense of hearing, what sounds were they listening to? No one was able to hear the sounds that guided the bats.

Today we know that Spallanzani was correct. Bats do navigate by sound. Not until the invention of machines that could detect extremely high-pitched sounds were men able to hear the sounds that guide bats.

summer
winter
both

northern oriole's range

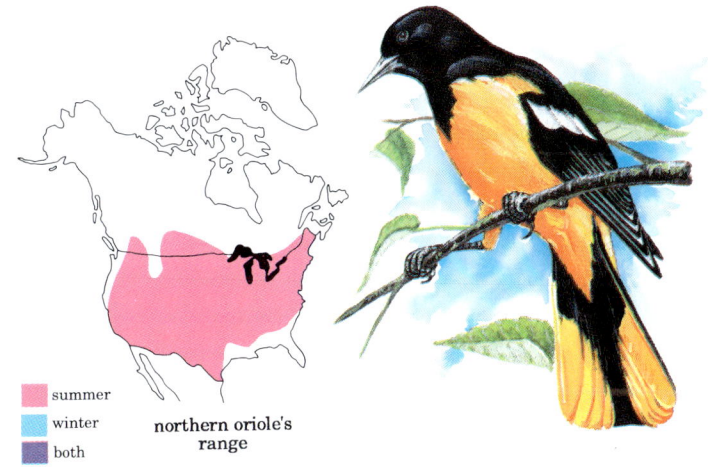

The strikingly beautiful Baltimore oriole will capture your attention with its brilliant plumage and sweet song. *Baltimore oriole* is the name for the type of northern oriole that lives in the East. The western variety is called *Bullock's oriole*. The Baltimore oriole is about seven inches long. The male's black and flaming orange plumage is eye-catching. Because black and golden orange were the colors of Lord Baltimore, Maryland's founder, Maryland's legislature chose the Baltimore oriole as their state bird. Orioles eat caterpillars, beetles, and wild fruit.

The northern oriole can be found from southern Canada to northern Mexico. In the fall it heads for southern Mexico and South America, where it spends the winter.

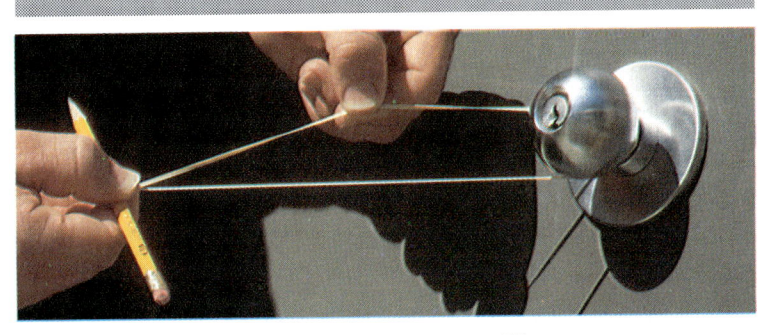

Frequency

Attach a rubber band to a doorknob. Loop the other end around a pencil. Stretch the band very tightly and pluck it. The vibrations of the rubber band are so rapid that all you can see is a blur. Next, allow the rubber band to become fairly slack. You can now see the vibrations, because they are much slower. Scientists use the term **frequency** with reference to *how many times* an object vibrates in each second.

Energy

When an object vibrates very rapidly, a large number of sound waves are produced each second. Such a sound is called a high-frequency sound. **High-frequency sounds have a high pitch.** **Pitch** is the highness or lowness of a sound. If an object vibrates more slowly, it produces fewer sound waves each second, and the sound is a low-frequency sound. **Low-frequency sounds have a low pitch.**

Keep in mind that frequency always means how many vibrations an object produces each second. Frequency has nothing to do with the speed of sound. Low-frequency sounds travel through the air at the same speed as high-frequency sounds.

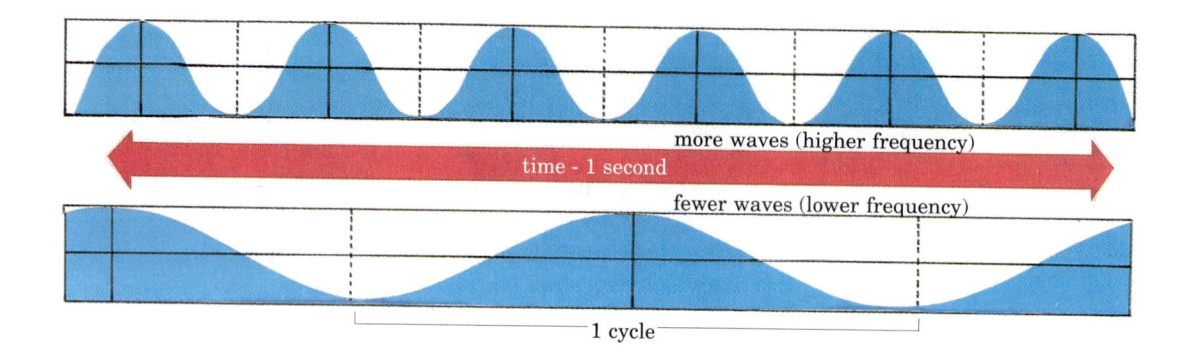

more waves (higher frequency)
time - 1 second
fewer waves (lower frequency)
1 cycle

Low-frequency sounds   *High-frequency sounds*

Your ears are not designed to hear every sound in the air around you. The nodding of your head, the movements of your muscles as you walk, the movement of blood through your body—all of these motions produce sounds with frequencies too low for you to hear. **An object must vibrate at least 20 times per second for your ears to pick up the sound.**

Wave your hand back and forth as fast as you can. Are you causing sound waves to form in the air? Why are you not able to hear the sound? Why can you hear a housefly but not a butterfly?

Just as there are sounds too low for you to hear, there are also sounds too high for you to hear. No one can hear the sounds bats make to guide them in their flight because **people are not able to hear sounds made by objects vibrating more than 20,000 times per second.**

Many animals are able to hear the high-frequency sounds that people cannot hear. Dogs can hear sounds made by objects vibrating 50,000 times per second. Cats have even keener ears. They hear sounds with a frequency of 65,000 vibrations per second. Bats and dolphins are able to hear sounds of even higher frequencies. They hear sounds that have a frequency of 120,000 vibrations per second.

182   *Understanding God's World*

SOMETHING TO DO *Make a straw instrument*

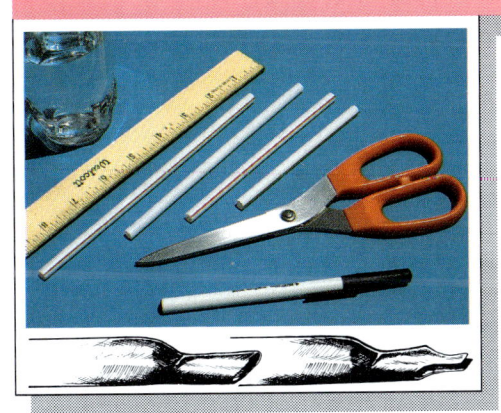

You will need four paper straws, a pair of scissors, a ruler, a pen, and a small container of water.

Use the ruler and pen to measure and mark off one inch at one end of one of the straws. Flatten that end of the straw by pressing your scissors two or three times across both sides of it.

Cut a small piece off each side of the flattened end of the straw. You have made a reed for your instrument.

Moisten the reed and blow through the straw. Can you feel the vibrations? You should hear a note produced by the vibrating reed. (You may need to try a few times.)

Cut the three remaining straws so that you have four straws of different lengths. Make a reed at the end of each of the remaining straws.

What do you notice about the pitch of the notes made by each of the instruments? Which straw produces the highest note? The lowest? Why?

Sometime when you are outdoors, you can make an "instrument," using your hands and a wide, thin blade of grass. Put your thumbs together side by side with the blade of grass between them. Put your lips against your thumbs and blow. The blade of grass acts like a reed.

SOMETHING TO DO *High and low sounds*

You will need a funnel, a balloon, a rubber band, and a pair of scissors. Cut the balloon so that it can be stretched over the large end of the funnel. Fasten the balloon in place with the rubber band. Cut a narrow slit in the balloon.

Blow into the small end of the funnel and listen to the sound. Now stretch the balloon so that it is tighter and blow again. Is the sound higher or lower than the first sound? Why?

Comprehension Check 6.4
1. What is meant by a sound's frequency?
2. How are high-frequency sounds produced? Low-frequency sounds?
3. What is pitch? How does pitch relate to frequency?
4. Do low-frequency sounds travel through the air more slowly than high-frequency sounds?
5. What is the lowest frequency that the human ear can hear? Highest frequency?
6. What two animals are able to hear the highest frequency sounds?

Energy 183

6.5 Sounds That Bounce Back

As a sound wave travels through the air, the water, or a solid object, its path can be changed. Some kinds of materials absorb sound waves. Others reflect sound waves, or cause them to bounce back. Materials with soft, uneven surfaces tend to absorb sound waves. Materials with hard, smooth surfaces tend to reflect sound waves.

Think of what happens when you throw a ball against a soft surface such as sand. The ball lands in the sand and stays there. What happens if you throw the ball against a hard surface, such as concrete or a brick wall? The ball bounces back to you. Sound waves also bounce back toward their source when they hit a smooth, hard object.

How would you describe the sounds you hear during a basketball game in a large gymnasium? The hard, smooth surfaces of the room reflect sounds and make it a very noisy place. Imagine all the unwanted and distracting sounds there would be in churches and concert halls if they were designed like gymnasiums! Materials that absorb sounds can be used to cut down on unwanted sounds. This is called **soundproofing.** The soft materials used in carpets, draperies, and cushioned seats absorb sounds, helping to soundproof the room.

184 ■ Understanding God's World

Echoes

When sound waves bounce back, they sometimes can be heard a second time. This reflected sound is called an **echo.** We do not hear an echo every time a sound is reflected. If the sound is weak or if the surface that it bounced off is too small, no echo is produced.

At other times, a single sound may produce many echoes. Repeating echoes occur in places such as canyons where there are many surfaces to reflect the sound. As sound waves bounce repeatedly from surface to surface, multiple echoes are produced.

SOMETHING TO DO

You will need a long spring or slinky and a chair.
Hook one end of the spring over the back of a chair. Hold the other end in one hand. Stand far enough away from the chair so that the spring is extended but not pulled tight. Pull some of the coils toward you so that you are holding a compact group of coils. These coils contain potential energy.

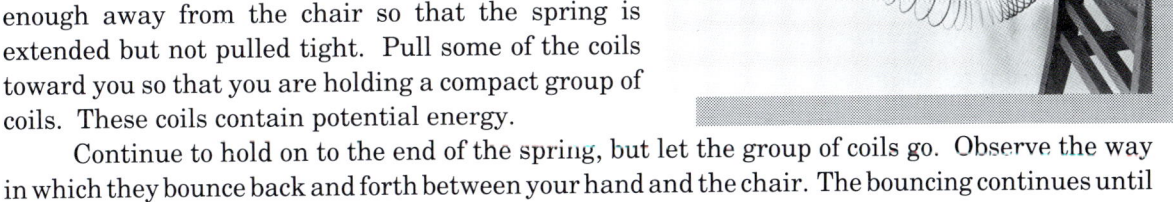

Continue to hold on to the end of the spring, but let the group of coils go. Observe the way in which they bounce back and forth between your hand and the chair. The bouncing continues until all of the potential energy has been converted into moving energy.

Sound energy also bounces back and forth.

Ultrasound

You will remember that there are sounds that are of frequencies too high to be heard by the human ear. Scientists call these sound waves **ultrasonic** waves. Ultrasonic waves echo more easily than sound waves of lower frequencies.

Some animals use ultrasonic waves. Bats, dolphins, and a few other animals use the echoes of ultrasonic waves to navigate, or find their way around.

You will remember that in the 1790s, Spallanzani thought that bats use their ears to "see." He was unable to prove his idea because no one could hear the sounds that the bats were using. In the 1930s, scientists used machines that were able to detect ultrasonic waves and make them audible

Energy 185

to human ears to prove that the bat does indeed "see" with its ears.

As bats fly, they emit (give off) ultrasonic cries. The ultrasonic waves bounce off a tree, a cave wall, or an insect. When the bat hears the echo, it knows how to steer itself around—or toward—the object. A bat can fly through a maze made up of wires that are less than 4/100 of an inch thick. A bat can also tell if a small object is a delicious insect or only a twig.

The dolphin also can locate objects by sound. Scientists do not know exactly how the dolphin's system works, because the dolphin does not have any vocal cords.

People use ultrasonic waves. Men have learned how to use ultrasonic waves in order to produce echoes. Naval vessels use an ultrasonic device called **sonar.** *Sonar* stands for *so*und *n*avigation *a*nd *r*anging. Sonar is used to determine the depth of the water beneath the ship and to locate objects such as icebergs, schools of fish, or submarines.

Recently, machines have been invented that use ultrasonic waves to "see" inside the human body. The ultrasonic waves reflect, or echo, off the structures inside the body. A machine converts the echoes to electrical impulses. The electrical impulses create a picture called a **sonogram** on a screen. Doctors use the sonogram to help them find diseased tissue, to diagnose tumors, and to check the progress of unborn babies.

Other machines use ultrasonic waves to clean watches, mix chemicals, weld metals, clean teeth, and homogenize milk.

> ### Comprehension Check 6.5
> 1. Soft, uneven surfaces usually _?_ sound waves.
> 2. Hard, smooth surfaces usually _?_ sound waves.
> 3. A reflected sound that is heard again is called an _?_.
> 4. Sound waves that are of frequencies too high to be heard by the human ear are called _?_ waves.
> 5. Ultrasonic waves cause echoes _?_ easily than sound waves of lower frequencies.
> 6. Two animals that navigate by listening for the echoes of ultrasonic waves are the _?_ and the _?_.
> 7. An ultrasonic device used by ships is called _?_.
> 8. Doctors use ultrasonic waves to "see" inside the human body by creating a picture known as a _?_.

6.6 Preserving Sound

It was almost time for the church Christmas program to begin. Snow had been falling steadily all day. Kathy worried that Grandma and Grandpa would not be able to come for the program and hear her sing her first solo. From her seat in the choir loft she looked at the people coming into the church. Grandma and Grandpa were not among them.

Kathy's grandparents arrived the next day, too late for the program.

"I wish you could have heard my solo," said Kathy ruefully.

"They will hear it," said Dad bringing out a small tape recorder. "Didn't you notice me taping the program?" He put a tape into the recorder and soon Kathy's solo could be clearly heard. She was delighted. What a wonderful thing a tape recorder is!

The phonograph

Preserving sound was not possible until 1877 when Thomas Edison invented the phonograph. The first sound recording ever made was a recitation of "Mary Had a Little Lamb" by the inventor himself. Edison's first phonograph was a machine that recorded the patterns of sound waves on small metal cylinders covered with tin foil. The sound waves caused a fine needle to scratch grooves on the foil. The pattern of the grooves matched the pattern of the sound waves. When the recording was played back, the needle retraced the grooves and the sound waves were reproduced.

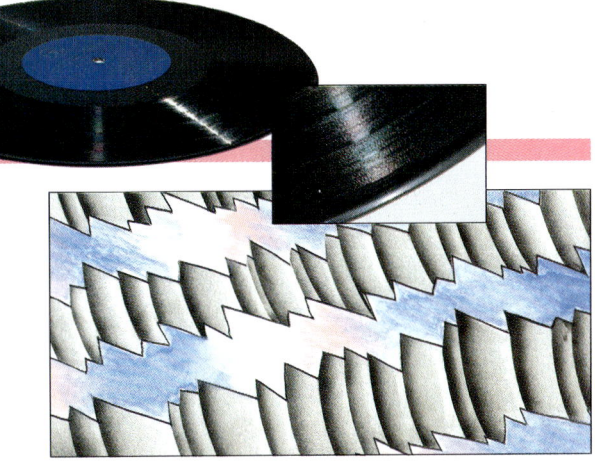

Today's records are made by a much more complicated process, but the principle is the same. The tiny grooves on the plastic surface of a record are made to match the patterns of the sound waves being recorded. Today, sound is more often recorded on tape and on compact discs than on records.

Energy 187

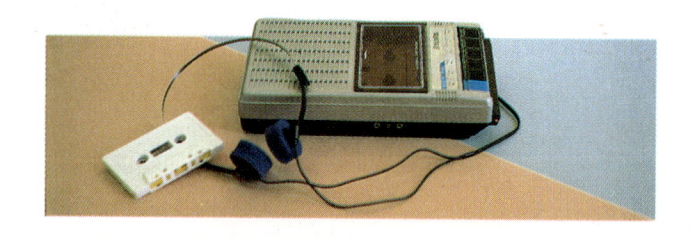

Two ears and stereo

Two ears are better than one because they help you tell which direction a sound is coming from. If a sound is made on your right, it will sound louder in your right ear than in your left. Because it sounds louder in your right ear, you know the sound is coming from the right. Sounds coming from the left will sound louder in your left ear. A sound made behind or in front of you will sound equally loud in both of your ears. If you turn your head, you will be able to tell from which direction a sound is coming.

The first records had only one sound track and were played on one loudspeaker. They were called *monaural* recordings (mono for short), which means one. Listening to a monaural recording is like hearing with only one ear. Since live music comes to our ears from all directions, mono recordings did not have the same quality of sound as live music.

Later *stereophonic* recordings were invented. Engineers make two or more separate recordings and combine them on one disk or tape. You hear the music through two or more loudspeakers. Stereo recordings make the sounds seem to come from different parts of the room as they would in real life. There is a sense of depth in stereo music.

A link with the past

Through recordings we can hear the voices of people who have left this world. This is very important not only for families but also for nations. Great preachers such as Dr. M. R. DeHaan and Charles E. Fuller can be heard

188 ■ *Understanding God's World*

today even though they have been gone from the earthly scene for some time. They are still being used of God because their voices were recorded for future generations. Recordings of speeches made by great leaders of the past such as Sir Winston Churchill help to preserve our history in a special way.

Comprehension Check 6.6
True or *False*

1. The pattern of the grooves on a record matches the pattern of specific sound waves.
2. Two ears are better than one because you can hear sounds twice as loud with two ears.
3. Sounds coming from your left sound louder in your right ear.
4. Sounds coming from behind you sound louder in your right ear.
5. Stereo recordings sound more like live music than monaural recordings.

17 Ruffed Grouse

summer
winter
both

The ruffed grouse is a hardy game bird found over much of North America. It is an attractive, chickenlike, ground-dwelling bird, about nineteen inches long. Rarely will it come out into the open, unless its cover is disturbed. Then it will fly up, suddenly and noisily. Even if you never see him, you may hear the male ruffed grouse. At any time of the day and all seasons of the year, but especially in the spring, he drums by beating the air with his wings.

The ruffed grouse lives from Alaska and northern Canada south to California, South Dakota, and the Carolinas. It eats the berries and fruits of forest plants in the summer. In the winter it goes to the treetops in search of buds, catkins, and twigs to eat.

SOMETHING TO DO
Sound difference

Make a recording of your speaking and singing voice. Play it back and listen carefully. Do you sound the way you thought you did? Why not?

When you hear yourself speak, some of the sound you hear travels through the bones of your head. When you listen to a tape, the sound waves travel only through your ears and not through the bones of your head.

Play a mono record and then a stereo record. What difference do you notice?

Energy

Alexander Graham Bell
demonstrating his telephone

6.7 Alexander Graham Bell: Inventor of the Telephone

Whenever you answer the telephone, think of its inventor: a Scottish-American scientist who wanted only to be remembered as a teacher of the hearing impaired. As much as any great scientist about whom you have read, Alexander Graham Bell sought to understand the wonders of God's world in order to help others, especially the hearing-impaired people whom he loved so much.

Aleck Bell, as his family called him, was born in Edinburgh, Scotland, in 1847. Bell's father and grandfather were noted public speakers. Aleck's father also taught people who could neither hear nor speak, how to speak. To help them, he invented a system known as "Visible Speech," a code in which written symbols represent sounds by indicating the position of the throat, the tongue, and the lips.

Aleck's mother, who was partially deaf, was an accomplished artist and musician. She was a devout Christian and taught Aleck and his two brothers the Bible as well as reading, writing, and arithmetic. His father saw to it that his boys learned how to speak correctly. As teenagers they began going with their father on lecture tours to demonstrate the usefulness of Visible Speech in teaching the hearing impaired to speak and in learning foreign languages.

Aleck, who now was called Graham,

190 Understanding God's World

also began teaching music and speech to children and working with people who could neither hear nor speak. When his family moved from Scotland to Canada, Graham went to Boston, giving his own lectures on Visible Speech and opening a school for training teachers of the hearing impaired. The next year he became a professor at Boston University, where he taught how the organs of speech function. Bell also continued the experiments with electricity and sound which he had started some time earlier. He was attempting to find a way to send several telegraph messages over a single wire at the same time and to transmit sounds of any sort over a wire.

Two wealthy men who were interested in Bell's work with the hearing impaired also became interested in his inventions and offered to pay the cost of his experiments. Bell later married Mabel Hubbard, the hearing-impaired daughter of one of these men. Shortly after his friends began to finance his experiments, Bell met a young repair mechanic and model maker, Thomas Watson, who was eager to help him with both the "harmonic telegraph" and the telephone. Bell and Watson worked long into the night almost every evening until success crowned their efforts. At first, the new machine could only transmit the sound of a plucked reed. More experiments followed until they were able to transmit human vocal sounds, but not words, over the harmonic telegraph. On March 10, 1876, Bell and Watson were in different rooms in a Boston boardinghouse trying out a new transmitter. Bell clumsily spilled battery acid all over his clothes and called for his assistant. Watson heard the first words to be transmitted by telephone: "Mr. Watson, come here. I want you!"

The telephone achieved widespread recognition that summer when Bell demonstrated it to the emperor of Brazil at the Centennial Exposition in Philadelphia. Bell's invention soon became a worldwide sensation. From the royalties which he received from the telephone, Bell set up an experimental sound laboratory and established the American Association to Promote the Teaching of Speech to the Deaf (now the Alexander Graham Bell Association for the Deaf). Bell's laboratory eventually became the Bell Telephone Laboratories, responsible for such wonders of the electronic age as stereophonic sound and the transistor. Bell became interested in the new science of aviation and helped finance experiments with heavier-than-air machines that became the airplanes we know so well. Alexander Graham Bell became an American citizen and spent the remainder of his seventy-five years on earth promoting the cause of science and invention and education for the hearing impaired.

Chapter Check-up

A On the lines below, write the name of the ear part represented by each number.

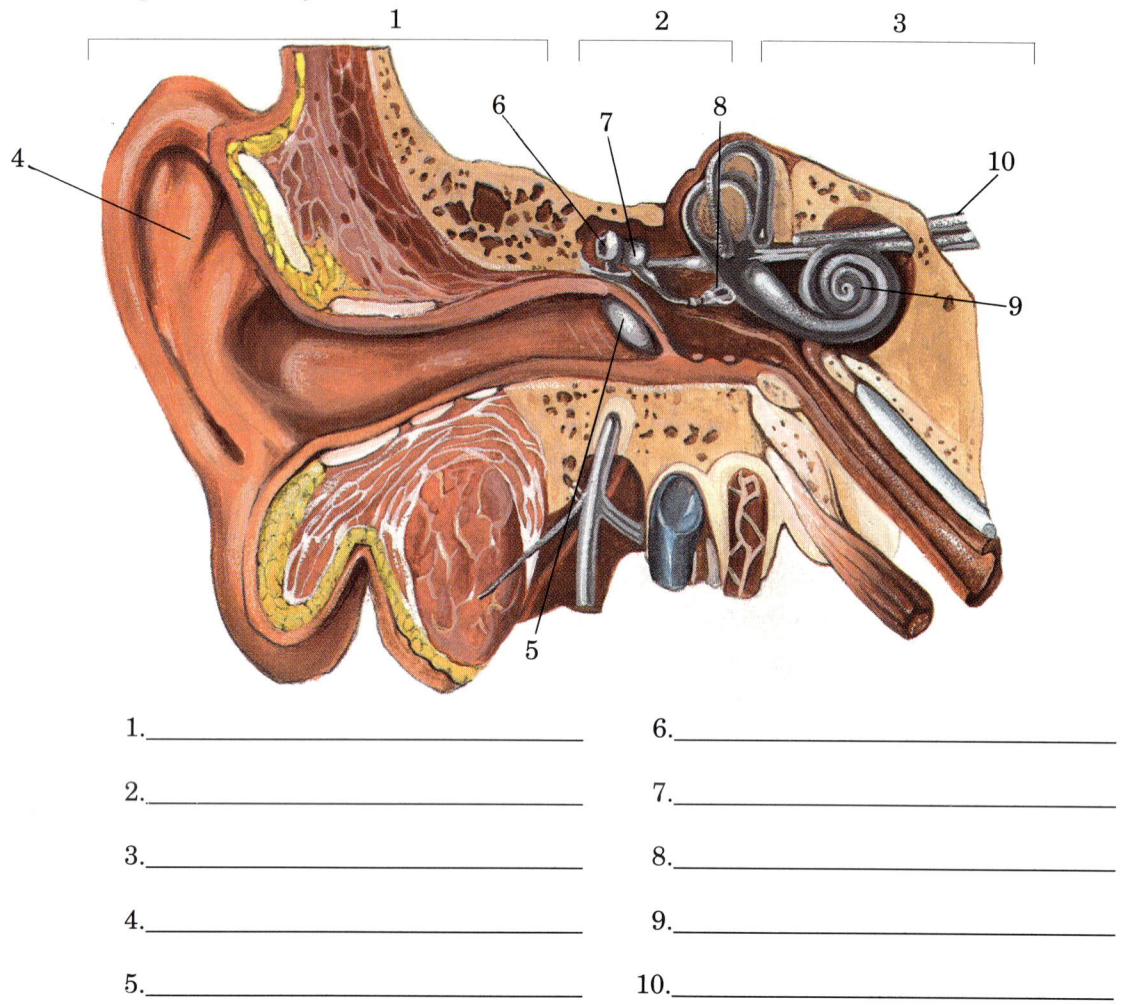

1. _____   6. _____

2. _____   7. _____

3. _____   8. _____

4. _____   9. _____

5. _____   10. _____

B Think about these questions and answer them as clearly as you can.

1. Adam was watching a display of fireworks. As each skyrocket exploded, he saw a brilliant flash of colored light. Then he heard the sound of the explosion. Why?
2. Explain how a sound travels through your ear to your brain.
3. When you hear sounds, do the molecules of air move all the way from the place where the sound began to your ears? Explain your answer in three or four good sentences.

192 ■ *Understanding God's World*

C *Match each term with the phrase that identifies it.*

_____ 1. vibrate
_____ 2. sound waves
_____ 3. supersonic
_____ 4. larynx
_____ 5. auditory nerve
_____ 6. auricle
_____ 7. eardrum
_____ 8. cochlea
_____ 9. vocal cords
_____ 10. frequency
_____ 11. pitch
_____ 12. echo
_____ 13. ultrasonic
_____ 14. resonance

A. a reflected sound that is heard again
B. stretchy bands of tissue that vibrate and produce the human voice
C. sounds that are too low for human beings to hear
D. reinforcing sound by prolonging it and making it louder
E. the outer, fleshy part of the ear
F. to move back and forth rapidly
G. the highness or lowness of a sound
H. sound vibrations
I. the snail-shaped structure in the inner ear
J. faster than the speed of sound
K. sounds that are too high for human beings to hear
L. carries the message of sound to the brain
M. the thin membrane separating the outer ear from the middle ear
N. the number of sound waves that a vibrating object produces each second
O. the structure that contains the vocal cords

D *Fill in the answer(s) to complete each sentence.*

1. Sound usually travels through the air at the speed of about _____ feet per second.
2. An object must vibrate at least _____ times per second to be heard by the human ear.
3. If an object vibrates more than _____ times per second, it cannot be heard by the human ear.
4. A low-frequency sound has a _____ pitch.
5. Two animals that locate things by echoes are _____ and _____.
6. The tighter your vocal cords are pulled, the _____ your voice will be.
7. A hearing-impaired person can learn to speak by feeling _____ and copying them.
8. The three small bones in the middle ear are the _____, the _____, and the _____.
9. The only animals that have auricles are the _____.

E *Can you read this message?*

Energy ■ 193

7 GEOLOGY: Planet Earth

7.1 Our Home, the Earth

He stretcheth out the north over the empty place, and hangeth the earth upon nothing. – Job 26:7

When God created the universe and all that is in it, He planned a special place for man to live. That special place is our planet, the earth.

The circle of the earth

The earth is round like a ball, or **sphere.** You probably already knew this, but did you know that the Bible told us this about the earth long before men figured it out? Isaiah 40:22 says, "It is He that sitteth upon the circle of the earth."

Because the earth is like a sphere, special maps called globes can help us to understand what the earth is like. A globe is a sphere-shaped map that looks like a miniature earth. To make it easier to find places on the earth, most globes are marked with points and lines. These markings are not actually on the earth, but they are on globes and maps to help us to find places that are north, south, east, or west of other locations. Find the following markings on your classroom globe.

194 ■ *Understanding God's World*

At the top of the globe is the **North Pole.** The **South Pole** is at the bottom. The imaginary line around the earth that is exactly halfway between the North and South Poles is called the **equator** [ē-kwā′tẽr]. The equator divides the sphere of the earth in half. Each half is called a **hemisphere,** which means half of a sphere. The half of the earth between the North Pole and the equator is the Northern Hemisphere. The half between the South Pole and the equator is the Southern Hemisphere. Which hemisphere do you live in?

The diameter [dī-ăm′ē-tẽr] of the earth at the equator is about 8,000 miles. The diameter measured from the North Pole to the South Pole is a little shorter. This means that the earth is not perfectly round. It is slightly flattened at the poles. However, the difference is so small that when the earth is viewed from space, it appears round.

If you could see the earth from space, you would also see what holds it up—nothing! Long before men traveled in space and could see this for themselves, God told us in the Bible that He "hangeth the earth upon nothing" (Job 26:7).

Maps and globes are often updated as new information about the earth becomes available. Satellites orbiting the earth have been very useful to mapmakers. The Landsat series of satellites began mapping the earth in 1972. Landsat photographs have revealed new information about our planet. A photograph taken in 1976 showed an island, which was previously unknown, off the coast of Labrador, Canada. The island has been named Landsat Island.

Geology ■ 195

SOMETHING TO DO   *Measuring the earth*

One measurement we can make of a sphere is its **circumference** [sĕr-kŭm′fĕr-ens]. The circumference is the distance around the outside of an object. You may want to try this demonstration to measure the circumference of a sphere. *You will need an apple, a long piece of string, scissors, a ruler, and a friend.*

Have your friend hold the apple with one hand at each end while you put the string around the center of the apple. Try to get the string where the equator would be if the apple were the earth. Cut the string where the ends meet. Measure the string with your ruler. How many inches long is it? That measurement is the circumference of your apple.

You could not measure the circumference of the earth with a string, because you would need a piece of string almost 25,000 miles long! That is the circumference of the earth at the equator.

Another measurement of a sphere is its **diameter.** To find the diameter of a circle, begin at one point of the circle and draw a straight line through the center of the circle, ending up at a point exactly opposite from where the line began. You may try this demonstration to measure the diameter of an apple. *You will need the same equipment which you used for the preceding demonstration, plus a knife. Do not try this demonstration without the permission of an adult.*

Cut the apple in half through the "equator." Lay the string across the cut side of the apple. The end of the string must be even with the edge of the apple. Make sure that the string goes directly over the center of the apple. Cut the other end of the string so that it is even with the opposite edge of the apple. Remove the string and measure it. This is the diameter of your apple. How does it compare in length to the circumference?

Comprehension Check 7.1
1. The earth is shaped like a ball or _____.
2. What is the imaginary line around the earth which divides it in half?
3. What is the name for the part of the earth marked *a*? the part marked *b*?

7.2 The Earth's Motion

The earth rotates

Although you cannot feel it, the earth is moving right now. Have you ever watched a top spin? The earth spins in much the same way that a top does. We call this spinning motion of the earth its **rotation**.

Notice how your globe rotates. There is a stick going through the globe. One end of the stick is at the North Pole, and the other end is at the South Pole. The globe rotates on this stick. The stick represents an imaginary line which runs through the earth. This imaginary line is called the earth's **axis** [ăk′sĭs]. The axis does not point straight up and down; it is tilted.

The surface of the earth near the equator rotates at a speed of about 1,000 miles per hour. *It takes about twenty-four hours for the earth to rotate once on its axis.* What name is given to a twenty-four hour period of time?

The earth rotates from west to east. This is why the sun seems to rise in the east each morning and set in the west each evening. However, the sun is not really moving across the sky each day. Because the earth rotates, people on one side of the earth face the sun and have day while people on the opposite side of the earth are facing away from the sun and having night. As the earth spins, the parts of the earth having night gradually rotate until they are facing the sun. Then the other parts of the earth have night.

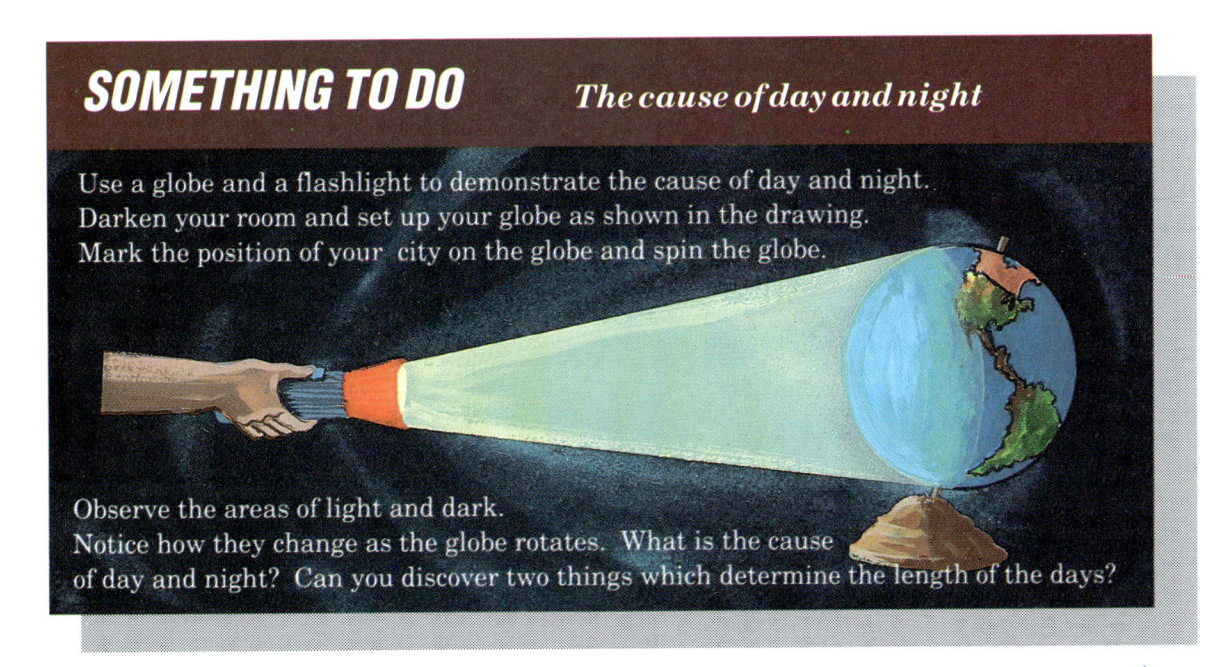

SOMETHING TO DO — *The cause of day and night*

Use a globe and a flashlight to demonstrate the cause of day and night. Darken your room and set up your globe as shown in the drawing. Mark the position of your city on the globe and spin the globe.

Observe the areas of light and dark. Notice how they change as the globe rotates. What is the cause of day and night? Can you discover two things which determine the length of the days?

Geology 197

*The earth **revolves** around the sun once every year...*

*...as it **rotates** on its axis once a day.*

The earth revolves

As the earth rotates on its axis, it also travels in a path around the sun. We say that the earth **revolves** around the sun. The pathway, or **orbit,** which the earth follows is 595 million miles around. The earth travels at a speed of 66,000 miles per hour as it orbits the sun. It takes 365 1/4 days for the earth to revolve once. What measurement of time is 365 days long? We have an extra day in February every four years during leap year to use up the extra quarter of a day left over each year.

How is it that the earth stays in its orbit day after day? As you know, the force that draws things toward the center of the earth is called *gravity*. If it were not for the earth's gravity, we would fly off into space. Did you know that the sun has gravity, too? Because the sun is so much bigger than the earth, it has a much stronger pull of gravity. The sun's gravity not only holds the sun together; it also pulls at the earth and all the other planets, keeping them from going off into space. The sun's gravity keeps the earth in its orbit day after day, year after year. We can be thankful to God for setting up such an orderly, faithful system as this.

The seasons

We have seasons of the year because, as the earth revolves around the sun, its axis remains tilted at an angle which does not change. This tilt causes heat and light from the sun to strike the earth in different ways at different times of the year.

Look at the diagram on page 199. In December, the people in Canada, the United States, and other parts of the Northern Hemisphere are having winter because the northern end of the earth's axis is tilted away from the sun and thus the sun's rays strike the Northern Hemisphere at an angle. Therefore, less heat and light reach the Northern Hemisphere in winter than in summer. Winter days are colder and have fewer hours of daylight than summer days.

The people in Australia, South Africa, Chile, and other parts of the Southern Hemisphere are having summer in December, because they are

198 ■ *Understanding God's World*

receiving the full rays of the sun. Days are warmer than in the Northern Hemisphere, because the Southern Hemisphere is receiving more hours of daylight and more direct sunshine.

Summer begins in the Northern Hemisphere in June. Notice that the northern end of the earth's axis is tilted toward the sun. Is the Northern Hemisphere receiving the full rays of the sun? What season are the people in the Southern Hemisphere having in June?

In March and September, the earth is positioned in such a way that neither hemisphere receives direct sunlight. The days are divided quite equally between hours of daylight and hours of darkness. The Northern Hemisphere has spring in March and autumn in September. What seasons are people in the Southern Hemisphere having at these times?

Keep in mind that the seasons change slowly as the earth rotates around the sun. Days gradually get warmer and longer as summer approaches, and colder and shorter as it gets closer to wintertime.

If you lived near the equator, you would not notice much of a temperature change throughout the year. The tilt of the earth at the equator is not great enough to affect the way the sun's rays hit the earth at this spot. There are seasons near the equator, however: a wet season and a dry season.

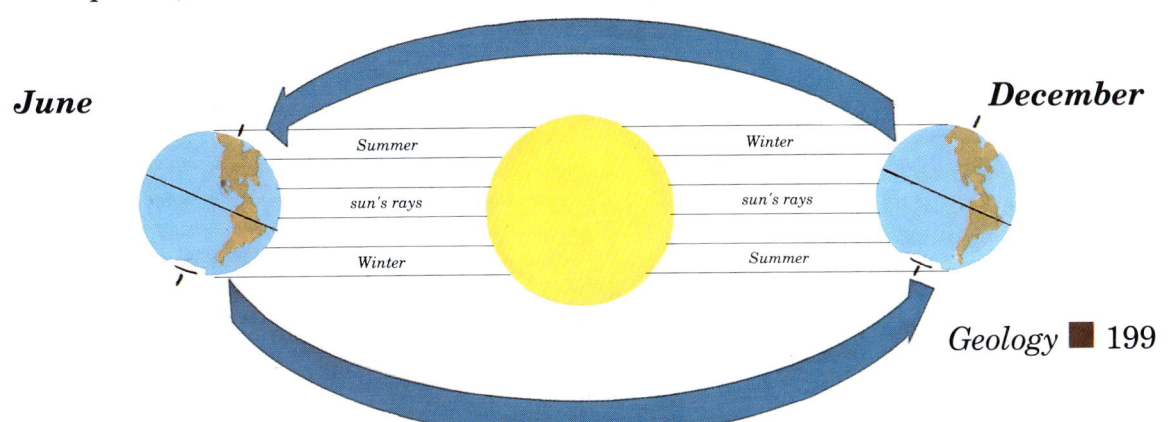

18 California Quail

summer
winter
both

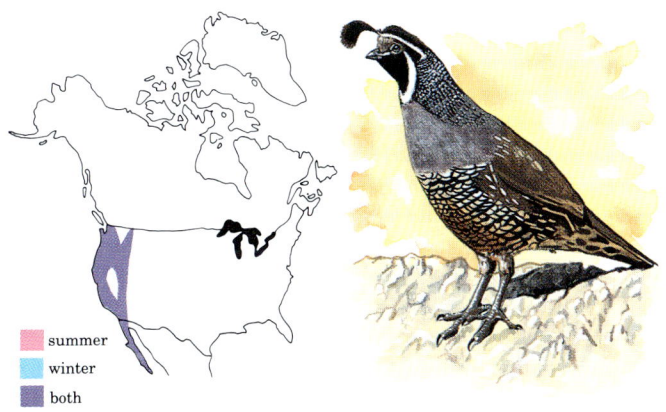

The California quail is a plump, chicken-shaped bird that is very colorful. It is a small member of the pheasant family, usually about eleven inches long. Its plumage is distinctively marked in a very detailed pattern. A black, teardrop-shaped plume rises from its crown and curves forward over its forehead. The California quail is a swift runner and only flies when it must.

A native of California, the California quail has spread into southern Oregon and northern Nevada. It has been successfully brought to the southern part of Vancouver Island and to Hawaii. It is a friendly bird, often seen in populated areas, although its natural home is in the open countryside with some brush and thickets of live oak for cover. Seeds, buds, and berries are its favorite foods, although it will eat some insects, especially in winter.

June   *December*

Summer   Winter
sun's rays   sun's rays
Winter   Summer

Geology ■ 199

SOMETHING TO DO — *Why winter is cold*

For this activity *you will need a flashlight, a globe, and a piece of cardboard with a one-inch-square hole cut in it.* Darken the room so that you will be able to see the results of the experiment better.

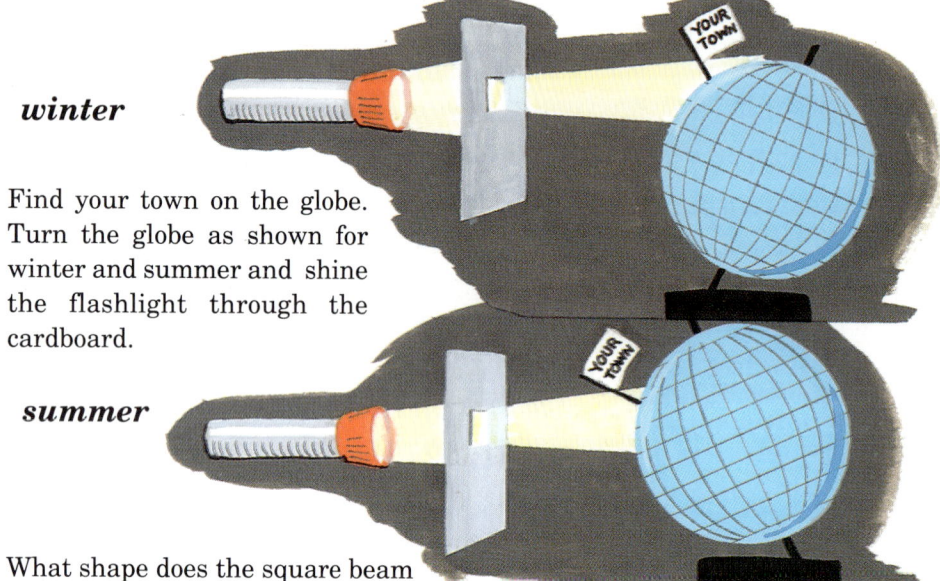

winter

Find your town on the globe. Turn the globe as shown for winter and summer and shine the flashlight through the cardboard.

summer

What shape does the square beam of light make on the globe in winter? Is the shape different in the summer position? Do you see that winter is cooler because the same amount of light is spread over a larger surface?

Comprehension Check 7.2

1. What is the spinning motion of the earth called?
2. Explain what the earth's axis is.
3. What is the earth's orbit?
4. What amount of time is measured by one rotation of the earth? One revolution?
5. What is the name of the force which keeps the earth in its orbit?
6. Why are there seasons?
7. Where on earth would you not notice a seasonal change of temperature?

Pacific Ocean *Atlantic Ocean* *Indian Ocean* *Arctic Ocean*

Understanding God's World

7.3 The Oceans and Continents of the Earth

The oceans

The sea is his, and he made it: and his hands formed the dry land.
— Psalm 95:5

The oceans, which are the earth's largest bodies of water, are all connected with each other, forming one vast body of water which we often call "the sea." The sea is rich in animal and plant life. Valuable oil reserves lie in the crust of the earth beneath the sea.

There are four oceans—the Pacific Ocean, the Atlantic Ocean, the Indian Ocean, and the Arctic Ocean. Locate them on the map.

The Pacific Ocean. The Pacific Ocean is **the world's largest ocean.** It is much larger than all of the lands of the earth put together. The Pacific Ocean covers more than one third of the earth's surface and is two times larger than any other ocean. In many places, the Pacific Ocean is 10,000 miles wide.

The Pacific Ocean is also **the world's deepest ocean.** The Mariana Trench, near the island of Guam, is 36,198 feet deep, the deepest known spot in any ocean. Many small islands dot the surface of the Pacific Ocean. The famous explorer Magellan gave the Pacific Ocean its name. Despite its name, which means "peaceful," raging storms often arise in the Pacific Ocean.

The Atlantic Ocean. The Atlantic Ocean is about half the size of the Pacific and about 3,000 miles wide. It is the world's second largest body of water and **the saltiest ocean.** The world's richest fishing areas are in the Atlantic Ocean, and it has long been an important route for trade between countries.

The Indian Ocean. The Indian Ocean is **the warmest ocean.** It is about one third the size of the Pacific Ocean. It touches the shores of the warm lands of Africa, India, and Australia.

The Arctic Ocean. Around the North Pole is the ice-covered Arctic Ocean, **the coldest and smallest ocean.** Huge icebergs float in the parts of the Arctic Ocean that are not frozen over. The Arctic Ocean is so cold that it hardly ever receives rain or snow.

Geology

The continents

The largest areas of dry land that rise out of the oceans are called **continents.** There are seven continents on the earth—Asia, Africa, North America, South America, Antarctica, Europe, and Australia. Locate the seven continents on the map and on your classroom globe. Did you notice that most of the continental land areas of the world are in the Northern Hemisphere?

Asia. Asia is *the largest continent.* The highest mountain, Mt. Everest, is located in Asia. Mt. Everest rises 29,028 feet above sea level! Because Asia is connected to Europe, Europe and Asia are often referred to together as Eurasia. Some of the countries of Asia are China, India, and Korea. A large part of the Soviet Union is also in Asia.

Africa. Africa, *the second largest continent,* was once connected to Asia by a narrow strip of land. The Suez Canal now cuts through this strip of land to make a waterway between the two continents. Egypt, Ethiopia, and Nigeria are a few of the many African nations.

North America. The next largest continent is North America. Can you name any North American countries? Canada, Mexico, the United States, and the Central American countries are found on the North American continent.

South America. The two Americas were once joined by a narrow strip of land. The Panama Canal now separates the two continents. South America is slightly smaller than North America. Some of the countries of South America are Brazil, Chile, and Peru.

Antarctica. *The only continent where no people (except researchers) live* is the frozen continent of Antarctica. It is at the "bottom of the world."

Europe. Although Europe is the next to the smallest continent, it has been a very important continent to

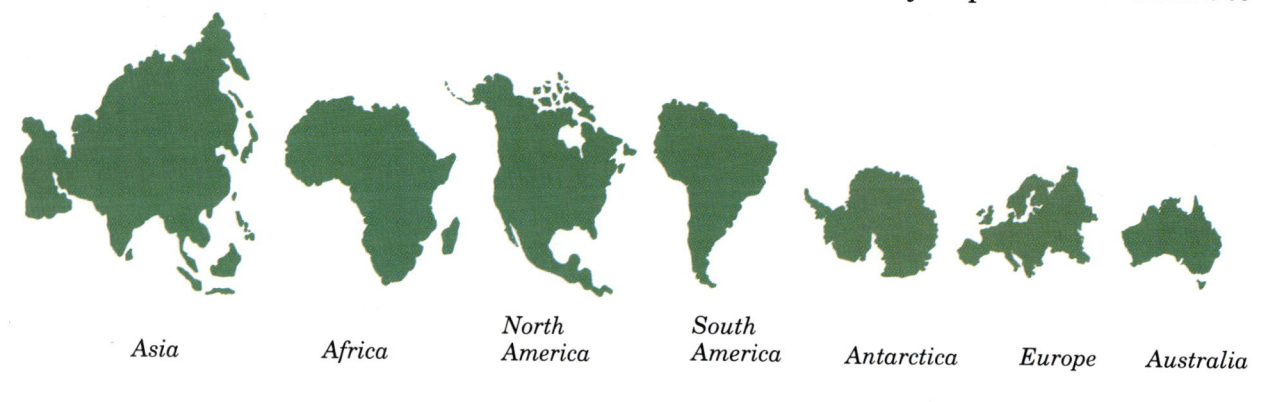

| Asia | Africa | North America | South America | Antarctica | Europe | Australia |

Understanding God's World

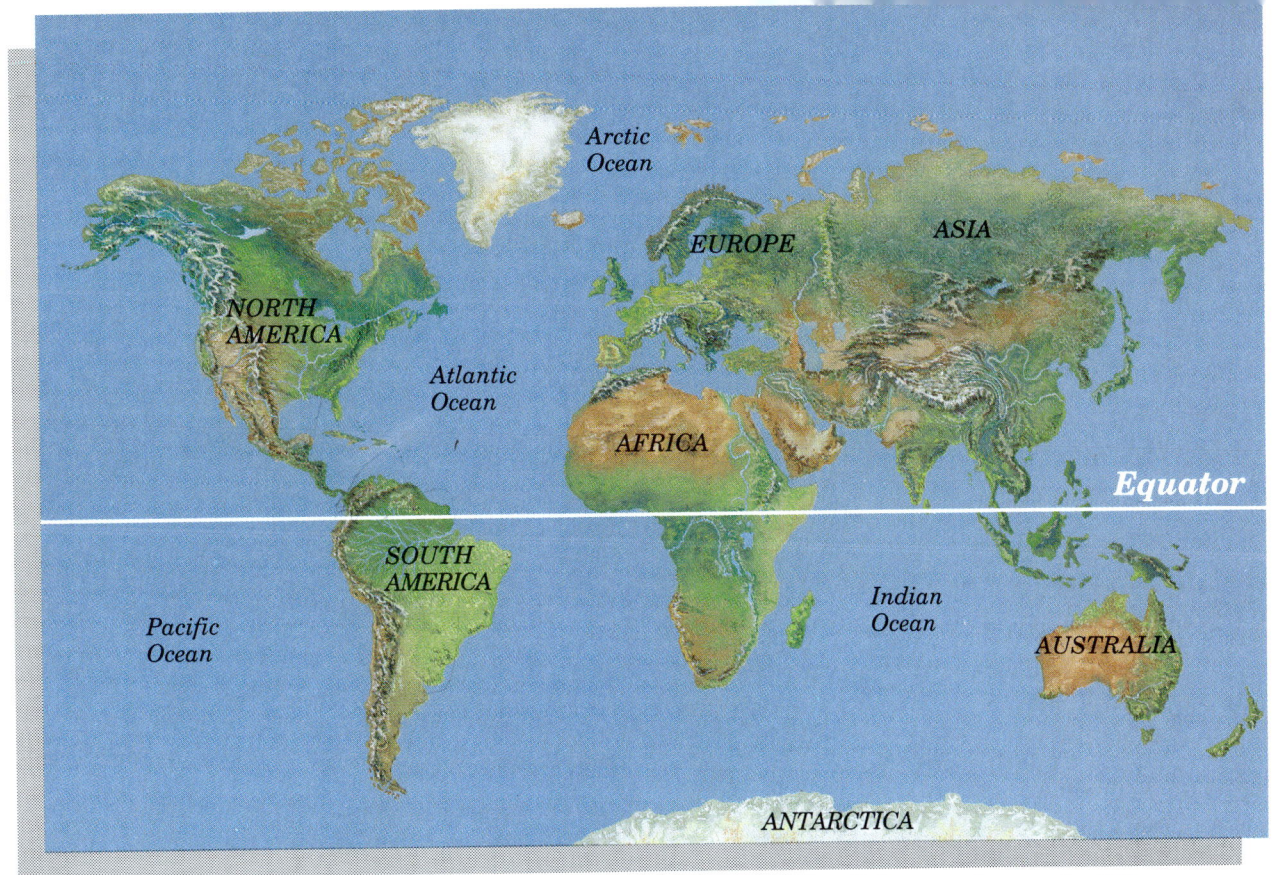

man. People from Europe were responsible for much of the settlement of the continents of North and South America in modern times. France, Germany, Italy, and Spain are a few of the many European countries.

Australia. *The smallest continent* is Australia. Because it is small for a continent, and because it is completely surrounded by water, it is sometimes called the "Island Continent." There is only one country, also called Australia, on the Australian continent.

Earth is a magnet

You are probably familiar with magnets, pieces of metal that attract iron, steel, and some other metals. Bar magnets have two ends or poles. These poles are known as the north and south poles. The earth is a giant magnet which has two ends or poles known as the North and South Poles. The north and south magnetic poles are near the North and South geographic poles. If you hold a bar magnet suspended horizontally from a string, its south pole (marked "N" for north-seeking) will point toward the magnetic north pole. Opposite poles of two magnets attract each other. A compass, which has a magnetized needle, helps us to find the north because the needle is drawn toward the magnetic north pole.

Geology ■ 203

SOMETHING TO DO — Making a Compass

You can make your own compass from items that you probably have at home. *You will need a needle, a cork, a shallow bowl with water in it, a bar magnet, and a pair of scissors or a knife.* Cut a piece of cork about 1/2 inch thick. Cut a groove large enough to hold the needle across the center of the piece of cork. Rub one end of the bar magnet across the needle in one direction only. Place the magnetized needle in the groove in the cork. Place the cork in the water so that the cork and needle are floating. Your needle should now point in a north-south direction.

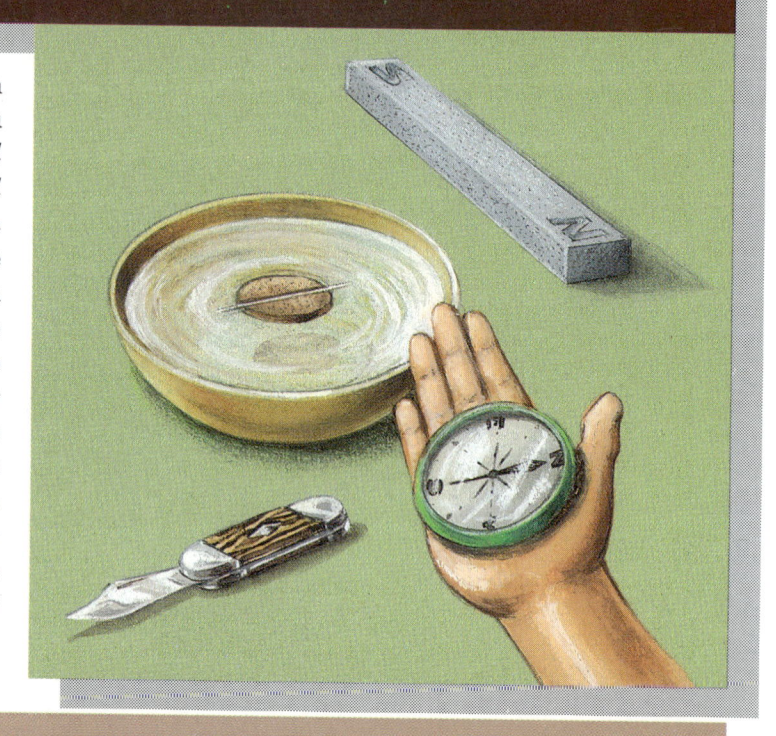

Comprehension Check 7.3

1. List the oceans in order of size from **smallest** to **largest**.
2. Which ocean . . .
    a. contains the world's richest fishing areas?
    b. contains huge icebergs?
    c. is the warmest ocean?
    d. covers 1/3 of the earth's surface?
3. List the continents in order of size from **smallest** to **largest**.
4. Why does the needle of a compass always point toward the magnetic north pole?
5. Which continent . . .
    a. is separated from Asia by the Suez Canal?
    b. contains the countries of Canada and Mexico?
    c. is called the "Island Continent"?
    d. has the highest mountain?
    e. is the only continent with no people except researchers?
    f. was the home of the people who were responsible for settling much of North and South America in modern times?
    g. contains the countries of Peru and Brazil?
    h. is north of Africa?
    i. is west of Europe?
    j. is south of North America?
    k. is east of South America?

7.4 Soil and the Earth's Layers

Soil's ingredients

Humus. Most of the earth which is not covered by water is covered by soil. Soil contains two ingredients: (1) minerals from tiny pieces of weathered rock and (2) decayed material from dead plants and animals. Rocks are broken down, or weathered, by exposure to air, water, plants, and animals. Temperature changes also are important to the process of weathering. The decayed material in soil is called **humus** [hū'mus]. Humus fills up some of the spaces between the pieces of weathered rock. Because humus is soft, it can soak up water. Humus also returns nitrogen to the soil. If the soil were not being constantly enriched by humus, it would lose its ability to provide nourishment for plants.

Minerals. According to **geologists** [jē-ŏl'ō-jĭsts], scientists who study the earth, a substance must have the following characteristics in order to becalled a **mineral:**

salt

geode

sulfur

(1) A mineral is never man-made, and it is never made of things which were once alive.
(2) A particular mineral is always made up of exactly the same kinds of atoms, no matter where on earth it is found.
(3) The atoms of a mineral are always arranged in an orderly pattern that forms a crystal.

Geology ■ 205

copper

gold

diamond

graphite

silver

A **crystal** is a substance with smooth, flat surfaces that meet in sharp edges and corners. If you look at salt with a magnifying glass, you will see its little boxlike crystals, or cubes. Other minerals form crystals in shapes like pyramids, diamonds, and needles. Snowflakes are tiny six-sided clusters of ice crystals. Crystals are beautiful examples of God's creativity.

There are about 2,000 different minerals in the world, but only about 100 of them are common. *Salt, sulfur,* and *copper* are common, useful minerals. The lead in your pencil is made from the mineral *graphite. Gold* and *silver* are beautiful and valuable minerals. Some very rare and costly minerals, such as *diamonds, rubies,* and *emeralds,* are called **gems.**

Valuable soil

Soil is important to us because it provides many of the materials which plants need in order to make food. We all depend upon green plants and good soil for our food.

Although there is soil the world over, not all soil is the same. Some soils are dark brown. Others are grayish, yellowish, or reddish. The color comes from the different minerals found in the soil. For example, reddish soil has large amounts of iron in it. It is part of God's plan to have different kinds of soil. The different soils are suited to the different crops they grow: rice needs to grow in soil that can hold a great amount of water, blueberries and cranberries grow best in acid soil, and so forth.

SOMETHING TO DO — *Making crystals*

You can see how crystals are formed by growing two kinds of crystals yourself. In order to grow salt crystals, *you will need a small saucepan, 1 cup of water, 1/3 cup of table salt or more, a drinking glass (use glass, not plastic), a long pencil, and a piece of cotton string.* Pour the water into the saucepan and bring it to a boil. After the water has started to boil, turn off the heat and remove the pan from the burner. Add the salt and stir until the salt is dissolved. Continue to add salt until no more salt will dissolve. Allow the solution to cool, then pour it into the glass. Be sure to pour only the solution into the glass and leave the salt that did not dissolve in the pan. Tie one end of the string to the pencil and drop the other end of the string into the solution. Rest the pencil across the rim of the glass. Place the glass in a cool area where it will not be disturbed. Be sure that you do not move it or lift the string from the glass for several days. Check it daily to see if your crystals are growing.

Another kind of crystal that you can grow is *alum*. Alum is a powder which is used to stop the bleeding of small cuts and can be found in your local drugstore. It makes clear crystals which form very rapidly. In order to grow alum crystals, *you will need alum, a drinking glass, one cup of warm water, a long pencil, a piece of cotton string, and a measuring teaspoon.* Measure eleven teaspoons of alum into one cup of *warm* water. Stir until the alum is dissolved. Suspend a piece of string into the water from a pencil that is placed across the rim of the glass. You should see some crystal formation within a few hours or less.

Geology ■ 207

Layers of soil

Although most land is covered by soil, soil is not the same depth the world over. In some places, the layer of soil may be only two inches deep. In other places, you could dig a hole ten feet deep before you came to the layer of rock underneath the soil.

In most places, there are two layers of soil. When holes are dug in the earth, you are often able to see where the two layers meet.

The upper layer of soil is called **topsoil.** This is the layer of soil which supports plant life. Topsoil is more fertile than the layer of soil beneath it, because topsoil contains more of the ingredients which plants need in order to make food. The best topsoil is a mixture of sand, silt, clay, and humus. *Sand* is made up of coarse particles of rock. It allows air into the soil. *Silt* is the name for medium-sized particles of soil. Very fine particles of soil are called clay. *Clay* holds water in the soil. Do you see how the sand, silt, clay, and humus work together to make the best topsoil?

Beneath the layer of topsoil is the **subsoil.** Since subsoil does not contain as much humus as topsoil, it is not as fertile. Subsoil often contains partly weathered rocks.

topsoil

subsoil

bedrock

layers of the earth's crust

Under the soil

Below the subsoil is a layer of rock which geologists call **bedrock.** It is part of the earth's **crust.** The crust of the earth is a solid layer of rock which begins beneath the soil and goes down about 5 miles to 25 miles below the earth's surface. The earth's crust is much thinner beneath the oceans than it is beneath land. Men have drilled and dug into the earth's crust, but no one has ever gone beneath the crust to the layers below. As far as we know, all of earth's creatures make their homes above the crust, on or near the earth's surface. If the earth were as small as an apple, the crust would be about as thin as the peel of the apple.

The layer of earth beneath the crust is called the **mantle.** If the earth were apple-sized, the mantle would be about as thick as the white part of the apple. Geologists believe that the mantle is made mostly of solid, hot, dense rock. In some places, however, the rock has melted. This hot, liquid rock is called *magma.* The mantle goes down about 1,800 miles. Scientists believe the temperature of the mantle is about 5,000° F, which is hot enough to melt rock.

Like an apple, the earth has a **core** at its center. Geologists think that part of the core is melted iron and nickel. The innermost portion of the core is probably solid because of the great pressure of all the rock above it. Some scientists think that the temperature reaches over 7,000° F.

19 Brown Thrasher

summer
winter
both

The brown thrasher is a shy bird that likes to live in thickets, brush, and hedgerows. It is able to run or hop speedily across the ground as it hunts for its food. It will even probe the dirt with its long bill, searching for insects. Because it eats so many harmful insects, the brown thrasher is a very helpful bird.

The brown thrasher is known for its varied and musical song. Like its relative the mockingbird, the brown thrasher is a clever mimic of other songbirds.

The brown thrasher is about 11 1/2 inches long, the size of a blue jay, but it is thinner than a robin. It lives east of the Rockies, from south central Canada and northern New England southward to the Gulf of Mexico.

Comprehension Check 7.4
1. What is a geologist?
2. What are the characteristics of a mineral?
3. What two things is soil made of?
4. Why do plants grow better in topsoil than in subsoil?
5. Of what is the earth's crust made?
6. Describe the layers of the earth below the crust.

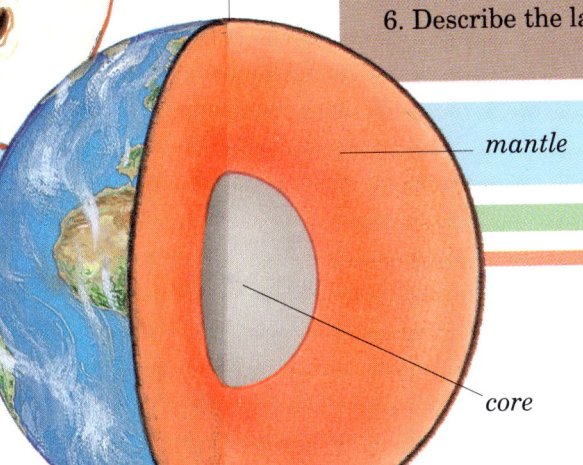

crust

mantle

core

Geology ■ 209

7.5 Water and Soil

Wearing away of topsoil

He cutteth out rivers among the rocks; and his eye seeth every precious thing.
— Job 28:10

One thing that keeps changing the earth's soil cover and crust is water. Perhaps you have seen the gullies that running water has made in the side of a hill that has been cut away. Water is seldom at rest. It is always seeking to get to a lower level because of the force of gravity. When water falls to the ground as rain, much of it runs off the surface of the ground to form tiny streams. The streams come together to form bigger streams. The larger streams often end in a pond, lake, or ocean, where the downward flow of water has finally stopped. Gravity gives moving water its energy. (You will remember that energy is the ability to do work.) As it travels, water easily carries away the soil from bare hillsides. Water has also carried away the rich topsoil from many farms. **Erosion,** the wearing away of the earth's topsoil, is a form of work done by water and by wind. Erosion is often harmful.

Soil conservation

The protection of soil from water erosion and other kinds of erosion is called soil conservation. **Conservation** is using nature's resources wisely. (A **natural resource** is a material helpful to man which is found in or on the earth.) Fertile soil and other natural resources are gifts of God and should be used with care.

Farmers use a variety of methods to conserve soil. Soil erosion is reduced when trees are planted and strips of grass are left between fields. The leaves of trees keep the rain from beating down directly on soil and washing it away. Decayed leaves form a rich soil which soaks up water easily. Root systems absorb water and hold the soil in place. Some farmers also plant crops such as alfalfa or clover to cover and protect the soil. (These crops also return nitrogen to the soil, making it fertile.)

Since the soil on hillsides erodes (wears away) easily, farmers pay special attention to the way hillsides are cultivated. Contour plowing is one way to conserve soil on hillsides. Plowing the slope across instead of up and down forms ridges which slow down the flow of the water. In other places, sloping land is terraced by building the land up into wide, flat areas which make the hillside look like an enormous stair-

contour plowing

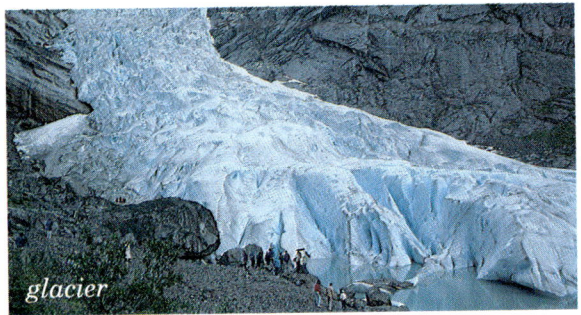

glacier

case. Soil built up in this way is able to hold the rain because terraces prevent running water from forming gullies.

Frozen water is also responsible for erosion. Water seeps into the cracks of rock. Do you remember that water, unlike other liquids, expands when it nears the freezing point? As the water freezes, it expands with enough force to crack the rock farther apart. **Glaciers** [glā′shĕrz] are massive rivers of ice that move very slowly, carrying with them broken rocks and soil.

Water as a builder

Water does not just tear things down. It also works to build things up. In the little coves and pools along the edge of a stream, the water does not move very fast, and it deposits some of the fine bits of rock, sand, and decaying plant and animal material it has been carrying. The stream slows down as it reaches lower levels, and more of the particles that it was carrying settle to the bottom or at the sides of the stream bed. Matter that settles to the bottom or sides of a body of water is called **sediment.** During the summer, the edges of a glacier will melt, leaving a load of sediment behind.

A river can carry its sediment all the way to its mouth and drop it there.

delta

After years and years, new land is built by the collecting sediment. This new land is called a delta. A **delta** is a deposit of sand and soil, usually in a triangular shape, at the mouth of some rivers.

Have you ever thought how powerful flowing water is? It is always working as it slowly tears down highlands and takes the material from them to build up lowlands.

Geology

Floods

Floods are caused when a great deal of water flows into an area, causing a river to overflow its banks. Floods are often caused when large amounts of snow melt quickly. Sudden heavy rainfall may also cause flooding. Floods can be both destructive and helpful. Flooding waters have changed the courses of rivers, left people homeless, destroyed crops, and caused death. But some people of the world depend upon floods, because these floods carry rich soils from higher lands down to lower lands used for farming. Men have found ways to control floods in order to prevent great damage. Sometimes channels are dug to allow excess water to flow quickly out to sea. In some places, the river banks are built up higher to protect the land on either side of the river. These high embankments are called levees [lĕv′ēz]. Dams are also built to hold back flood waters. When danger is over, the water behind the dam can be slowly released.

Consider!

Can you think of a time in the history of the world when the earth was completely covered with water? Look up Genesis 1:9, 10, which mentions a time before the continents had risen from the sea. Also read Genesis 7, which tells of a great flood. Where do you suppose all the water came from?

Comprehension Check 7.5
1. Why does water always seek to get to a lower level?
2. Define erosion.
3. What two forms of water erode the soil?
4. What is a delta? Where does its soil come from?
5. How can floods be helpful?

7.6 Rocks

He putteth forth His hand upon the rock;
He overturneth the mountains
by the roots.
— Job 28:9

The solid material which forms the earth's crust is **rock.** Thus, rocks are a very important part of God's creation. Can you remember the characteristics of a mineral? Rocks may be made up of one mineral by itself or of several minerals put together. Because of the different kinds of minerals found in rocks, rocks differ from one another in color, density, hardness, and texture. Geologists have divided rocks into three main groups, depending upon the way they can be formed. Although rocks are being formed and broken up today by natural processes, we know that God created rock in the beginning when He laid the foundation of the earth (Ps. 102:25). Much of the formation of rock may have taken place on the third day of Creation, when God pushed the dry land up out of the seas (Genesis 9, 10).

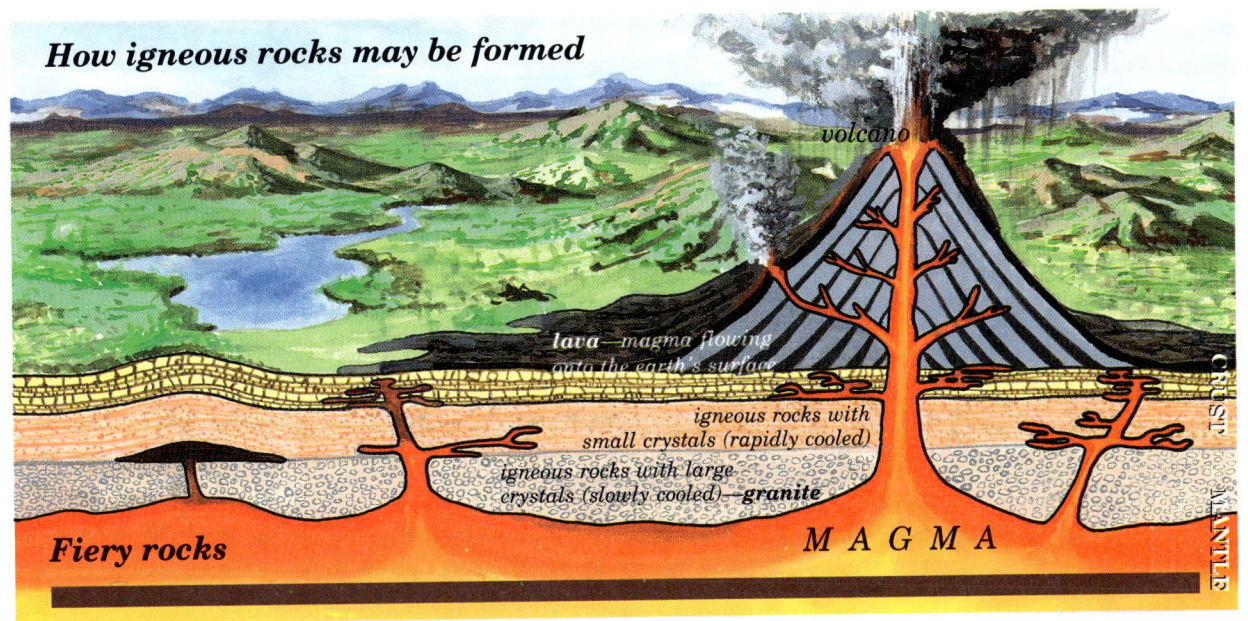

How igneous rocks may be formed

volcano
lava—magma flowing onto the earth's surface
igneous rocks with small crystals (rapidly cooled)
igneous rocks with large crystals (slowly cooled)—granite
Fiery rocks   M A G M A
CRUST
MANTLE

You will remember that geologists believe that beneath the crust, the earth's mantle contains some very hot liquid rock, or magma. Sometimes magma comes out of the earth through volcanoes. Sometimes it rises close to the surface of the earth underground and cools. When it cools, magma changes from liquid rock to solid rock. Rocks which can be formed from hot magma are called **igneous** [ĭg′nē-us] **rocks.** The word *igneous* means "fiery." (The word "ignite," which means "to set fire to," comes from the same root.)

Geology ■ 213

Granite (1) forms when liquid rock cools slowly, deep underground. Most of the earth's crust under the continents is granite. This abundant and useful rock is extremely hard and can be polished until it is very smooth. It is usually speckled with glittery crystals. It is used for monuments, tombstones, and the outsides of important public buildings.

Pumice [pŭm′ĭs] and obsidian [ob-sĭd′ĭ-an] are igneous rocks that form when liquid rock cools quickly after it comes out of a volcano. Both rocks are forms of lava. **Pumice** (2) is full of air holes, which make it so light that it will sometimes float on water. It can be ground up and used in soaps and scouring powders. The material that the dentist uses to clean your teeth contains pumice. **Obsidian** (3) is shiny and black and feels smooth and glassy, with sharp edges. Indians used it to make arrowheads. Obsidian is made of the same kinds of molecules as granite, but they cooled so quickly that crystals did not have time to form.

Settled rocks

You will remember that moving water slowly deposits *sediment,* or fine bits of humus and minerals, on the land over which it flows. If this sediment is pressed together under the earth so that it hardens, it forms **sedimentary rock.** Much sedimentary rock is formed from deposits that have settled under the ocean. Sediment, or material which is washed into the sea, is pressed together by burial under more sediment until it hardens into rock. Different materials such as sand, mud, or sea shells cause different kinds of sedimentary rock to form.

Sandstone (4) can be made of sand that is pressed down under the ocean. Its layers are often visible, and if you rub it, you can probably rub off some sand. If you look at sandstone with a magnifying glass, you can distinguish the many different kinds and colors of sand grains. Sandstone is used to make glass, concrete, and sandpaper. Some kinds of sandstone are so hard that they can be used to construct buildings. **Conglomerate** (5) contains pebbles or cobbles cemented together.

Limestone (6) can be made from the shells of sea creatures. After the animals die, their shells settle to the bottom of the sea. Here the shells are pressed together until they form

How sedimentary rocks may be formed

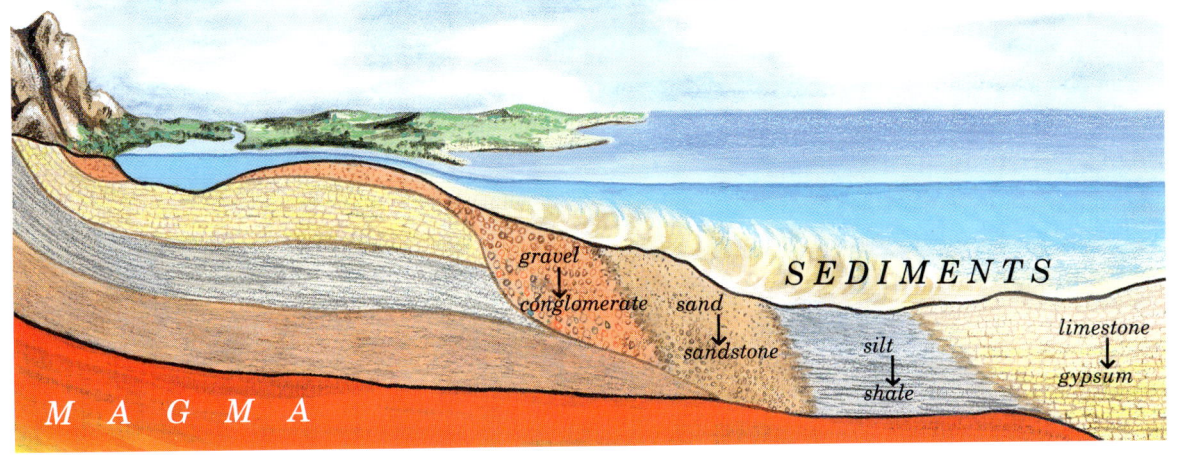

gravel
conglomerate *sand*
sandstone
silt
shale
SEDIMENTS
limestone
gypsum

MAGMA

solid rock. You may be able to see its layers, and sometimes you can find fossils in it. Limestone is often crushed and used to make cement.

The **chalk** in your classroom is made of white, fine-grained limestone that did not harden. If you rub a piece on something hard, some of the grains will come off, leaving a white mark. The famous white cliffs of Dover in England (7) are made of layers of chalk.

Shale (8) can be formed from mud or clay. It even smells like mud when it gets wet. Shale is the most common sedimentary rock. It is very soft and is often crushed to make tiles and bricks. It is often found with layers of sandstone or limestone.

Much sedimentary rock is formed in the sea, and yet it is found all over the earth, even in places far from the ocean. How can this be? Much of it was probably created by God in the beginning. Some could have been formed before the dry land appeared (Gen. 1:9). Some could have been formed during the great Flood of Noah's day (Gen. 6–8), and some could have been formed during the days of Peleg, when the earth was divided (Gen. 10:25).

4.

5.

6.

7.

8.

Geology ■ 215

Changed rocks

How metamorphic rocks may be formed

unchanged layers
changed by heat
changed by pressure
changed by pressure
changed by pressure
changed by heat
changed by heat

M A G M A

Do you remember what *metamorphosis* means? It means the change of form that insects (and amphibians) undergo from egg to adult. Rocks also can undergo a change of form, or metamorphosis. **Metamorphic rock** is rock which seems to have been changed by heat or pressure.

One of the most beautiful rocks is **marble** (9), a metamorphic rock. Marble may begin as limestone and be changed by heat and pressure. Like granite, marble can be highly polished. It is often used for statues and for very special buildings. The Washington Monument, the Lincoln Memorial, and the Jefferson Memorial are all made of marble. The finest deposits of marble are found in Italy, where the great artist Michelangelo carved his magnificent statues of David and Moses from large pieces of marble.

Slate (10) is another useful metamorphic rock. Slate, which may begin as shale, is very hard and smooth. You may have a large piece of slate in your classroom, because many blackboards, especially older ones, are made of slate. In colonial and pioneer days, children used a small piece of slate rather than paper for their schoolwork. Would you use an igneous rock or a sedimentary rock to write on slate?

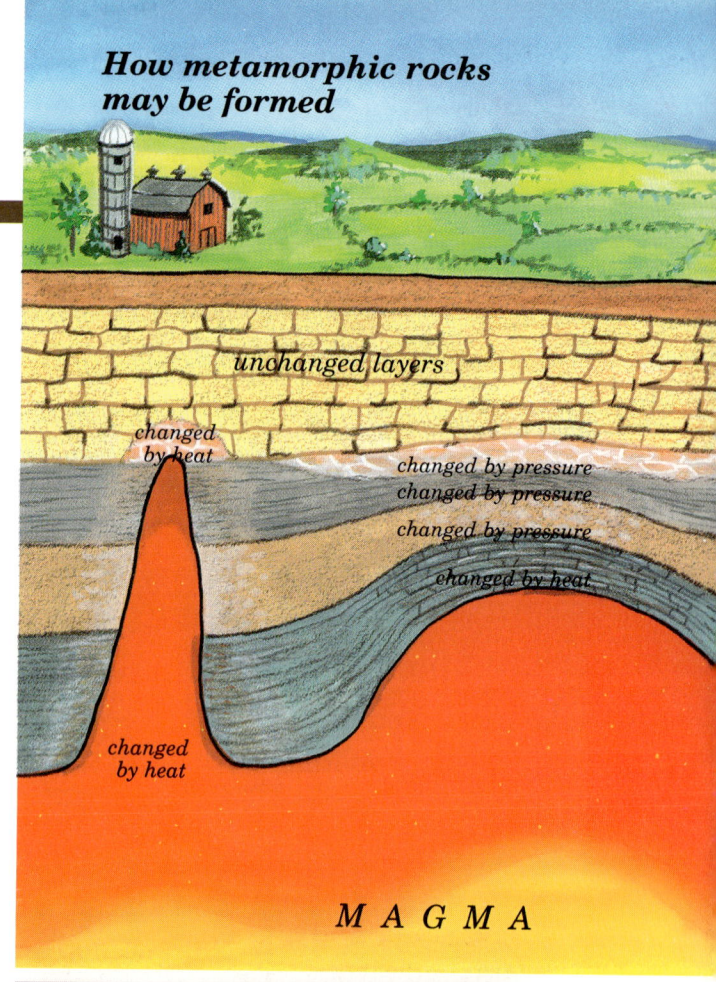

9.
10.

Understanding God's World

SOMETHING TO DO — Rock collections

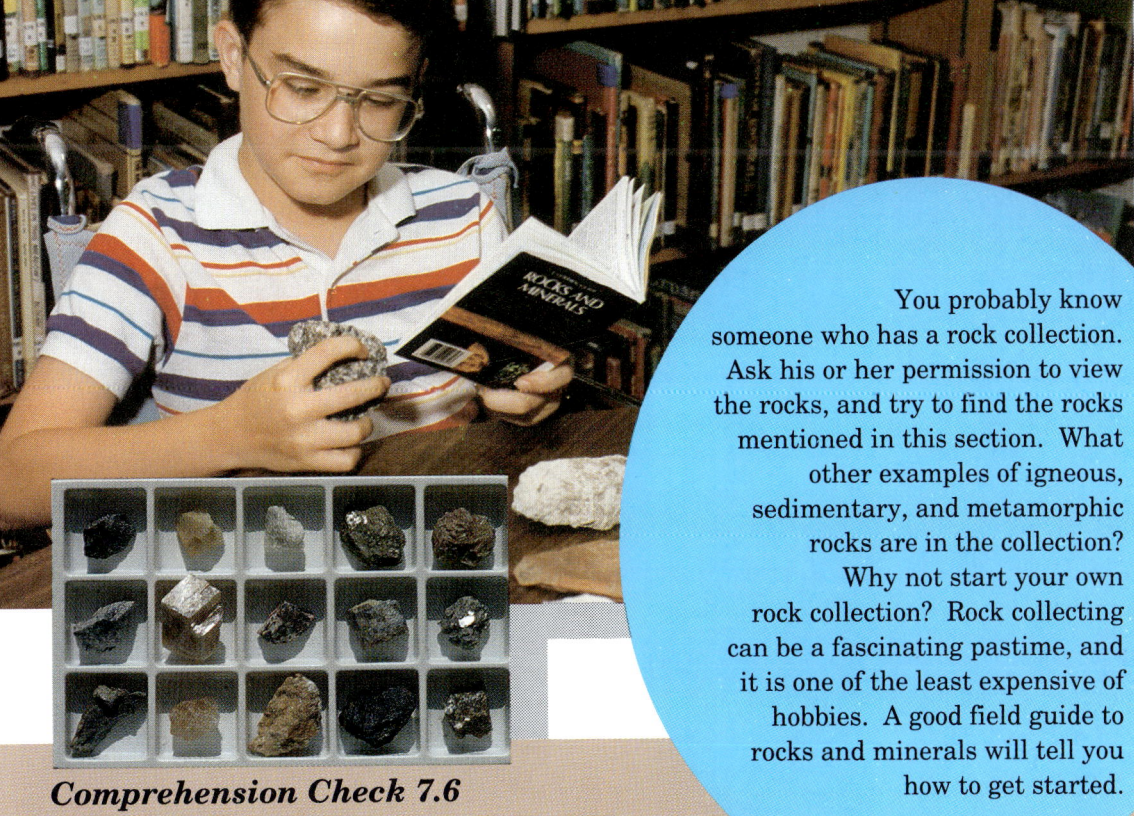

You probably know someone who has a rock collection. Ask his or her permission to view the rocks, and try to find the rocks mentioned in this section. What other examples of igneous, sedimentary, and metamorphic rocks are in the collection?

Why not start your own rock collection? Rock collecting can be a fascinating pastime, and it is one of the least expensive of hobbies. A good field guide to rocks and minerals will tell you how to get started.

Comprehension Check 7.6

1. What are rocks made of?
2. Which type of rock can be formed by heat?
3. How may sedimentary rocks be formed?
4. What main group of rock can be formed from rock which has undergone a change?
5. Identify each of these rocks:
   a. a shiny, black igneous rock from which Indians made arrowheads
   b. the beautiful metamorphic rock from which the Lincoln Memorial is made
   c. sedimentary rock made from layers of sand
   d. the igneous rock from which most of the earth's crust under the continents is formed
   e. the sedimentary rock that can be used for writing, and the metamorphic rock upon which it leaves a white mark
   f. the igneous rock that floats
   g. the sedimentary rock that can be made from seashells
   h. the sedimentary rock made from mud

Geology ■ 217

Chapter Check-up

A *Be able to identify each rock described in this chapter and to tell at least one thing about it.*

B *Write the name of the continent represented by each of the following groups of countries.*

1. India and China _____

2. Peru and Brazil _____

3. Nigeria and Egypt _____

4. no countries _____

5. France and Italy _____

6. only one country _____

7. Mexico and Canada _____

C *Write the letter of the phrase that identifies each term.*

_____ 1. equator
_____ 2. axis
_____ 3. rotation
_____ 4. orbit
_____ 5. gravity
_____ 6. topsoil
_____ 7. erosion
_____ 8. conservation
_____ 9. magma
_____ 10. glaciers
_____ 11. sediment
_____ 12. delta
_____ 13. rock
_____ 14. natural resource

A. a deposit of sand and soil found at the mouth of some rivers
B. the imaginary line running through the earth from North Pole to South Pole
C. a material useful to man found in or on the earth
D. rivers of ice that move very slowly
E. the imaginary line running around the earth exactly half way between the North and South Poles
F. decayed material that enriches the soil
G. the upper layer of rich soil
H. the solid layer of rock beneath the soil
I. the spinning motion of the earth
J. the solid material that forms the earth's crust
K. the pathway that the earth follows as it revolves around the sun
L. the wearing away of the earth's topsoil
M. the force that attracts all of the objects in the universe to each other
N. matter that settles to the bottom or sides of a body of water
O. using natural resources wisely
P. hot, partly liquid rock within the earth

D *Fill in the answer to complete each sentence.*

1. The warmest ocean is the

   _____ Ocean.

2. The largest and deepest ocean is the

   _____ Ocean.

3. The smallest ocean is the

   _____ Ocean.

4. The saltiest ocean is the

   _____ Ocean.

5. Rare and valuable minerals are called

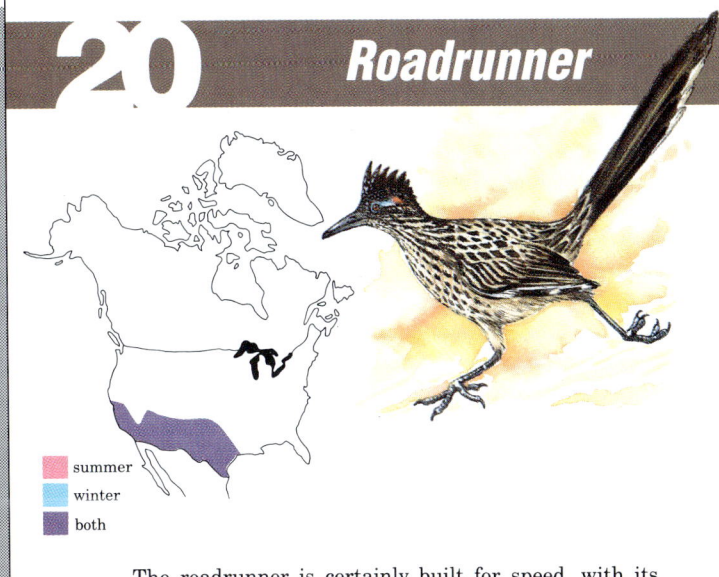

   _____.

20 Roadrunner

- summer
- winter
- both

The roadrunner is certainly built for speed, with its streamlined body and long, powerful legs. The roadrunner is about 24 inches long, and nearly half of that length is tail. This bird prefers running to flying any time, and has been clocked traveling as fast as 18 m.p.h.

The desert Southwest is the home of the roadrunner. It lives in open, dry places with scattered trees, cactuses, and stones. Its strong legs give it the ability to swiftly pursue its prey. It will eat just about any small creature, including grasshoppers, lizards, snakes, mice, and small gophers. The roadrunner beats its prey against a rock and then swallows it whole. When roadrunners are only three weeks old, they are able to catch their own dinners.

E *Write* true *or* false *in the space before each statement.*

_____ 1. The earth is shaped like a sphere.

_____ 2. The earth is slightly flattened at the poles.

_____ 3. Gravity is the force that keeps the earth in its orbit.

_____ 4. The earth rotates on its axis once every 365 1/4 days.

_____ 5. The earth's axis is tilted at a different angle at different times of the year.

_____ 6. When a region of the earth receives the sun's direct rays, it has winter.

_____ 7. Some man-made substances are minerals.

_____ 8. The subsoil supports plant life.

_____ 9. Floods can be both destructive and helpful.

_____ 10. Sedimentary rocks can be formed when magma cools to solid rock.

_____ 11. Igneous rocks can be formed by moving water.

_____ 12. Metamorphic rocks can be formed when igneous and sedimentary rocks are changed by heat and pressure.

Geology ■ 219

8 OCEANOGRAPHY: Wonders of the Sea

8.1 The Paths of the Seas

You learned in chapter one that there are at least four good reasons for studying science:

1. *God has made us curious about the world around us.*
2. *When God created us, He gave us minds that are able to think His thoughts after Him and thus learn to understand His creation.*
3. *God gave us the ability to enjoy His world and to use it wisely.*
4. *God gave us a desire to help others.*

A Christian man of science who had all of these reasons for studying science was **Matthew F. Maury** [mô'rĭ], *the first man to make an orderly study of the sea.*

Matthew Maury was born in Virginia in 1806. As a young boy, Matthew dreamed of going to sea aboard a navy frigate like the U.S.S. *Constitution.* At nineteen, Matthew's dreams came to pass when he became a midshipman in the U.S. Navy. He looked forward to years of active duty aboard navy vessels. Perhaps he would even command his own ship one day!

These hopes were shattered when he was seriously injured in a stagecoach accident and confined to bed. The doctors told him he would be lame for the rest of his life and would never serve aboard ship again. Instead of becoming discouraged, however, Maury spent much time praying and reading his Bible. One day, a phrase in Psalm 8, "the paths of the seas," set him to thinking seriously. What could be

Understanding God's World

The sea is His, and He made it.
—Psalm 95:5a

meant by "paths of the seas"? The Bible seemed to be saying that God created set patterns of movement in the ocean. Matthew Maury knew that if God said there were such paths, they must exist, for God never makes a mistake. ***Although the Bible is not a science book, it is always true when it talks about scientific things, just as it is true when it talks about other things.*** Believing this truth helped Matthew Maury to make important discoveries. He began to read and study everything he could find about winds and waves. Then he received the good news that he could return to duty as head of the navy's Depot of Charts and Instruments. At once Maury put together special logbooks that sea captains could take along on voyages to record information on wind patterns and ocean currents.

He also asked sailors to put messages into bottles and drop them into the sea. Each message was a record of a ship's location on a particular date. Later, when the bottles were picked up by other ships, the messages would help Maury to determine how objects travel through the sea. Within six years, Maury had collected enough information to make a whole new set of ocean charts for ships' pilots and to publish maps of the earth's major wind patterns.

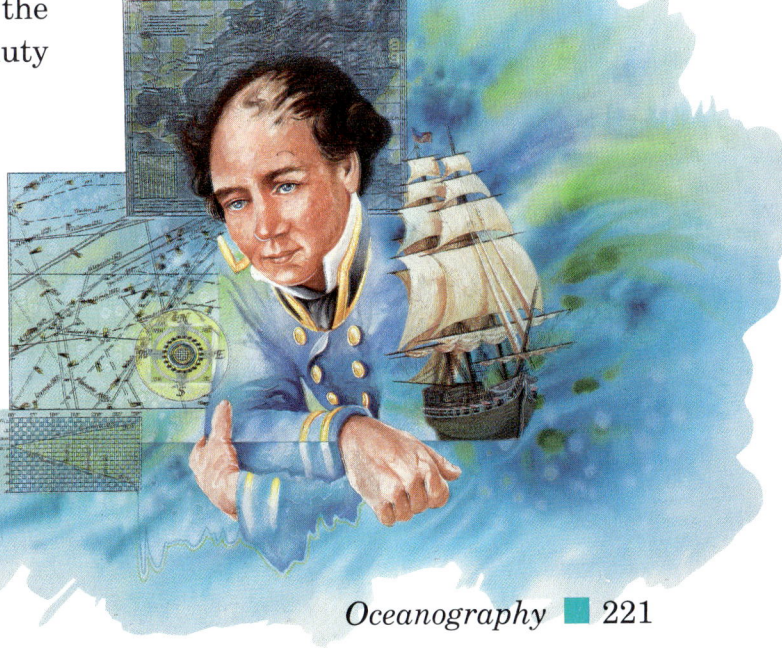

Oceanography 221

Ocean Currents: The Paths of the Seas

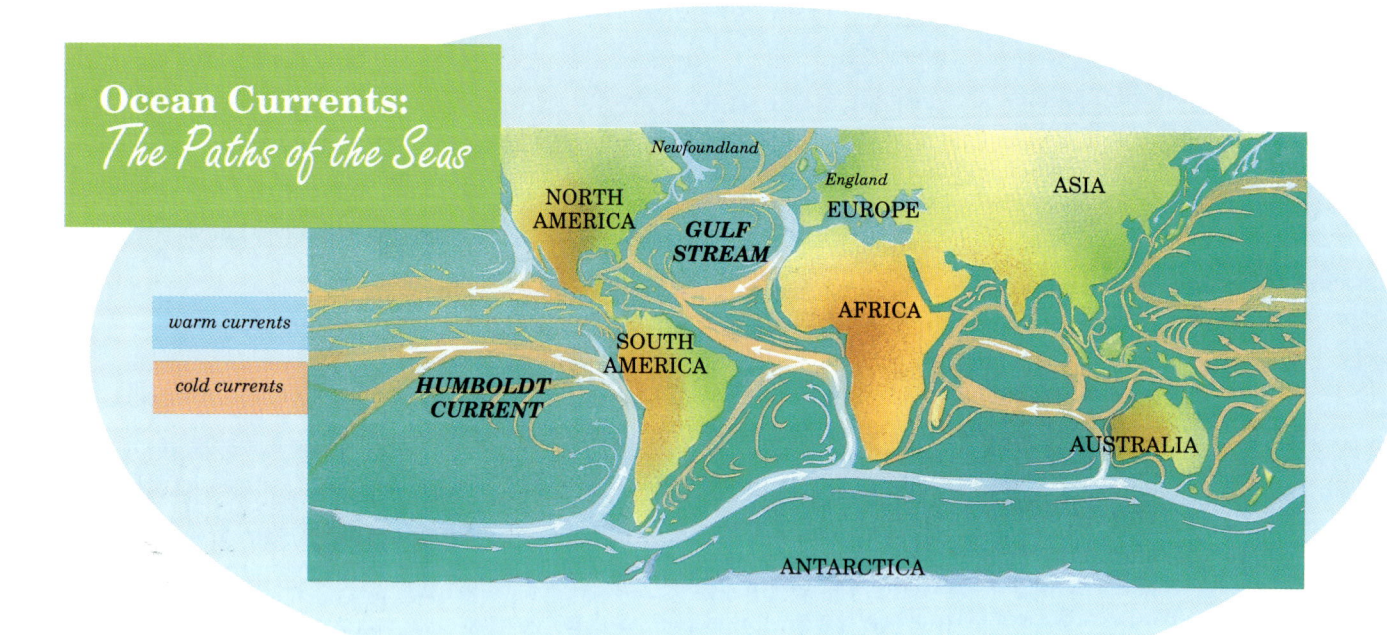

Maury's work led to a new science, **oceanography,** the scientific study of the ocean. When scientists met in Brussels, Belgium, in 1853, for the first international marine conference, Matthew Maury served as the American representative. From information provided by seamen and navigators of many countries, Maury compiled charts of the currents in the Atlantic, Pacific, and Indian oceans. Then, in 1855, Maury wrote and published the first textbook in the new science of oceanography, *The Physical Geography of the Sea.* Maury's work helped make sea travel safer and quicker, saving both lives and ships.

From Matthew Maury's research, as well as from other studies, scientists have learned that there are indeed "paths of the seas." These streams of water called **currents** are so large that they dwarf the mightiest land rivers. Ocean currents are moved primarily by winds. Those flowing from the equator carry warm water toward the Poles and help to warm land areas near the ocean. The people in England, for example, enjoy a moderate climate even though they live as far north as Newfoundland, because the great current called the **Gulf Stream** warms their air. Other currents moving away from the Poles carry cool water toward the equator. In general, therefore, we can see that currents help to moderate (make less extreme) earth's climate.

222 *Understanding God's World*

Many currents are home to large numbers of ocean creatures. The cold **Humboldt Current,** for example, which sweeps up from the South Pole along the western coast of South America, is full of plankton (tiny, floating plants and animals), small and large fish, dolphins, and whales. In certain years, however, the current mysteriously changes; warm waters from the equator shift it from its course, killing the plant plankton on which the fish feed. Then the beaches are strewn with dead fish, and fishermen's families face great hardship. There is much yet to be learned about the "paths of the seas."

SOMETHING TO DO — *Making Currents*

You will need a jug, a small jar, food coloring, and two pieces of string about 1 1/2 feet long. Tie one end of each string around the top of the small jar so that the knots are opposite each other. Fill the jar with *hot tap water* and add enough food coloring to make a dark color in the water. Fill the jug with *cold water.* Lower the jar carefully into the jug. What happened? Do you know why? The hot water rose to the top because when water is heated, it expands and becomes lighter than cool water. What do we call streams of warm or cool ocean water that do not mix with the surrounding water?

Comprehension Check 8.1
1. How did Matthew Maury know that there must be "paths of the seas"?
2. Describe the way in which currents circulate water through the ocean.
3. Name two currents.
4. What happens when a current changes?

Oceanography

8.2 The Continental Shelf and Slope

Oceanographers, scientists who study the oceans, have discovered that the land beneath the waters of the oceans is as varied as the dry land of the earth. A breathtaking view of valleys, mountain ranges, plains, and slopes can be found underwater. The land beneath the waves is divided into three main areas: the *continental shelf,* the *continental slope,* and the deep *ocean floor.*

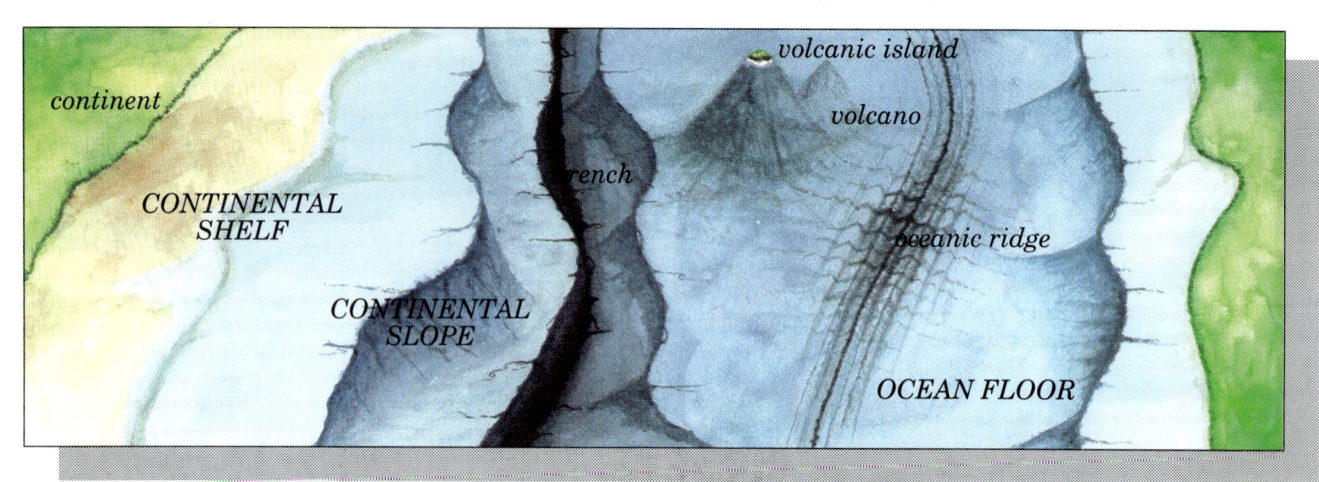

The continental shelf

Along the edges of the continents is an area of underwater land known as the **continental shelf.** It is made primarily of mud and sand deposited by rivers as they empty into the ocean. Many of the ocean's treasures are located along the continental shelf. Most marine life can be found there. Since the water is shallow enough for sunlight to penetrate easily, plants flourish, providing food for the small animals that are eaten by fish. Rich oil fields are also found in the continental shelf.

The continental slope

The **continental slope** lies between the continental shelf and the ocean floor. There is *no plant life* in the region of the slopes, but there are fish and other marine animals. The continental slope is irregular, containing valleys and canyons of varying depths. At the base of the slope are **trenches,** which are the deepest parts of the ocean. The deepest known spot in the ocean is located in the **Mariana Trench** near the island of Guam in the Pacific Ocean. If you placed the tallest mountain in the world, Mt. Everest, in the Mariana Trench, it would be covered by 1 1/2 miles of water!

Understanding God's World

Fish of the continental shelf

Almost all fish that are caught for commercial use (to sell to large numbers of people) come from the continental shelves. A number of fascinating game fish (fish caught for sport) also live in the rich waters above the shelves.

Over a million tons of **herring** (1) are caught each year in the waters of the North Atlantic and North Pacific oceans, making herring one of the world's most important food fishes. Nearly four million tons of **mackerel** (2) are caught each year in American, Canadian, and European waters. The mackerel's blue-green body, silvery white belly, and wavy, black-striped back make it a strikingly beautiful little fish. **Cod** (3) are caught for their meat and for *the oil in their liver,* which *is high in vitamins A and D.*

Flounders are called **flatfish** because they have **both of their eyes on the same side of the head**. Flounders prefer to live along the shore on the muddy or sandy bottoms of bays, where their camouflaged markings help them to blend in with their surroundings. The **winter flounder** (4) is about a foot long. The **halibut** (5) is a *coldwater flatfish* of the flounder group.

Salmon [săm′ un] (6) are unique because they live their adult lives in the ocean but return to the freshwater stream where they were hatched in order to *spawn* (lay eggs).

Comprehension Check 8.2
1. Define: *continental shelf, trench.*
2. In which of the three main areas of the ocean would you find the most marine life? Why?
3. Which fish migrates from salt water to fresh water in order to spawn?

8.3 Ocean Floor and Open Ocean

And God blessed them [Adam and Eve], and God said unto them, Be fruitful, and multiply, and replenish the earth, and subdue it: and have dominion over the fish of the sea, and over the fowl of the air, and over every living thing that moveth upon the earth.
— Genesis 1:28

The ocean floor

At the very bottom of the ocean is the **ocean floor,** where there are wide plains, great basins, and long mountain ranges called **oceanic ridges** (see page 224). There are also isolated underwater mountains called **seamounts.** Seamounts may have peaks or may be flat-topped. Volcanoes are numerous in the ocean, and often they form islands. The Hawaiian islands are volcanic islands. Sometimes underwater volcanoes erupt, and earthquakes are triggered deep in the ocean. These earthquakes cause the very dangerous waves called tsunamis. Oceanographers are now able to make very accurate maps of the ocean floor by using satellites that measure minute changes in the depths of the ocean.

Fish of the ocean depths

The fish that live on or near the ocean floor are very strange-looking creatures with huge mouths and many sharp teeth. Among them are grenadiers, viper fish, tripod fish, and deep sea anglers. Above them, in the dimly lit **twilight zone** of the ocean, are many oddly shaped fish with special glands that give off light to guide the fish through murky waters and attract prey.

226 ■ *Understanding God's World*

Upper level fish

The largest and fastest fish live in the upper level of the open seas. Since sunlight easily penetrates this level, it is rich in **plankton** (tiny, floating plants and animals), which provide abundant food for these large fish.

The **tuna** (7) is a large open-seas fish which can swim great distances and must eat much food on its long journeys.

Manta rays (8) *appear to fly through the water* by flapping their huge winglike fins. Mantas have been known to let men ride on their giant backs.

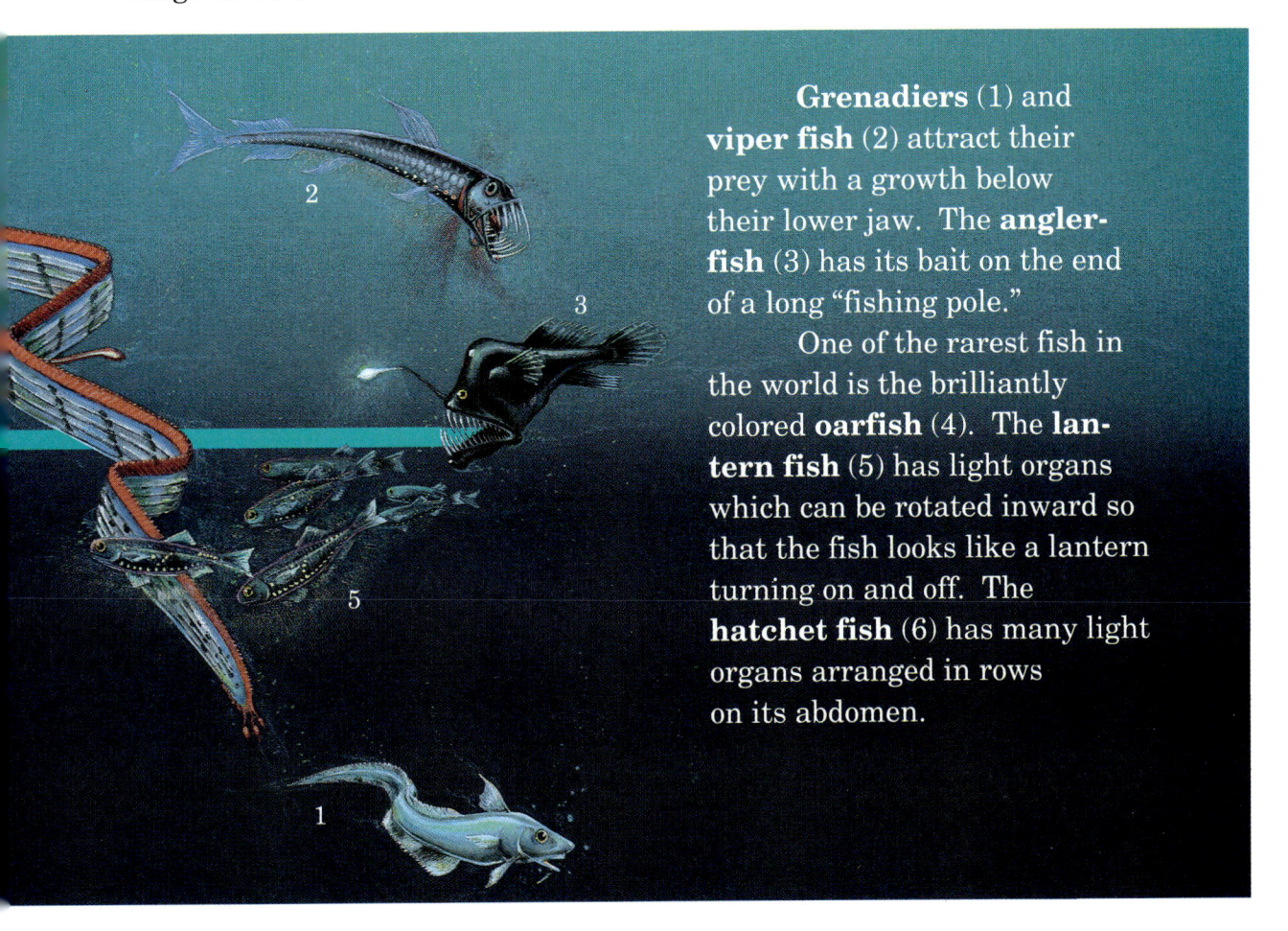

Grenadiers (1) and **viper fish** (2) attract their prey with a growth below their lower jaw. The **anglerfish** (3) has its bait on the end of a long "fishing pole."

One of the rarest fish in the world is the brilliantly colored **oarfish** (4). The **lantern fish** (5) has light organs which can be rotated inward so that the fish looks like a lantern turning on and off. The **hatchet fish** (6) has many light organs arranged in rows on its abdomen.

Oceanography 227

The **blue marlin** (9), which often makes spectacular leaps into the air, is popular with sport fishermen.

The **sailfish** (10) is easily recognized by its dark blue, fan-shaped back fin that looks like a sail and its swordlike bill.

The **flying fish** (11) gets its name from its ability to glide through the air for up to 1,000 feet.

The **swordfish** (12) is prized as both a food and sport fish. Since swordfish travel in pairs during breeding season, fishermen often catch two together.

The **ocean sunfish** (13) is a huge, strangely shaped fish found worldwide.

228 ■ *Understanding God's World*

Shark!

Unlike other fish, sharks *have skeletons made of cartilage rather than of bone.* Sharks have a rounded, torpedolike body that helps them glide swiftly through the water. Also unlike other fish, most sharks *give birth to live young which hatch from eggs inside the mother shark's body.* The shark must swim constantly from birth to death to keep from sinking.

Of the 300 or so types of sharks, all of which are carnivorous (meat-eating), the **whale shark** (14) is the most fearsome-looking. The whale shark is not only the biggest shark but also *the largest fish* of all. Whale sharks may grow to sixty feet in length and weigh as much as fifteen tons. In spite of their huge size, whale sharks feed mainly on plankton and small fish and are harmless to humans. Of the twenty-five kinds of **man-eating sharks,** the fiercest and most dangerous is the **white shark** (15), which is about twenty feet long and infests warmer waters. White sharks attack swimmers and bathers and even small fishing boats.

Oceanography

People who swim where there may be sharks need to follow these ***important safety rules***:

1. *Never swim or dive alone.*
2. *Never swim or dive with an open wound; blood attracts sharks.*
3. *Never swim or dive at night or in dirty water, where there is less chance of spotting a shark.*
4. *Leave the water immediately if a shark is sighted; swim as smoothly as possible because thrashing movements might attract the shark.*
5. *Never grab or injure any shark, even a small and apparently harmless one.*

A shark's mouth is filled with hundreds of molarlike, razorlike, or pointed teeth, designed for grinding, cutting, or tearing its prey. When a tooth is lost or worn out, another one moves in to replace it. Sharks have an extremely keen sense of smell; in fact, two thirds of a shark's brain is devoted to its sense of smell, with which the animal can detect a minute quantity of blood in the water a quarter of a mile away. Sharks also have a keen sense of hearing and are extremely sensitive to vibrations in the water 100 feet away. Because a shark can detect an electric field, it can sense the presence of fish and other animals by the tiny electric currents their bodies give off. All in all, the shark is a sea animal to be feared and respected.

Comprehension Check 8.3
1. Define: *ocean floor, seamount, oceanic ridge.*
2. Why do you think that the fish living at the top level of the seas are larger than the fish at lower levels?
3. Why do many fish in the lower levels of the ocean have glands that give off light?
4. Learn to recognize each fish described in this section, and be able to give at least one fact about each.

CONSIDER! *The wonders of fish*

The fishes of the sea shall declare unto thee. Who knoweth not in all these that the hand of the Lord hath wrought this?
Job 12:8b–9

The most numerous and varied animals of the ocean are the fish. Like birds, mammals, reptiles, and amphibians, fish are *vertebrates,* or animals with backbones. Although they live in an aquatic (watery) environment, fish breathe oxygen as you do. The oxygen they breathe is dissolved in the water. Fish use special structures called **gills** to remove dissolved oxygen from the water.

God designed fish to be able to move easily through the water. He made them *streamlined*—rounded at the front and tapering to a point at the tail. Since the fish's body is streamlined, water flows over it smoothly. God also gave fish a slippery layer of gel-slime to cover their bodies for protection and to help them to move through the water with little resistance. He gave them strong, sensitive *tail muscles* for propelling themselves forward and a wondrous variety of *fins* to help them to turn, stop, and move in many directions. He also gave them a *swim bladder,* which enables them to float at a chosen depth.

Fish are one of God's greatest provisions for mankind. He told the Israelites, "Whatsoever hath fins and scales in the waters, in the seas, and in the rivers, them shall ye eat" (Lev. 11:9; see vs. 9–12). Fish are among the most nourishing of all foods, providing as much protein as red meat as well as necessary vitamins and minerals.

Oceanography

8.4 Exploring the Sea

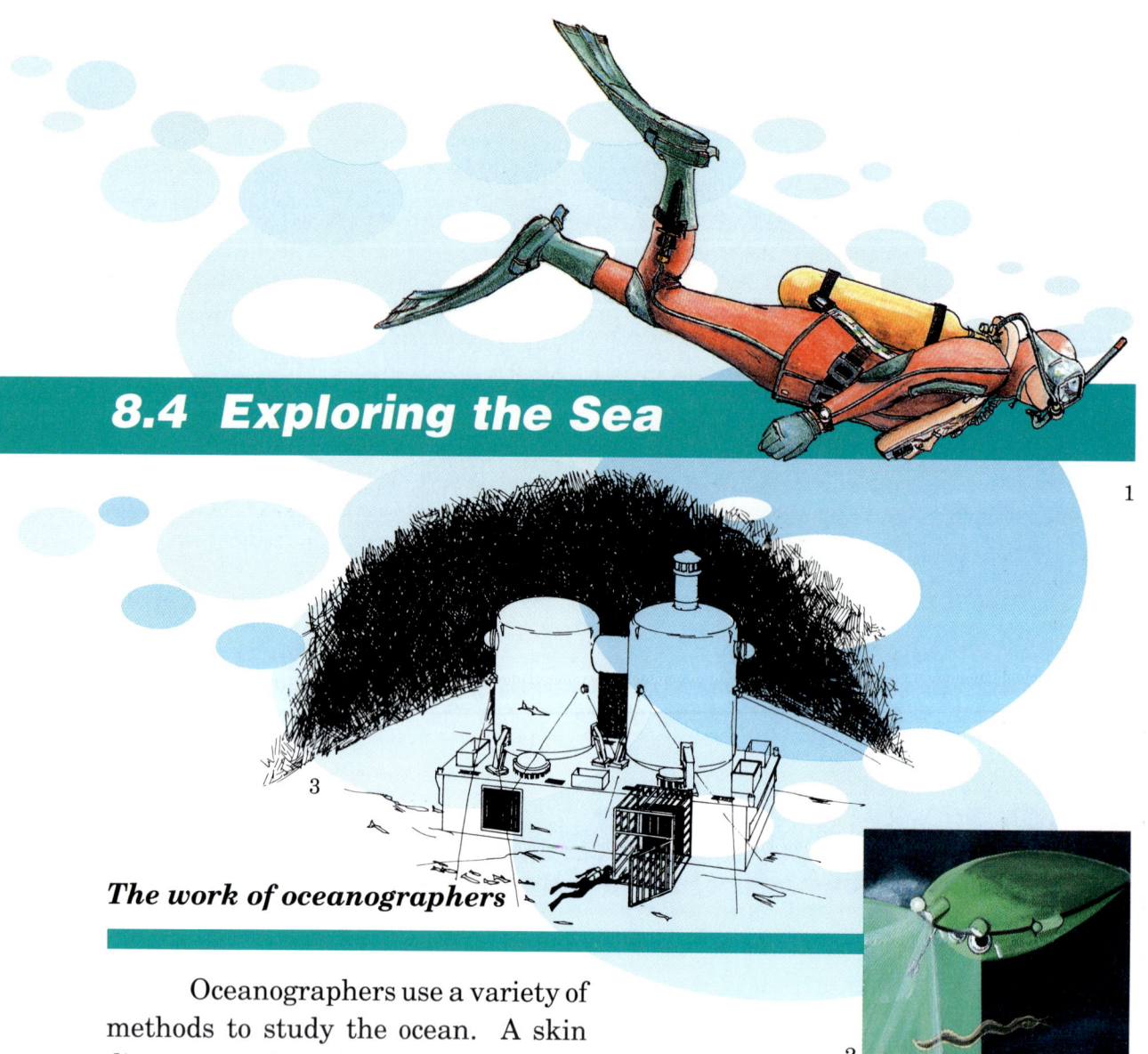

The work of oceanographers

Oceanographers use a variety of methods to study the ocean. A skin diver can explore shallow water simply by learning to hold his breath for a long time. A **scuba diver** (1) uses an **aqualung,** which is made up of one or more tanks of compressed air, an air hose, and a device that controls the flow of air so that air pressure in the diver's lungs is equal to the pressure of the water. Divers who need to stay underwater for more than an hour use a waterproof diving suit and helmet. If the water is too deep for diving suits to be used, scientists are able to explore the depths in a small submarine called a **submersible** (2). In submersibles, scientists can go to ocean depths where the temperature is too cold and the pressure too great for divers. Finally, **undersea labs** (3) allow scientists to live underwater for extended periods of time and may make possible deep-sea mining and farming in the future. Using all of these methods and others, oceanographers have been able to unlock many mysteries of the ocean.

232 ■ Understanding God's World

SCIENCE CONCEPTS — *What is water pressure?*

Have you ever dived to the bottom of a swimming pool and noticed the change in pressure in your ears? Water pressure is the weight of the water around you as it presses on your body. Water pressure increases with the depth of the water. Weight is the result of gravitation, which pulls you to the earth; so water pressure is also a result of gravity. You can see how water pressure works by doing this experiment at home. Take a quart or half gallon *milk carton* and punch three holes in one side of the carton with a *nail*. One hole should be near the top, one in the middle, and one near the bottom. Place a long strip of *masking tape* on the carton to cover all three holes. Fill the carton with water and place it in the sink or at the end of a long, shallow pan. Quickly remove the tape and notice where the water flows out the fastest. That is the point of the greatest water pressure.

Water pressure greatly limits how deep a man can dive and work. Even at 10 feet, it is possible for a diver to burst an eardrum if proper precautions are not taken. Most divers do not go deeper than 300 feet because of the pressure and problems related to it. The deepest that a free diver has ever gone was 1,400 feet, and that was only for a few minutes. Scientists can go much deeper, but they must do so in submersibles which are made of thick steel to protect them from the extreme pressures. Without submersibles, man would not be able to explore the ocean depths.

The fish that live in the great depths of the ocean seem to be unaffected by the pressure other than by having a flattened shape. Scientists do not know why they can survive at such extreme pressures.

The sea is extremely important to life on our world. First, all living things need water. Yet almost all of the water is in the ocean; only 3 percent is in the polar ice caps and the rivers. People cannot drink the ocean's water because it is too salty, but **the ocean provides water which we can drink.** As the ocean's water evaporates, leaving behind the dissolved materials, clouds form and move inland where they deposit rain. Rain fills the rivers and the lakes with fresh water, necessary to life. Second, **the ocean moderates the earth's climate.** Because the temperature of the sea does not change as quickly as the temperature of the land, the ocean helps to warm the land in winter and cool it in summer. Because of the ocean, the earth is neither too cold nor too hot for us. Truly, the ocean is a helper which God in His wisdom has given us.

Oceanography 233

The sandy sea

The sea is full of sand. It is constantly carrying sand about in its waves, building beaches or tearing them down and moving them somewhere else.

How does the sea make sand? As the earth's rivers empty into the sea, they carry with them soil, minerals, and rocks. The churning waves dash against the rocks and whirl them around until they are broken into pieces. Each of these pieces is then polished by the water until it is a small, smooth particle of sand.

Sand is a gift from the sea. Sandy beaches provide a beautiful place for recreation. Also, sand is used to make many important products such as sandpaper, cement, and glass. Just as a carpenter uses sandpaper to smooth wood, so the waves use sand to help them wear away rocks and cliffs. Tiny grains suspended in the water scour rock and leave their impact on the coast.

Comprehension Check 8.4
1. How do oceanographers study the sea?
2. What are two important things the sea does for us?
3. How does the sea make sand?

8.5 Salt and Waves

The salty sea

There are several reasons why God designed the sea to be salty. **Because it contains dissolved salt particles, sea water is denser than fresh water.** That is, there are more molecules in a cup of sea water than there are in a cup of fresh water. Since sea water has a higher density than fresh water, it can support weight better. If you have ever been swimming in the ocean, you may have noticed that you can float and swim more easily in salt water than in fresh water.

A second important property of salt water is that its freezing point is lower than the freezing point of fresh water. Fresh water freezes at 32°F, but sea water does not freeze until it is about 30° colder, at approximately 2°F. What do you think would happen to the oceans if salt water froze at 32°F?

Brown Pelican

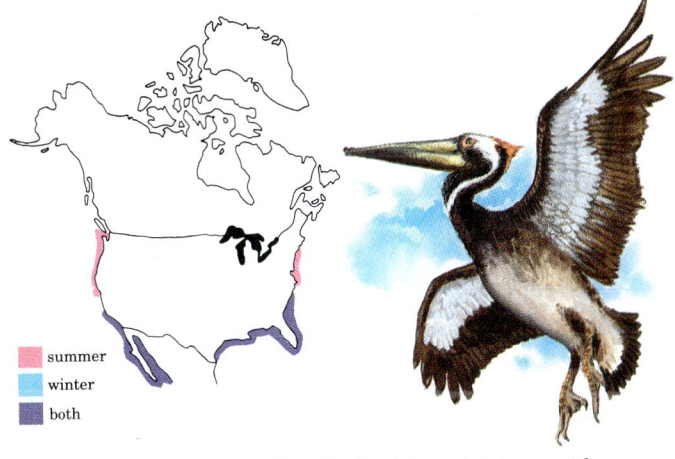

summer
winter
both

The brown pelican is about four feet long, with a wingspread of 6 1/2 feet. It lives along the Atlantic and Pacific Coasts of North and South America in salt bays, on beaches, and on islands close to the coast.

The brown pelican is a strong swimmer and an expert diver. Unlike the white pelican, the brown pelican plunges bill first into the sea after its prey, sometimes from heights of 30 feet. Using its large bill and expandable pouch, it scoops up fish along with twice its own weight in water. Then it shuts its bill, bobs up to the surface, and floats with its bill pointed down, draining out the water that was trapped in its pouch. After the water has drained out, the pelican swallows its catch.

SOMETHING TO DO
The floating crayon

You will need a glass, one cup of water, half a crayon, two tablespoons of salt, and a spoon. Pour the water into a glass; then put the piece of crayon into the water. What happened? Take out the crayon and stir in the salt until it is dissolved. Now put the crayon into the water again. What happened this time? Do you know why?

Oceanography

The salts and other minerals in sea water are helpful to living things in a variety of ways. The floating plants in the ocean get their mineral nutrients directly from the water, and some marine (sea) animals take other minerals from the water to build their shells. Sea water scatters sunlight better than fresh water, thus ensuring that marine plants get the light they need. Sound waves travel much farther in sea water than in fresh water. This is important to animals such as whales and dolphins that communicate underwater by echolocation. Scientists have also found that salt spray from the sea cleans the air of pollutants.

SOMETHING TO DO — *An icy glue*

To prove that salt water freezes at a lower temperature than fresh water, try the following experiment. *You will need a glass full of cold water, an ice cube, a salt shaker, and six inches of string.* Put the ice cube in the glass of cold water; then place one end of the string on the ice cube and shake some salt on the ice cube. After waiting twenty seconds, pull carefully on the string. What happened? Do you know why the string stuck to the ice? When you put salt on the ice cube, you lowered its freezing point and caused it to melt. As the ice cube melted, however, the salt solution on top of it became more diluted with fresh water. The ice refroze, trapping your string inside.

The moving sea

Waves. The water in the oceans moves constantly. You have already learned about the ocean currents. A more familiar movement of sea water is **waves.** ***Winds cause waves and determine the type of wave produced.*** Do you remember how sound energy travels through the air in waves? The molecules of air are pushed together and then return to their original positions so that only the disturbance travels; the sound wave does little to affect the positions of the molecules of air. Waves of water move in much the same way. When a wave passes, the wave form moves forward, but the water itself does not. You can see this by watching a floating object in the waves. Notice that when the wave passes, the floating object will be in almost the same place as it was before the wave passed. The floating object did not move to the shoreline with the wave.

Understanding God's World

Comprehension Check 8.5
1. Why is salt water denser than fresh water?
2. Tell four properties of sea water.
3. What causes waves?

8.6 Giants of the Sea

And God created great whales, and every living creature that moveth, which the waters brought forth abundantly, after their kind, and every winged foul after his kind: and God saw that it was good. –Genesis 1:21

1

Marine mammals

Do you know what animal is as big as a ten-story building and weighs as much as thirty-three elephants? The **blue whale** (1), measuring 90 to 100 feet long and weighing 200,000 pounds, is *the largest animal that has ever lived.* Whales, dolphins, and porpoises are part of a group of animals known as **marine mammals,** mammals which are designed to live in the sea. Mammals are warm-blooded vertebrates which have at least some hair and are usually born alive and fed milk by their mothers. All mammals, including marine mammals, breathe air through their lungs. Whales and dolphins breathe through **blowholes** at the top of their heads.

Marine mammals can stay underwater anywhere from ten minutes to over an hour, depending on their type. Since the calves (young) of whales and dolphins are born underwater, they are usually born tail first to prevent drowning. Their mothers help them to the surface so that they can take their first breath.

Baleen whales

Blue whales belong to a group of whales known as *baleen* [bə-lēn′] *whales.* Baleen whales have sheets of **baleen** (a hard but flexible substance like fingernails) in their mouths. The sheets of baleen strain *krill* (small, shrimplike animals) and other kinds of animal plankton from the water for the whale to eat.

Oceanography ■ 237

The **humpback whale** (2) has huge, white flippers and emits long songs of high-pitched sounds and whistles, heard for many miles underwater. The humpback gets its name from the humped appearance it has when it dives.

Toothed whales

The second group of whales is made up of the toothed whales. Most toothed whales are smaller than baleen whales. Toothed whales eat fish and other animals such as squid and sea lions.

The **sperm whale** (3), largest of the toothed whales, feeds on giant squid that live deep in the ocean. In the eighteenth and nineteenth centuries, the sperm whale was hunted because it produces two kinds of oil. One kind was used in lamps; the other became the main ingredient in candles. Sperm whales also produce in their intestines a substance called **ambergris** [ăm′ bĕr-grēs] which is used to make certain expensive perfumes.

The **beluga** [bə-lōō′gə] **whale** (4), which lives in the Arctic, is the only truly white whale. Belugas have been trained in captivity and perform at some oceanariums.

The **narwhal** (5) is an odd-looking whale found only in the Arctic Ocean. The male narwhal has one tooth—a very long tusk that grows out of the left side of its head. No one knows what the strange creature does with its tusk.

238 ■ *Understanding God's World*

Pilot whales (6) get their name from their habit of following a stray member of their group, or pod. If one of the pilot whales swims off course, the whole pod will follow him.

Killer whales (7) are toothed whales which get their name from their keen hunting ability. Killer whales can be trained to perform in captivity and appear to enjoy human companionship.

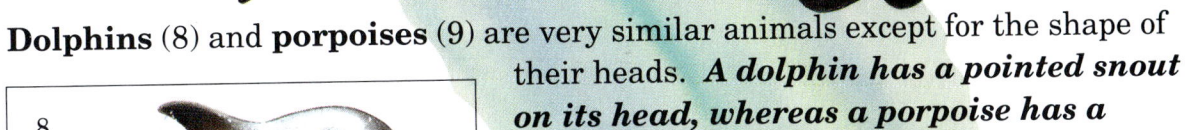

Dolphins (8) and **porpoises** (9) are very similar animals except for the shape of their heads. *A dolphin has a pointed snout on its head, whereas a porpoise has a blunt head.* Dolphins are very intelligent and friendly, and are easily trained in captivity. The "porpoises" that you see in "porpoise shows" are really dolphins.

Comprehension Check 8.6
1. All marine mammals breathe air with their __?__.
2. Some whales strain their food from the water with the sheets of __?__ in their mouths.
3. The largest animal that has ever lived is the __?__ whale.
4. The only white whale is the __?__ whale.
5. The whale with the long tusk is the __?__.
6. Although the __?__ whale is a good hunter, it can be trained to perform in captivity.
7. The dolphin has a __?__ snout; the porpoise's head is __?__.

Oceanography ■ 239

8.7 Three Invertebrates

Although fish and whales are the most obvious animals in the ocean, they are not the only animals which live there. Corals, octopuses, squids, sponges, starfish, jellyfish, crabs, lobsters, clams, and oysters are a few of the many fascinating *invertebrates* (animals without backbones) of the sea. Marine invertebrates have many unusual shapes and living habits. Some of them do not even look like animals, but they are.

Octopuses

Down through the years, one of the most feared sea creatures has been the **octopus** (1). It has **eight long tentacles,** each covered with many round muscles which act like **suction cups.** The octopus uses its tentacles to move about on rocks and hard surfaces and to catch its prey. After the octopus has made its catch, it cuts up its prey with the **hard beak in its mouth.** Some octopuses secrete poisonous saliva to paralyze the prey. Octopuses feed on crabs, fish, and other small marine animals. One octopus was observed catching twenty-five crabs at once and then eating them one at a time.

In spite of its fierce reputation, the octopus is actually a shy creature that would rather flee than fight. **When threatened, it changes colors, squirts an inky "smoke screen," and uses jet propulsion to quickly dart away from its predator.** If the octopus is attacked and loses one of its tentacles, the tentacle can regenerate, or grow back.

Some octopuses are as small as a dime, but others are twenty-five feet across. The only one known to be poisonous is the *blue-ringed octopus* of Australia. Although it is only four inches in diameter, its poison is strong enough to kill a man in less than five minutes.

Of all the invertebrates, octopuses have the largest brains. Many scientists think they are the most intelligent of the invertebrates. Octopuses in captivity can be trained to do some simple tricks and can tell the difference between colors and shapes.

Key to Marine Invertebrates

1. octopus
2. squid
3. jellyfish
4. Portuguese man-of-war
5. cowrie shell
6. conch shell
7. sea snail
8. oyster
9. giant clam
10. mussel
11. shrimp
12. lobster
13. crab
14. barnacle
15. starfish
16. sea anemone
17. coral
18. horseshoe crab
19. sand dollar
20. sea urchin
21. sea slug
22. scallop
23. clamworm
24. sponge
25. chambered nautilus

Oceanography ■ 241

SCIENCE CONCEPTS

What is jet propulsion?

The octopus has no fins for swimming. Instead, God has equipped it with a special means of moving through the water: jet propulsion. You can see how this works by making a jet-propelled toy. Blow up a long *balloon* and clip it closed with a *spring clip*. *Tape* the balloon to a lightweight *plastic truck* with the clipped end of the balloon facing the rear of the truck. Remove the clip and notice the direction that the truck moves. As the air escapes the balloon from the rear, the truck moves forward in a direction opposite the escaping air. Jet airplanes work on the same principle by moving forward when hot gases escape through the rear of the engines. The octopus uses water rather than air for jet propulsion. Water is forced through a tube under the octopus's head. The water escapes forward, thereby forcing the octopus to move through the water backward.

Squid

The **squid** (2) is an invertebrate similar to the octopus, but it has **ten tentacles** instead of eight. Squids are more aggressive than octopuses, although they defend themselves in much the same way. When threatened, the squid ejects a blob of blue-black ink that is about its own size. Then, while the predator attacks the ink blob, the squid changes its color and makes its escape. Squids, as well as octopuses, are able to assume a wide variety of colors in order to blend in with their background.

The smallest adult squids are less than one inch long. The biggest squid ever seen measured fifty-seven feet from top to bottom; however, there is evidence that giant squids grow much larger than that. These giants of the deep ocean are the primary food for the sperm whale.

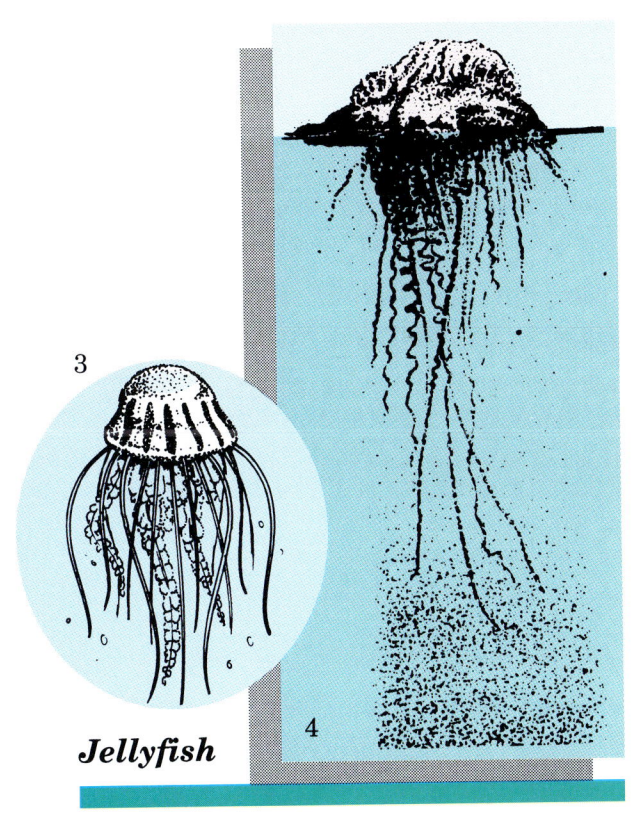

Jellyfish

Jellyfish (3) are invertebrates whose bodies are ***shaped like bells or bowls. Many stinging tentacles*** hang down from their bodies. The jellyfish uses its tentacles to catch fish and other small marine animals and pass them up to its mouth. There are many types of jellyfish. Some are the size of peas, but the huge Arctic jellyfish can be seven feet across. All jellyfish contain stinging cells in their tentacles. The stinging cells are like tiny harpoons. When they are touched, they uncoil and shoot a stinging poison into the victim. It is never wise to pick up a jellyfish with your bare hands even if it is dead, because the tentacles can still sting.

One jellyfish found in Australia, the **sea wasp,** is more poisonous than any snake. The sea wasp's poison is so potent (strong) that it can kill a man in 3 to 8 minutes. Fortunately, the sea wasp feeds offshore and is seldom encountered by man.

A more common jellyfish is the **Portuguese man-of-war** (4). It was named by sailors who thought that the float of the jellyfish looked like a kind of sailing ship that was commonly called a man-of-war. The body of the Portuguese man-of-war is a beautiful blue, with tinges of pink, purple, and orange. ***Its tentacles can be 100 feet long.*** The strong poison from the man-of-war's stinging cells can inflict great pain on a person.

Comprehension Check 8.7
1. Which of the following animals have tentacles: *octopuses, squids, jellyfish?*
2. What do octopuses use their tentacles for?
3. How does the squid distract its enemies and make its escape?
4. How does a jellyfish get its food?
5. Name a common jellyfish.

Oceanography

Chapter Check-up

A *Learn to recognize each sea creature pictured in this chapter, and be able to give at least one fact about each.*

B *Write the letter of the phrase that identifies each term.*

_____ 1. continental shelf
_____ 2. current
_____ 3. gills
_____ 4. ocean floor
_____ 5. oceanographers
_____ 6. plankton
_____ 7. seamount

A. tiny plants and animals that float in the upper regions of the ocean
B. special structures that allow fish to remove dissolved oxygen from water
C. an isolated underwater mountain
D. mollusks with two matching shells
E. underwater land along the edges of the continents
F. the bottom of the ocean
G. scientists who study the ocean
H. a flowing stream within the ocean

C *Write each of the marine animals listed below under the correct heading.*

cod	blue marlin	white shark	clam
grenadier	coral	beluga	salmon
jellyfish	starfish	octopus	blue whale
narwhal	sperm whale	porpoise	dolphin
flounder	manta	squid	oyster

Mammals *Fish* *Invertebrates*

244 ■ *Understanding God's World*

D *Fill in the answer(s) to complete each sentence.*

1. The deepest area in the sea is the _____ _____ in the Pacific Ocean.

2. The area between the continental shelf and the ocean floor is the _____ _____.

3. Like all other mammals, whales breathe with _____ _____.

4. Water pressure _____ _____ as the depth of the water increases.

22 Nene

summer
winter
both

The nene [nā′nā], or Hawaiian goose, is a rare bird. It is native to Hawaii and is not found naturally in any other part of the world. The nene is about 28 inches long with gray, brown, black, and white plumage. Its strong legs and toes help it live high on the slopes of volcanoes on old lava flows, where the terrain is very rugged. Unlike most geese, the nene does not go into the water because its feet are only partially webbed. The nene eats grass and a few berries.

In 1950 there were only about 50 nene left. Conservation measures, however, have helped save it from extinction. Three nene were caught and transported to the Wildfowl Trust in England, and 200 of the offspring of these captured birds were later returned to Hawaii. By 1978 there were over 1,000 nene.

E *Write* true *or* false *in the space before each statement.*

_____ 1. Salt water scatters sunlight and carries sound waves better than fresh water does.
_____ 2. The best fishing areas are in the deepest parts of the ocean.
_____ 3. Most undersea oil fields are found in the continental slope.
_____ 4. The Gulf Stream carries cool water toward the North Pole.
_____ 5. Objects float more easily in fresh water than they do in salt water.
_____ 6. Octopuses and squids are able to camouflage themselves.
_____ 7. Octopuses and squids both have eight tentacles.

F *Think about these questions and answer them as clearly as you can.*

1. Why are submersibles valuable in deep sea research?
2. Explain how the octopus uses jet propulsion to move itself.

Oceanography ■ 245

9 ASTRONOMY: Consider the Heavens

9.1 Wonders of the Night Sky

When I consider Thy heavens, the work of Thy fingers, the moon and the stars, which Thou hast ordained; what is man, that Thou art mindful of him? And the son of man, that Thou visitest him?

Psalm 8:3, 4

The message of the heavens

How radiantly the stars shine on a clear night! As we gaze at them, our eyes are almost dazzled by their number and splendor. At first, it seems as if these gleaming ornaments of the night are flung haphazardly through the skies. But God Who made them does nothing by chance. Rather, he has placed each one in its proper place in the sky. He has arranged many into **constellations,** or star pictures. Throughout the centuries, people have found the constellations mysterious and fascinating. They have thought that the constellations told stories.

Indeed, the Bible tells us that the stars do have a message to tell the world. They speak of the power and glory of God, and *"there is no speech nor language where their voice is not heard"* (Psalm 19:3).

The star of Bethlehem

God created one special star as a sign—the star of Bethlehem. Do you remember that the Wise Men followed the star of Bethlehem to find the Christ child? This sign told the Wise Men which direction to follow.

But the star of Bethlehem was not like the other stars we now see in the night sky. If you watch the stars for an evening, you will notice that, like the sun, they seem to rise in the east and set in the west. This, of course, is because the earth is turning on its axis. However, the star of Bethlehem was different. All night long, as the Wise Men journeyed south from Jerusalem to Bethlehem, the star they were following went before them. It did not rise or set. And then as the Wise Men approached the house where Jesus was, the star stopped in the sky and "stood over where the young child was." This was a very special star which God must have made just to guide the Wise Men to Jesus.

Astronomy ■ 247

the Milky Way with our solar system marked by an X

The immensity of the heavens

All of the stars that you can see without a telescope are in a huge star group, or **galaxy,** called the **Milky Way.** Besides being home to our Earth, the Milky Way may contain around 200 billion other stars. The sun, orbiting the center of the Milky Way, travels a path so huge that 225 million years would be needed to complete it. Yet the Milky Way extends far beyond the region where the sun travels. And the Milky Way is only one of billions of galaxies, each containing innumerable stars. These billions of galaxies make up the **universe,** or *all the things which God created.* It is impossible for us to understand the size of the universe, but as we begin to think about the immensity of God's creation, we are filled with wonder. We feel a sense of our smallness as well as an admiration for God's handiwork. God not only created the heavenly bodies, but He calls them all by name (Psalm 147:4). Truly we serve a great God! Perhaps the greatest wonder is that this God loves weak and sinful people.

The universe is made up of billions of galaxies.

our solar system

1　2　3　4　5　6　7　8　9

The beauty of the solar system

The glory of the night sky is only a small part of the beauty we would see if we could take a rocket trip through the heavens. As we soared through our **solar system,** the part of our galaxy made up of our sun and the nine planets, we would encounter many magnificent sights. The stark beauty of barren planets would be awe inspiring. **Planets** are heavenly bodies which revolve around the sun. The nine planets of our solar system, in order from the sun, are ***Mercury*** (1), ***Venus*** (2), ***Earth*** (3), ***Mars*** (4), ***Jupiter*** (5), ***Saturn*** (6), ***Uranus*** [ū′rə-nus] (7), ***Neptune*** (8), and ***Pluto*** (9).

Astronomy ■ 249

On *Venus,* we would behold the fury of continuous lightning storms crashing over a desolate landscape. *Mars* would reveal a red surface scarred with gigantic craters and crisscrossed by plunging canyons three times deeper than the Grand Canyon. As we passed *Jupiter,* the spectacle of white, pink, and orange clouds swirling across the face of the planet would dazzle our eyes. Amid these clouds of gases whirls the Great Red Spot—an enormous hurricane larger than two Earths. Next, we could see *Saturn's* majestic, banded rings. Perhaps we would fly so close to the planet that the rings would rise above us like a gigantic rainbow. Making a large loop back to the sun, we would find its glory too great to look at

250 ■ Understanding God's World

without special instruments. Its burning surface would show us a fantasy of dancing gases with sprays hurtling thousands of miles upward before arching gracefully down again.

But none of these sights would please us as much as the most beautiful planet of all—a lovely, blue world clothed with a life-giving atmosphere. As we approach, patches of green appear—continents of fertile and welcoming land—surrounded by oceans. Nowhere else have we seen water, which nourishes and sustains life. Drawing very near, we delight to see rivers, forests, and gently rolling hills instead of the savage barrenness of other worlds. Our spaceship settles upon the surface of this rich world. We have returned to *Earth,* the beautiful planet specially designed by God to be the home of His creatures.

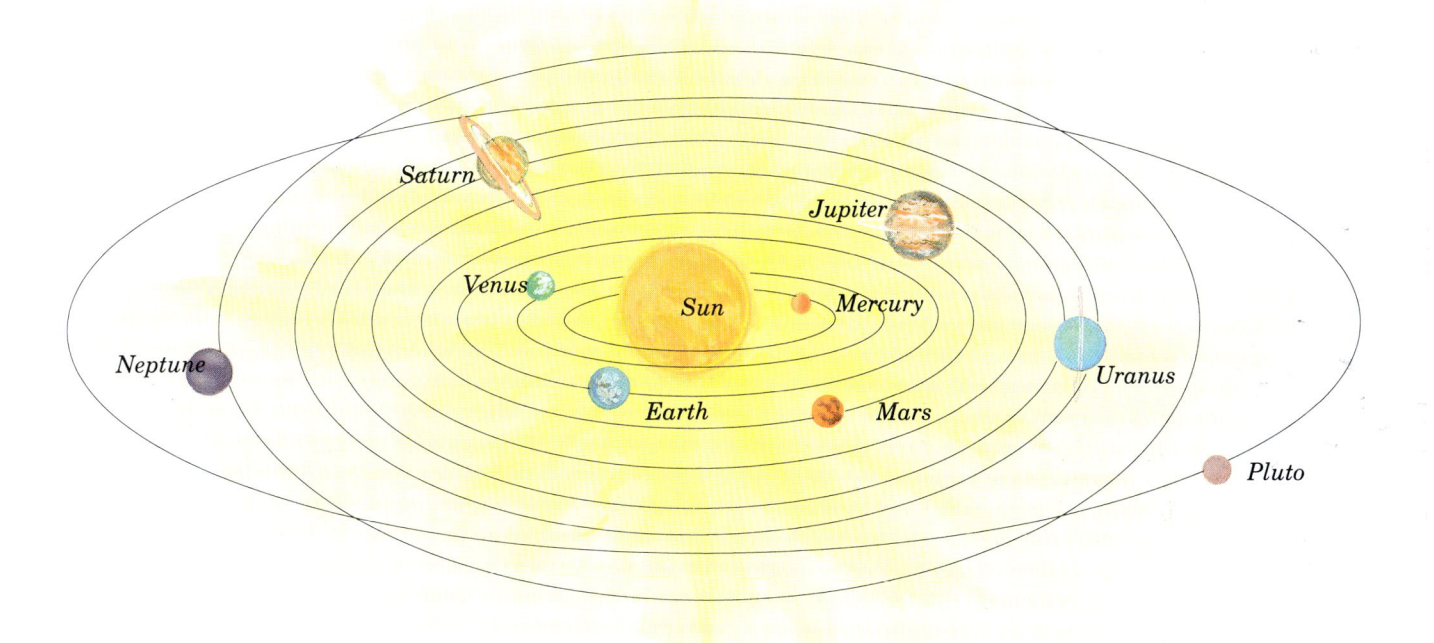

Comprehension Check 9.1
1. What are star pictures called?
2. What important message do the stars have for the world?
3. Name the galaxy in which our sun is located.
4. What do we call all the things which God created?
5. What do we call the sun and the nine planets?
6. Name the nine planets in order from the sun.

9.2 Seasons, Days, and Years

> *And God said, Let there be lights in the firmament of the heaven to divide the day from the night; and let them be for signs, and for seasons, and for days, and years.*
> –Genesis 1:14

Have you ever wondered what life would be like if there were no calendars? How would you know when it was time for you to have another birthday? How would anyone know when it was time for school to be over and summer vacation to begin? What if there were no clocks? Would you be able to tell the time? Although our modern time-measuring devices are convenient, we would not be lost without them. We would simply do what ancient peoples did—depend on the sky and on the heavenly bodies.

The year and the day

God has caused the earth to move in two different ways in regard to the sun. First, the earth revolves around the sun in 365 1/4 days, the period which we call a **year.** Second, the earth rotates on its axis every 24 hours. During this rotation, the sun shines on the earth, giving periods of light and darkness which we call **days** and **nights.** Ancient people often told time by using an instrument called a sundial. The position of the sun's shadow on the dial told them what time it was.

God has caused us to have a day and a year of exactly the right length. If our day were as short as Jupiter's day (less than ten hours), we would not have time for all the things we wanted to do. If it were as long as Mercury's day (59 earth days), we would have to sleep many times before the day was over. Instead, we have a 24-hour day, which gives us just enough time to work or play and just enough time to sleep. Similarly, if our year were as short as Mercury's (88 days), we would not have adequate growing seasons. If it were as long as Mars's (687 days), some countries would suffer from very severe winters. Everywhere we look, we see evidence of a loving God Who created the world. He knows what is best for us.

Months and seasons

The moon passes from new to full approximately every 30 days, 12 times a year. Therefore, we have 12 **months** ("moonths") in a year. Ancient peoples could determine the time of the month by watching the phases of the moon. Often, these people considered the beginning of the month to be the appearance of the first thin sliver of moon after a short time when the moon could not be seen.

Our seasons occur because of the tilt of the earth's axis as it orbits the sun. Another way for our ancestors to determine months and seasons was by watching the stars. As the seasons change, different constellations become visible. Twelve important constellations called the **zodiac** (called **Mazzaroth** [măz′ə-rŏth] in Job 38:32) encircle the earth as it orbits around the sun. As the earth travels its pathway around the sun, the sun appears to pass through these constellations, one per month. In the past, farmers knew that when the sun "entered" a particular constellation, it was time to plant a particular crop. They could tell which constellation the sun was in by watching to see which one was above the eastern horizon when the sun rose.

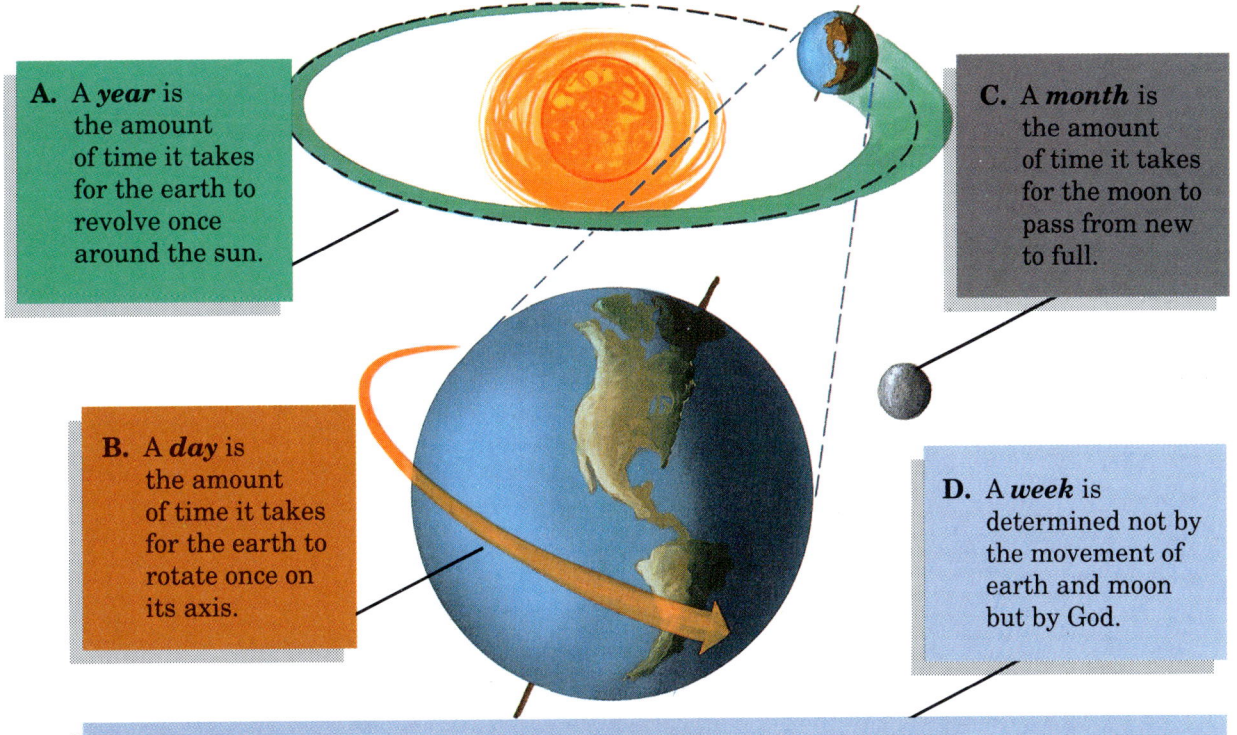

A. A *year* is the amount of time it takes for the earth to revolve once around the sun.

B. A *day* is the amount of time it takes for the earth to rotate once on its axis.

C. A *month* is the amount of time it takes for the moon to pass from new to full.

D. A *week* is determined not by the movement of earth and moon but by God.

For in six days the Lord made heaven and earth, the sea, and all that in them is, and rested the seventh day: wherefore the Lord blessed the sabbath day, and hallowed it. –Exodus 20:11

Astronomy ■ 253

Weeks

There is no orbit of planets or heavenly bodies that gives us the **seven-day week.** That was given to us directly by God to help us remember that He is the Creator of all the marvels of the universe. God created our world in only 6 days, and on the seventh day He rested.

Astronomy or astrology?

Perhaps now you understand better how important the heavens were to people of the past. Unfortunately, this importance was one reason that people, in their sinfulness, began to worship the heavenly objects. Instead of worshiping the Creator of the universe, they turned to **idolatry,** *the worship of false gods,* and to astrology. Do not confuse the science of astronomy with the false belief of astrology. **Astronomy** is *the scientific study of the stars, planets, and all other heavenly bodies* to discover their size, makeup, motion, and position. **Astrology** is *a false belief, or superstition, which claims to tell people's futures by studying the influence of the sun, moon, and stars on people's lives.* God warns us against believing in astrology. Read Isaiah 47:13, 14 and Daniel 2 to find out what God thinks of this false belief. When we look up at the heavens, we should think about God, not about fortune telling and luck:

> *The heavens declare the glory of God; and the firmament sheweth His handiwork.*
> –Psalm 19:1

Comprehension Check 9.2
1. What movement of the earth gives us a year?
2. What movement of the earth gives us a day?
3. What heavenly body gives us our seven-day week?
4. Which heavenly body helps us to divide our year into 12 months?
5. Name a group of 12 important constellations.
6. What is the difference between astronomy and astrology?
7. What evidence of God's goodness do we see in the length of the year and of the day?

9.3 Pictures in the Sky

You do not need to be familiar with the constellations in order to make important decisions about your life. You have parents, prayer, and God's Word to give you guidance. Knowing more about the stars, however, will help you to grow in your appreciation of the greatness and glory of God. Also, you will have fun learning how to recognize some of the "star pictures."

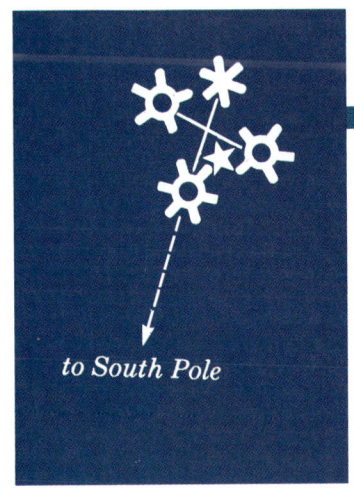

The Southern Cross

Fewer constellations can be seen from the Southern Hemisphere than from the Northern Hemisphere. One of the most famous is the smallest constellation of all, the **Southern Cross.** Its four most brilliant stars form the shape of a cross with the long crossbar pointing to the South Pole. What a beautiful picture for God to place in the southern sky!

The Big Dipper

One of the most familiar groups of stars seen in the Northern Hemisphere is the **Big Dipper.** It is made up of seven stars which are *part of the constellation called the Great Bear.* The Big Dipper got its name because its stars are in the shape of an old-fashioned, long-handled cup, or dipper. Locating the Big Dipper will help you to find other stars.

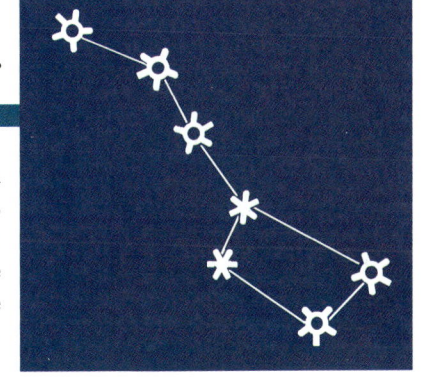

The Little Dipper

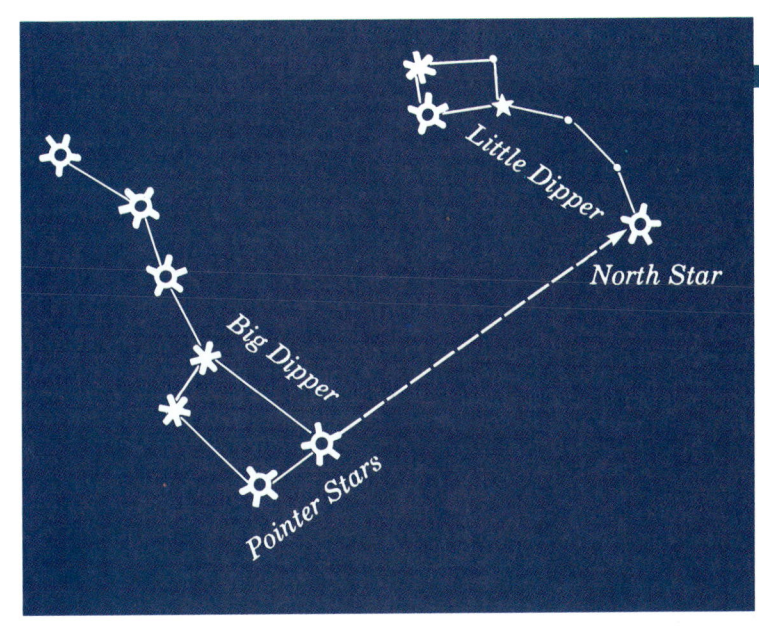

The North Star is at the end of the "handle" of the **Little Dipper,** another familiar group of stars. The Little Dipper, which looks like a smaller, fainter version of the Big Dipper, is most easily seen on a clear night. Finding the North Star will help you to see it. The Little Dipper seems to rotate around the North Star as if it were being swung by its handle. Both the Big and Little Dippers can be seen all year long.

Astronomy 255

The North Star

On the side of the cup of the Big Dipper are two very bright stars. They are called the *Pointer Stars* because they point in a straight line to the **North Star.** The North Star is a bright star that seems always to be in the same place. It is almost directly above the earth's axis at the North Pole. Because the earth rotates on its axis, other stars seem to rotate around the North Star. This star's position above the North Pole gives it its other names: *Polaris* and the *Pole Star*. For centuries, the North Star has been used for navigation. Explorers on land and sea have used it to find directions, and so can you! ***When you face the North Star, you are facing north. South is behind you. East is to your right, and west is to your left.***

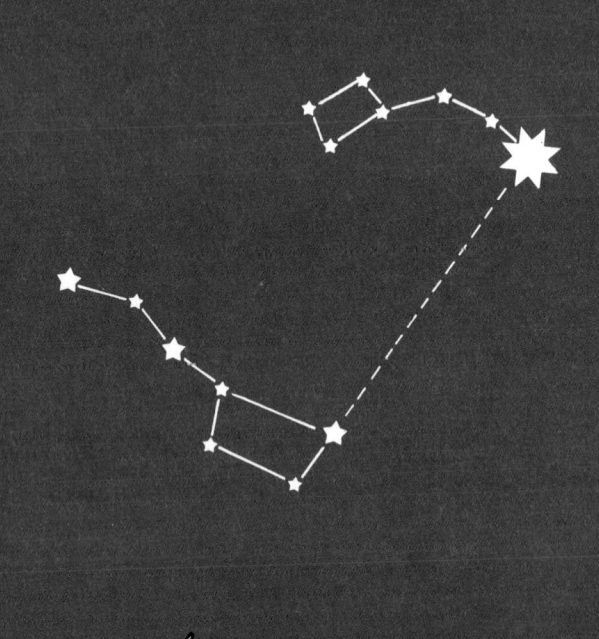

Connect the Stars!

1

1. Can you find the Big Dipper, the Little Dipper, and the North Star in the above picture?
2. Connect the stars below to show the Big Dipper, and then complete the Great Bear.

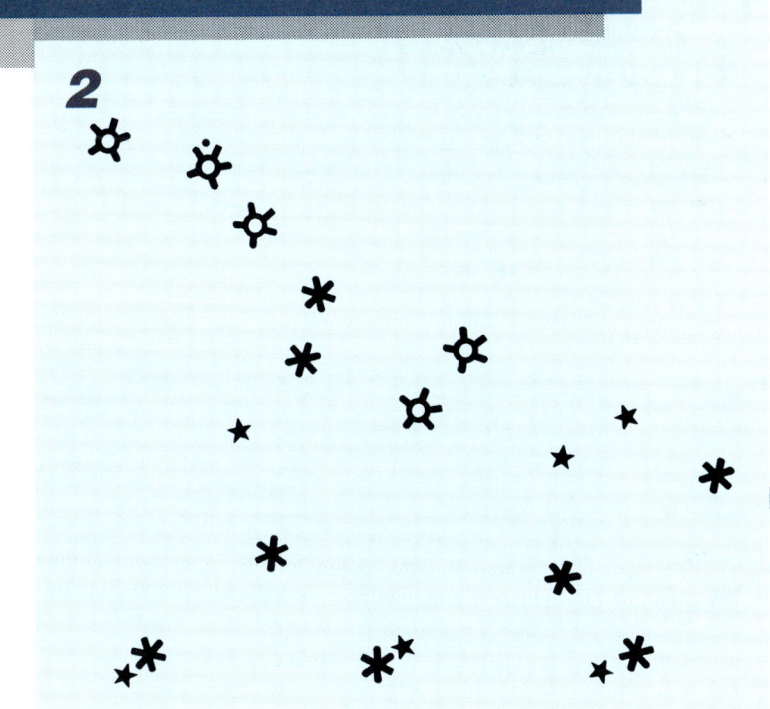

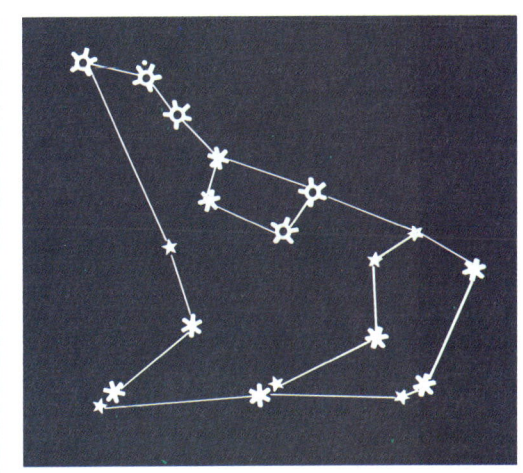

2

The Great Bear

The last star in the handle of the Big Dipper is the nose of the **Great Bear.** The other handle stars form the back of the bear's head, and the bowl of the Dipper is the bear's saddle. This huge bear of the northern skies looks very much like a polar bear, as it should, since it is near the North Pole. It can be seen best from February through June. In the Bible, the Great Bear constellation is called *Arcturus* [ärk-tū′rus] (Job 9:9; 38:32).

Astronomy

Leo the Lion

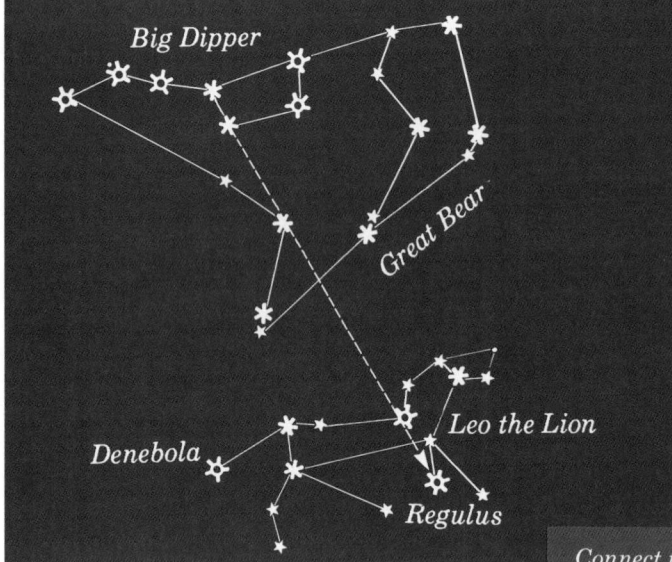

Not far from the Great Bear is another powerful mammal, **Leo the Lion.** You can see Leo in March, April, and May. First, locate the Big Dipper's cup. Now, trace a straight line from the two stars closest to the handle through the front leg of the Great Bear to two very bright stars. The brighter star, *Regulus,* [rĕg′ū-lus] is Leo's front paw. Another bright star, *Denebola* [dĕ-nĕb′ō-lə], is at the tip of Leo's tail.

Connect the stars below to form the Big Dipper, the Great Bear, and Leo the Lion.

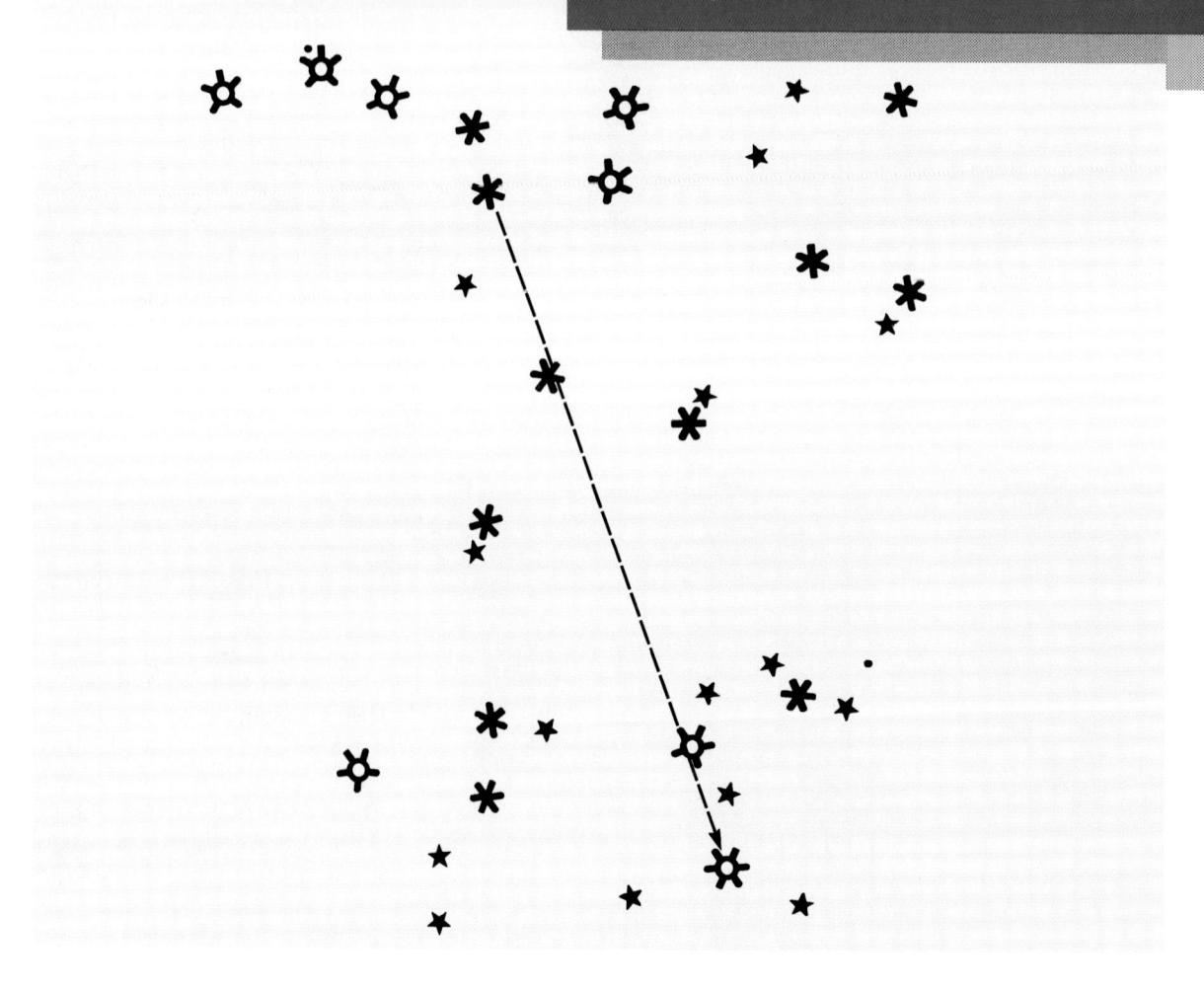

258 ■ Understanding God's World

The Herdsman

The Great Bear is looking at the horn of the **Herdsman,** a person who tends a herd of animals. Perhaps the Herdsman is a picture of the Good Shepherd who protects His sheep. The herdsman has a pointed hat, and he looks as if he is sitting on a grassy bank blowing his horn. You can see the Herdsman best from April through August.

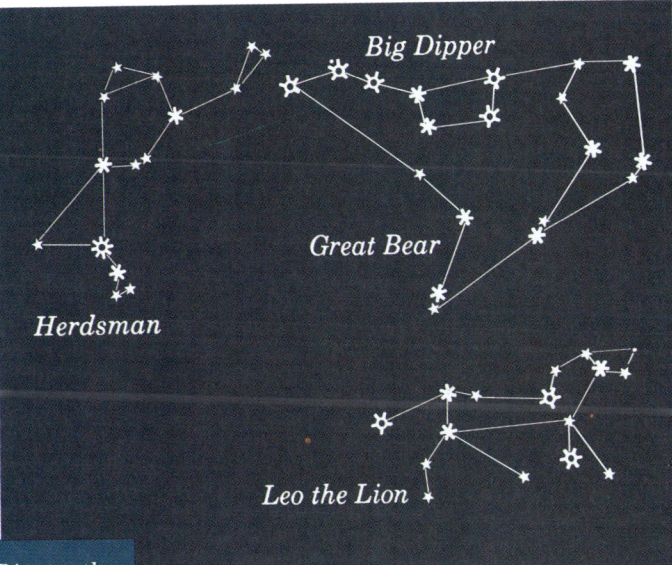

Connect the stars below to form the Big Dipper, the Great Bear, Leo the Lion, and the Herdsman.

Astronomy 259

Seek him that maketh the seven stars and Orion. . . .
—Amos 5:8

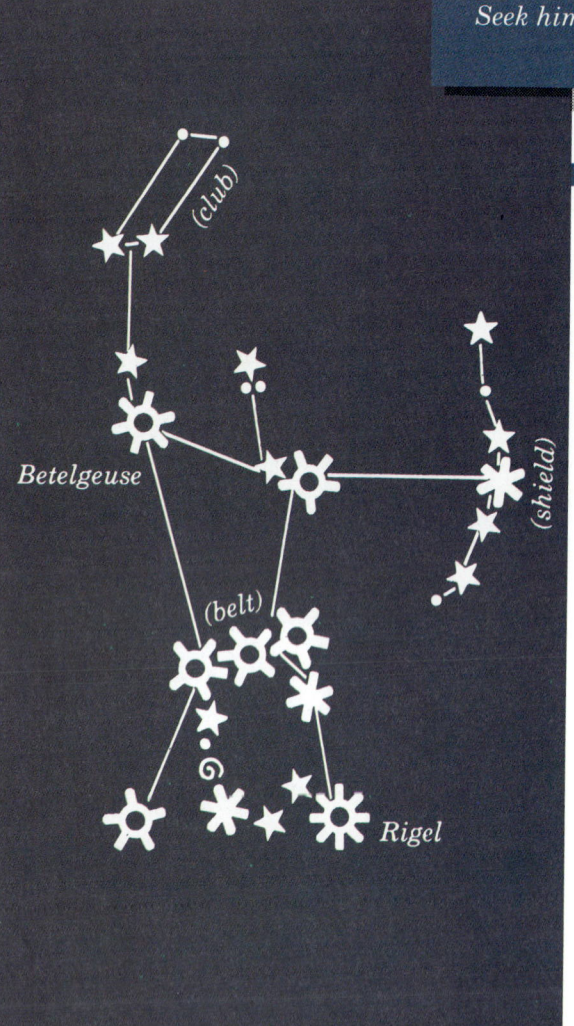

Orion

During the winter, one of the most spectacular constellations in the southern sky is **Orion** [ō-rī′ on], the hunter. This star group, which is mentioned three times in the Bible (Job 9:9; 38:31; Amos 5:8), has more bright stars than any other constellation. You can easily recognize Orion by finding the three brilliant stars which are aligned side-by-side, forming his belt. Orion appears to be holding a shield and raising a club high above his head. A sword hangs from Orion's belt. You may not be able to see Orion's sword nor his head without binoculars unless you live in a place where the sky is very dark at night. You will certainly be able to see his belt and his two bright stars, however.

SOMETHING TO DO — Making a star viewer

You will need a large shoe box, black construction paper, a pencil, tape, and a flashlight.

Construct a star viewer like the one you see in the picture. Mark the constellations given in this chapter by putting a dot on the black construction paper where each star is located. Then make small holes by pushing the tip of a pencil through the dots on the paper. Tape the constellation pictures, one at a time, on the open end of the shoe box, so that the light shines only through the small holes. In a darkened room, turn on the light and show your star pictures on the wall or ceiling.

260 ■ Understanding God's World

2-3 Chicken

Why do we see the stars only at night?

Have you ever wondered why we see the constellations and the other stars only at night? During the daytime, the earth's atmosphere scatters the light from the sun. This scattering makes the sky appear blue, and it also makes the sky so bright that we cannot see the stars. If you were on the moon, where there is no atmosphere, you could see the stars all day long.

Rhode Island and Delaware have chosen two different varieties of the chicken, a most useful bird, as their state birds. The Rhode Island red, a medium-sized chicken with brilliant red feathers, is one of the five top American breeds. Cocks (males) usually weigh about 8 pounds, hens 6 pounds. Like all other American breeds, the Rhode Island red has yellow skin, no feathers on its lower legs, and red ear lobes. It is a general purpose chicken, a meaty chicken that is also a good egg layer.

During the American Revolution, the militia from Kent County, Delaware, took some fighting gamecocks along with them to war. These chickens were supposedly descended from a famous blue hen (female) brought to the colony by the earliest settlers. The soldiers were nicknamed "Blue Hen's Chickens." The nickname stuck, and in 1939, Delaware adopted the legendary blue hen chicken as its state bird.

SOMETHING TO DO
Stars in sunlight

Make several pinholes in a piece of *white construction paper* and in a piece of *black construction paper*. Hold them up to lights in the room or up to the sunlight. Which paper makes the light shining through the holes more noticeable? How does this demonstrate what happens to the starlight during the daylight hours?

Comprehension Check 9.3
1. Which star is used to help find direction? Why?
2. Which group of stars will help you to find the North Star?
3. Which constellation points to the South Pole?
4. How does the atmosphere keep us from seeing the stars during the day?

Astronomy

9.4 The Sun: The Greater Light

The light that rules the day

God made two lights; the greater light to rule the day, and the lesser light to rule the night: He made the stars also.

— Genesis 1:16

The greater light that God made is the sun. God made the sun to shine on the earth on the fourth day of creation, and it has been shining ever since. The sun is **about 93 million miles from the earth.**

The sun is a star similar to the other stars you see at night. Because the sun is **the closest star to Earth,** it is the most important star to us. Its closeness to the earth makes it appear to us to be a very large star, but compared to some stars, it is only medium sized. When we compare the sun to the earth, the sun is huge, however. If we had a large ball the size of the sun, we could drop more than one million balls the size of the earth into it.

Although the sun is one million times the size of the earth, it is not one million times heavier than the earth. The earth is made of solids, liquids, and gases, but the sun is made entirely of **hot, glowing gases,** and gases are less dense than solids or liquids. Although one million Earths could fit inside the sun, it would take only about 333,000 Earths to equal the weight of the sun.

You must never, ever, look directly at the sun. The sun sends out powerful rays that can permanently damage your eyes if you look at it directly. It is also unsafe to use binoculars or an ordinary telescope to look at the sun. **These instruments increase the power of the sun's harmful rays and, therefore, increase the damage that the rays can do, even causing blindness.** When scientists study the sun, they use special telescopes which filter out the sun's harmful rays and enlarge the sun's image.

The sun's energy

God has designed the sun in such a way that it gives off a steady supply of energy but does not burn up. Scientists think that it produces its energy by atomic reaction. That is, the atoms in its center join together to produce energy. Day after day, the sun gives off almost exactly the same amount of heat and light. Sometimes the sun seems much brighter than at other times, but this is because of

Understanding God's World

changes in the earth's atmosphere, not because of changes in the sun.

Many other stars do not give off steady amounts of energy. We can be thankful that our sun does not behave as those stars do. If the sun were not dependable, the earth would suffer very harsh changes in climate. For example, if the sun increased its output of energy by a fairly small amount, the ice and snow in the Arctic and Antarctic regions would melt. Then the oceans would rise about 100 feet. If that happened, one fourth of the people on earth would be flooded out of their homes.

Only a very tiny amount of the sun's energy ever reaches the earth. Most is lost in space because the sun pours out its light and heat in all directions. Even though most of the sun's energy does not travel to earth, the energy that does reach the earth is very powerful—powerful enough to supply our need for heat and light. Do you remember how the sun affects the weather? Why is sunlight important to green plants?

Heat. The sun is so hot that nothing can exist there without changing into a hot gas. Knowing this, do you think that scientists would want to explore the sun in a spaceship? A spaceship could not go near the sun without being changed into a glowing, hot gas.

SCIENCE CONCEPTS — *A dark shirt on a hot day*

When heat and light travel to the earth from the sun, things on earth **absorb,** or *soak up,* much of the heat and light. But not all of the sun's energy is absorbed. Some of it is **reflected,** or *bounced back.* Dark things absorb a lot of heat but reflect very little. Light-colored objects are good reflectors; that is, heat and light bounce off them.

You can observe how this works. *You will need a flashlight, a piece of white paper, and a piece of black paper.* Darken the room. As you shine your flashlight on the white paper, hold your other hand about a foot above the paper. Notice how much light is reflected from the paper back to your hand. Now do the same thing with the black piece of paper. You should notice that much less light was reflected back to your hand. The dark paper absorbed most of the heat and light from the flashlight.

When you wear a dark shirt on a hot day, much of the heat and light from the sun is absorbed by the dark material. You will feel hot. What will happen to the heat and light from the sun if you wear a light-colored shirt instead?

Astronomy 263

Light. If we could drive by car without ever stopping, it would take us about two hundred years to travel the 93 million miles from the earth to the sun. Fortunately, light travels much faster than we can. Light travels from the sun to the earth at the speed of **186,000 miles a second.** It would take a ray of light about one second to travel around the earth seven times. The sunlight you see as you look out the window began to travel to Earth **eight minutes** ago.

The sun's gravity

As you know, **gravity** is the force or pull that holds us to the earth. The sun has gravity, too. Because the sun is much bigger than the earth, it has a much stronger pull of gravity. The pull of gravity on the sun is so much stronger than the pull of gravity on the earth that an object weighing 100 pounds on Earth would weigh 2,800 pounds on the sun! Of course, nothing on Earth could exist on the sun. The sun is far too hot. But these figures give us an idea of the strength of the sun's gravity.

The sun's gravity keeps the planets circling the sun. Without the sun's gravity, the earth and the other planets would move in straight lines, and would not curve to circle the sun.

SCIENCE CONCEPTS
The movements of the sun

Did you know that the sun travels through space at a speed of about twelve miles per second? As it moves, it carries the earth and the other eight planets with it. The sun also rotates, or spins like a top, completing its rotation in about 25 days.

Before astronomers knew about the sun's movement through the sky, the Bible told us about it. Psalm 19:6 says that the sun's "going forth is from the end of the heaven, and his circuit unto the ends of it . . . ." Many unbelievers have used this verse to try to disprove the Bible, because they thought that the sun stands still. How wrong they were! We should always believe the Bible. Even though we may not understand every part, someday God will make all things clear.

The sun and the planets move together in perfect harmony. They were created and set in their courses by the wise Designer of the universe. Do you know Him?

Comprehension Check 9.4
1. Why does the sun appear to be much larger than the other stars?
2. What is the sun made of?
3. Why must you never look directly at the sun?
4. How far is the earth from the sun?
5. Explain why dark clothing is not a good choice for a hot day.
6. What fact about the sun did Psalm 19 tell us long before scientists discovered it?

9.5 The Moon: The Lesser Light

When God created the sun to rule the day, He also created a lesser light to rule the night. We call that light the moon.

Our nearest neighbor

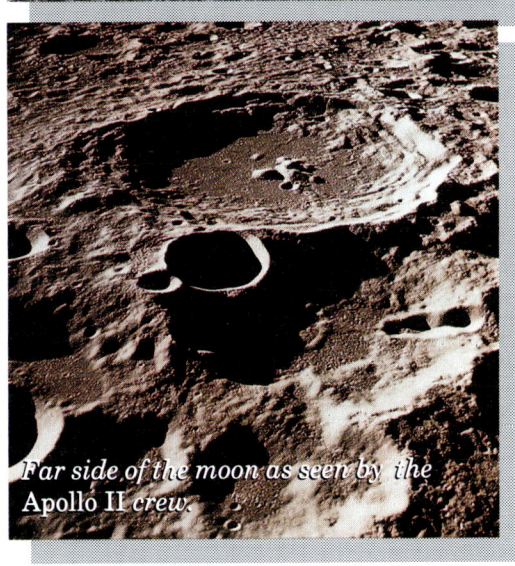

Edwin Aldrin on the moon.

Far side of the moon as seen by the Apollo 11 crew.

The moon seems to be the largest heavenly object that we can see in the sky, but it is actually quite small compared to the sun and the earth. The earth is four times larger than the moon, and the sun is about 400 times larger than the moon. You may ask, "Why does the moon look about the same size as the sun?" It is because the moon is much closer to us than the sun. Remember, the sun is about 93 million miles away from us. The moon is only 240 thousand miles away. But as seen from the earth, they seem to be about the same size.

In July 1969, the spacecraft **Apollo 11** landed American astronauts **Neil Armstrong** and **Edwin Aldrin** on the moon. Armstrong and Aldrin were the first men to walk on the moon.

Moonlight

On some nights, the moon is so bright that it seems to light up the whole sky. It even casts shadows. Yet the moon does not produce any light of its own. The light that we see from the moon comes from the sun. Since ***the moon reflects sunlight,*** it *appears* to be shining. If the sun were to be darkened suddenly, we would not see the moon.

Astronomy ■ 265

SCIENCE CONCEPTS
Why does the moon shine if it cannot produce light?

In order for our eyes to see, they must have light. Some objects can make their own light. The sun and the other stars are called **luminous** [lū′mi-nus] objects because they give off their own visible light. Any object which does not make its own visible light is a *nonluminous* object. The moon is nonluminous; so are trees, houses, most animals, and people.

Then how is it that we can see nonluminous objects, since they do not give off any visible light of their own? **We see all nonluminous things because of reflected light.** Light that is reflected is light that is bounced back in the direction from which it came. Light travels from its source, some luminous object, and comes in contact with nonluminous objects. **These objects may absorb, or soak up, the light; or they may reflect, or throw back, the light. Most objects absorb some light and reflect the rest.** The reflected light bounces back to your eyes, and you are able to see the object. Smooth things such as mirrors, jewels, water, glass, and metals are good reflectors of light. Objects which are seen as the result of reflected light are called **illuminated** objects.

Suppose you have gone for a walk in the woods at night. You have brought your flashlight along as a source of light. As light from your flashlight falls on the trees and rocks around you, you are able to see these objects, because they reflect the light from your flashlight back to you.

The moon receives rays of light from the sun. Some of these rays are reflected back from the surface of the moon. This is the moonlight or *illuminated* light that we see. The earth and the other planets also reflect light from the sun. When astronauts travel into space and look back at the earth, they can see the earth shining from its reflected light.

The moon moves

The moon is the earth's only natural satellite. A **satellite** is a smaller object that travels around a larger one. Today there are also man-made satellites which **orbit,** or travel in a path, around the earth. Some of them provide us with useful information about the weather, and some broadcast radio waves or take pictures of the earth. **The moon is a natural satellite, created by God.** *It takes the moon **about 30 days** to revolve, or travel, around the earth.*

Besides *revolving* around the

earth, the moon also *rotates,* or turns, on its axis. It takes almost the same amount of time for the moon to rotate once on its axis as it does for the moon to revolve once around the earth. For this reason, there is a side of the moon that we never see. Spaceships that have been sent to the moon to photograph the far side have shown us that the far side of the moon looks very much like the side we can see.

24 Pheasant

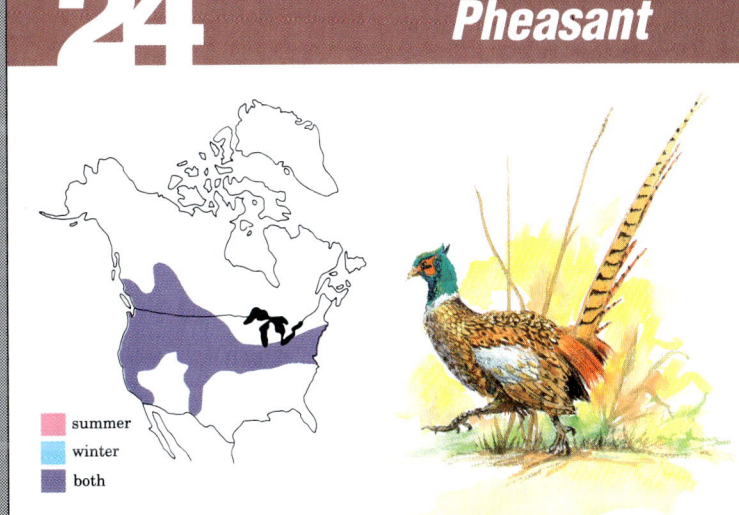

summer
winter
both

The ring-necked pheasant is a favorite game bird. It is not only beautiful to look at—it is also delicious to eat! The cock is a very handsome bird, usually about thirty-six inches long. His sweeping, pointed tail is 20 inches long. The hen is smaller, about twenty-four inches long, with a ten-inch tail. The pheasant is a swift runner and a strong flier.

The ring-necked pheasant lives in southwestern Canada, most of the western United States, throughout the Midwest, and in New England.

Pheasants live in pastures with brush close by for cover, along the grassy edges of woods, and even on the outskirts of large cities. You may see one roosting in an orchard or in a tree by the side of the road. Pheasants eat grain, berries, seeds, and some insects.

Does the moon change shape?

The moon is shaped like a sphere. Although you probably already knew this, you may have wondered why it looks as though the moon changes its shape. The moon appears to change because we see different amounts of the sunlit section of the moon as it travels around the earth. When the moon is directly between the sun and the earth, we cannot see the moon, because the sunlit side is facing away from the earth. This position is called the **new moon.** (A *new moon* looks like *no moon.*) As the moon changes position, we see more and more of the sunlit side. When the earth is directly between the sun and the moon, we see the **full moon.** Each night after we see a full moon, we gradually see less and less of the moon until the moon is between the earth and the sun again, and there is another new moon. As you know, it takes about 30 days, or one month, for a full moon to become a new moon.

Astronomy 267

What is the moon like?

Have you ever looked up into the sky at night and seen "the man in the moon"? When you look at the moon without a telescope, you can see a pattern of light and dark areas on the moon's surface. The pattern reminds some people of a man's face. If you look at the moon through a pair of binoculars some clear night, you will be able to see some of its features, such as **high mountains,** deep **craters** (holes), and flat **plains.**

There is no air on the moon. Therefore, there is no weather, because there is no air to be stirred up. The earth's sky is a pretty blue because of air. The moon's sky is black because it has no air. **There is also no water on the moon. There are no plants or animals on the moon,** because they need air and water.

Because there is no air on the moon, sound waves cannot travel as they do on Earth. You could not hear any sounds on the moon. (Do you remember Robert Boyle's experiment with air and sound from chapter 6?)

A day on the moon lasts about two weeks. The daytime temperature is about 216° F, which is hotter than boiling water. Of course, this temperature would be much too hot for us to live. At night, the moon's temperature drops to about -250° F. What would happen to you at that temperature?

Temperatures on the moon are extremely high and extremely low because the moon has no atmosphere. Do you remember how the earth's atmosphere protects us from the rays of the sun and helps to keep us warm at night? Astronauts who travel to the moon wear special clothing to protect themselves from the moon's extreme temperatures.

Because the moon is smaller and lighter than the earth, it has less gravity. The moon's gravity is about 1/6 of the earth's gravity. If you weighed 60 pounds on Earth, you would weigh 10 pounds on the moon. Because the force of gravity is less, you would also be able to jump much higher on the moon than you can on Earth.

Comprehension Check 9.5
1. What is the difference in the ways that the sun and the moon produce light?
2. Why does the moon appear to change shape?
3. What two things that are necessary for life are not found on the moon?
4. How are temperatures on the moon affected by the moon's lack of atmosphere?
5. Who were the first men on the moon?

9.6 The Origin of the Universe

Think of the earth, our home, and of all of the things—living and nonliving—that are on it. Then think of the sun and the moon, the lights that rule the day and the night, the innumerable stars in the millions of galaxies. Where did all these things come from? Do you think that scientists can tell us?

Scientists can prove some things by observation and careful experiments; we can learn many wonderful things through a study of science, and we have learned many such things as we have studied this book. If a thing cannot be observed, however, scientists cannot tell us much about it. If a hypothesis cannot be tested by experiments, then scientists cannot prove that it is true.

Science cannot tell us about the beginning of the world and the beginning of life. Was any scientist present to observe what happened when the universe came into existence? Can we send rocket ships back in time to find out what happened? Can we do experiments to show where the first life came from? Is there any way to make and to test a hypothesis about how something happened so long ago? No! Scientists cannot really prove what happened before there were any people.

Some things that we cannot learn through science we learn by believing someone we can trust. Do you know the date of your birth? You probably do, but not by your own observation. You know it by trusting someone who was there or by reading written medical records. We can know about God's creation of the universe because He has told us about it in His Word. No other person was there in the beginning; the Bible contains God's true and reliable written record of what happened at creation, and we accept this record by faith (Hebrews 1:3).

Genesis 1:1 says, "In the beginning God created the heaven and the earth." Before the creation of the universe, there was only God. God made matter and energy out of nothing. He spoke, and it was so. You have learned many things about matter and energy this year. Can you name some of them? God also made the waters, and His Spirit "moved upon the face of the waters" to bring into existence the wonderful world that we know today.

Astronomy

1 On the first creation day, God created light and divided the light from darkness, making day and night. What special characteristics of light can you recall? Why do we have day and night?

2 On the second day, God created the firmament, which He called *heaven*. The firmament is the atmosphere that surrounds the earth. What special things about the air can you recall that make life on our planet possible?

3 God gathered the waters together to make the dry land appear on the third day. There was evidently only one huge continent at that time, to be divided later. Can you name the continents and oceans that we have today? On the third day, God also commanded the earth to bring forth in abundance the wonderful variety of plants we enjoy today, each with the ability to reproduce new plants of the same kind.

You have learned the names of many plants this year. How many can you still recall? In creating the plants, God was preparing the earth to be man's home. The Bible tells us that twice on the third day—after God separated the seas and the land, and after He created the plants—God saw that His work was good. Can you explain why plants are especially important to life on Earth?

4 The sun, moon, stars, and other heavenly bodies appeared on the fourth day. God made them to divide day from night, to give light to the earth, and to be for signs, seasons, days, and years. How many heavenly bodies can you name? Again, God saw that His work was good.

5 On the fifth day, God created the birds and all the animals that live in water. How many of these can you name? He created each bird and each water animal with the ability to reproduce after its own kind, and He commanded them to fill the earth and the seas. At the end of the fifth day, God again pronounced it good.

6 The sixth day was the last day of creation. God made the land-dwelling animals, from the largest elephant to the smallest insect. For His final act of creation, God made man, the only creature that He made in His image (Genesis 1:24–31). God made man's body from the same matter He had used to create the earth, but man received his soul and spirit directly from God. All the living things upon the earth were made to benefit man; it was part of God's wise design for man to rule over the rest of creation. At the end of the sixth day when God surveyed all that He had made, He saw that it was very good.

7 On the seventh day, God rested. He blessed the seventh day and sanctified it; that is, He set it apart as a special day. God could have created everything at once, but He chose to do it in six days and to rest on the seventh in order to give us a pattern for the way He wants us to do our work (Exodus 20:9–11). Just recently, scientists have discovered that people are healthier if they rest for one day each week. How wise is our God, who formed us for Himself!

Throughout history there have been people, even scientists, who have thought up their own stories of how things came to be. Many myths, hypotheses, and theories of creation have been developed and discarded, but no one but the Designer and Creator of the universe is qualified to tell us how our magnificent universe *really* came into existence.

25 Willow Ptarmigan

summer
winter
both

The willow ptarmigan (tär′mĭ-găn) makes its home on the tundra and mossy bogs of Alaska and northern Canada. Most other birds would not be able to survive in this climate, but God has given the willow ptarmigan special characteristics which enable it to live in the Arctic. Its white feathers camouflage it as it roosts in a snowbank. They also help it to stay warm in winter because the cells of white feathers are filled with air, providing insulation for the ptarmigan.

In summer, the willow ptarmigan eats shoots of plants, berries, and leaves. In winter, it lives mostly on twigs and buds from the willow tree, which it is able to digest because it was created with special bacteria in its digestive system which break down these woody materials.

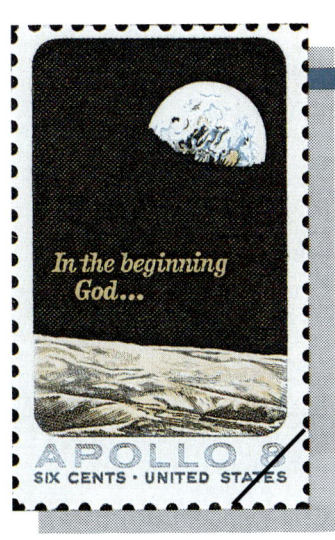

By late 1968 the American space team was almost ready to make a landing on the moon, but before making an actual landing they wanted to be certain everything was working perfectly. Consequently, they sent up three astronauts in **Apollo 8.** Their mission was to circle the moon without landing, check out all of the equipment, and then return to earth. It was almost Christmas time in December of 1968 before the *Apollo 8* mission was launched. Everything went well. Millions of people all over the world were watching their television sets as the astronauts circled the moon.

Astronomy ■ 271

And as Christmas day approached, the astronauts started reading from the Bible: "In the beginning God created the heaven and the earth." They took turns reading, and read the first ten verses of Genesis. "And God called the dry land Earth, and the gathering together of the waters called He Seas: and God saw that it was good." And then they finished with, "And from the crew of Apollo 8, we close with good night, good luck, and Merry Christmas, and God bless all of you—all of you on the good earth."

Throughout history, from the age of Adam to the age of the astronauts, people who have really wanted to know how our great universe came to be have looked to the Creator for the answer. And those who have searched for Him sincerely have found Him. Jesus said, *"Blessed are the pure in heart, for they shall see God"* (Matthew 5:8). Have you seen Him this year as you have sought to understand God's world?

How Well Can You Think?

All the statements below are true.
We know about some of them through observing.
We know about some of them through experimenting.
We know about some of them through believing someone we trust.
Read each statement and tell whether you know it by **observing,**
by **experimenting,** or by **believing.**
Sometimes more than one answer is correct.

1. The sun always rises in the east.
2. The name of the place where I was born is _____.
3. God made the world.
4. Cats can climb trees.
5. Columbus discovered America in 1492.
6. When grass is covered by a board for a few weeks, it turns white.
7. The moon sets in the west.
8. Oil will often stop a squeak in a wheel.
9. Plants cannot grow without water.
10. To balance a teeter-totter, the lighter person should be farther from the center.

Chapter Check-up

A *Match each term with the phrase that identifies it.*

_____ 1. absorb
_____ 2. astronomy
_____ 3. constellation
_____ 4. galaxy
_____ 5. gravity
_____ 6. orbit
_____ 7. reflect
_____ 8. solar system
_____ 9. zodiac
_____ 10. Milky Way

A. the force that holds the planets in orbit
B. to soak up
C. to bounce back
D. to spin on an axis
E. a large group of stars
F. the study of the stars and the planets
G. our galaxy
H. a picture made by stars
I. the sun and the nine planets with their satellites
J. twelve constellations that encircle the earth, called Mazzaroth in the Bible
K. the pathway that a planet follows around the sun

B *Write true or false in the space before each statement.*

_____ 1. The sun is made of solids, liquids, and gases.
_____ 2. The sun is about 93 million miles from the earth.
_____ 3. It is safe to observe the sun with binoculars.
_____ 4. The sun gives off a fairly steady amount of energy each day.
_____ 5. The moon gives off its own light.
_____ 6. We get our seven-day week from the orbiting of the moon around the sun.
_____ 7. On the moon, you would see the stars even in the daytime.
_____ 8. People living in the Southern Hemisphere can see the same constellations as the people living in the Northern Hemisphere.
_____ 9. Astrology is the science which studies the universe.

C *Fill in the answer to complete each sentence.*

1. The closest star to the earth is the_____.
2. Scientists who study the planets and stars are called_____.
3. The holes on the surface of the moon are called_____.
4. Our galaxy is the_____.
5. The Pointer Stars in the_____ help you find the North Star.
6. If you face the North Star, the direction to your left will be_____.

Astronomy ■ 273

D Name the planets.

a. _____ d. _____ g. _____
b. _____ e. _____ h. _____
c. _____ f. _____ i. _____

E Identify these constellations.

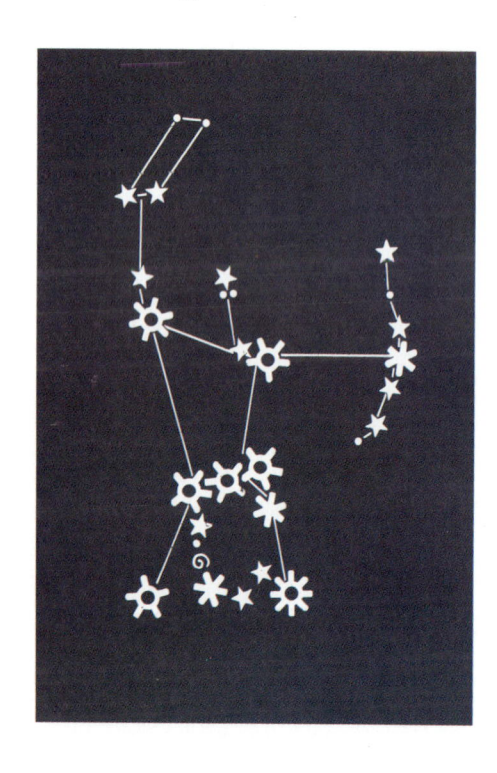

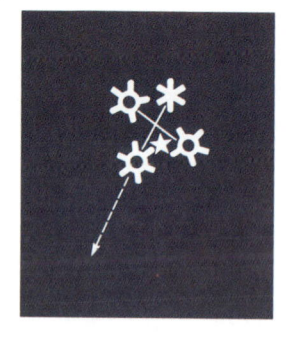

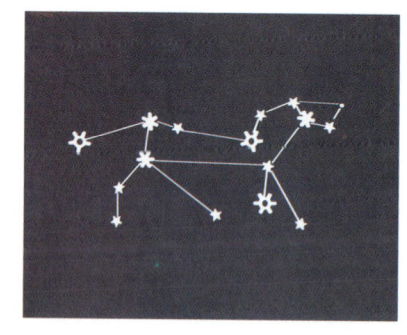

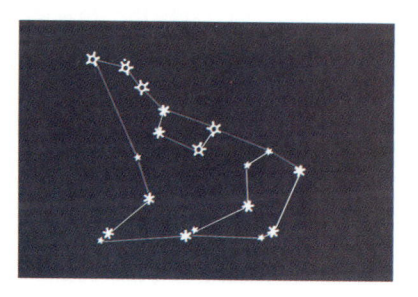

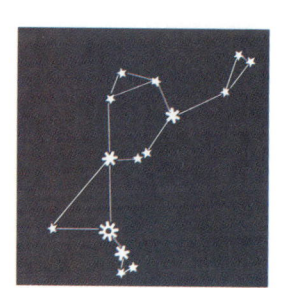

b. _____ c. _____

a. _____ d. _____ e. _____

274 ■ *Understanding God's World*

Glossary

Index

Glossary

Pronunciation Key

ā	āte	hw	what	o͞o	bro͞od
â	châotic	ī	īce	o͝o	bo͝ok
â	dâre	ĭ	ĭt	ou	out
ă	făt	i	clar*i*ty	sh	shark
ä	fäther	j	jog	th	thin
a	*a*bsorb	ks	perplex (ks = x)	t̶h̶	t̶h̶ere
ə	ago (ə·gō′)	kw	quart (kw = qu)	t͡u	virt͡ue
ch	chin	ng	song	ū	ūnit
ē	ēven	ō	ōver	û	ûnited
ê	fêar (a sound between ē and ĭ)	ô	ôbey	û	ûrn
ẽ	rẽsist	ô	côrd	ŭ	ŭp
ĕ	ĕgg	ŏ	sŏft (pronounced ô or ŏ)	u	foc*u*s
e	rec*e*nt	ŏ	nŏt	zh	azure (zh = z)
ẽ	pondẽr	o	*o*bscure	′	trifle (trī′f′l; shows that the vowel is not sounded)
g	good	oi	boil		
gz	exalt (gz = x)				

Abbreviation Key

adj. adjective   *n.* noun   *v.* verb   *pl.* plural   *sing.* singular

Note: *The terms are defined according to their use in the text. For more complete definitions, refer to a dictionary.*

A

abdomen [ăb′dô·men], *n.*
the last body part of an insect; it contains the insect's heart and stomach

absorb [*a*b·sôrb], *v.*
to soak up

acorn [ā′kôrn], *n.*
the fruit of an oak tree

agriculture [ăg′rĭ·kŭl′tûr], *n.*
the science of farming

air mass
a large body of air which has the same temperature and humidity

altocumulus [ăl′tô·kū′mû·l*u*s], *n.*
a high, puffy cumulus cloud

altostratus [ăl′tô·strā′t*u*s], *n.*
a high layer of clouds

ambergris [ăm′bẽr·grēs], *n.*
a substance produced in the intestines of sperm whales; it is used to make certain expensive perfumes

annual rings [ăn′û·*a*l rĭngz]
the layers of wood showing the growth of a tree

antenna [ăn·tĕn′ə], *n.*
a large "feeler," or sense organ, on the head of insects (and certain other invertebrates); *pl.* antennae [ăn·tĕn′ē]

anvil [ăn′vĭl], *n.*
a tiny bone in the middle ear

276   ■ *Understanding God's World*

aqualung

aqualung [ăk′wə·lŭng′], *n.*
an underwater breathing device

aquatic [ə·kwät′ĭk], *adj.*
watery

Arcturus [ärk·tū′rus], *n.*
the Biblical name for the Great Bear constellation

astrology [as·trŏl′ô·jĭ], *n.*
a false belief, or superstition, which claims to tell people's futures by studying the supposed influence of the sun, moon, and stars on people's lives

astronomy [as·trŏn′ô·mĭ], *n.*
the scientific study of the stars, planets, and all other heavenly bodies

atmosphere [ăt′mos·fêr], *n.*
the layer of air surrounding the earth

atom [ăt′um], *n.*
a particle which makes up molecules; the smallest part of matter

auditory canal [ô′di·tō′rĭ kə·năl′]
the tube which guides sound waves to the middle ear

auditory nerve
the nerve that carries the message of sound to the brain

auricle [ô′rĭ·k'l], *n.*
the outer ear

axis [ăk′sĭs], *n.*
the imaginary line that runs through the earth from pole to pole

B

baleen [bə·lēn′], *n.*
a hard, flexible substance like fingernails found in the mouths of some whales

baleen whale
a whale that has sheets of baleen in its mouth

chrysalis

barb [bärb], *n.*
a soft, hairlike branch attached to the quill of a feather

barbule [bär′būl], *n.*
a tiny, threadlike part of a feather having tiny hooks which keep the barbs in place

bedrock [bĕd′rŏk′], *n.*
the layer of rock below the subsoil; part of the earth's crust

beluga whale [bə·lōō′gə]
the only true white whale; a toothed whale

blowhole [blō′hōl′], *n.*
a breathing hole in the top of the head of whales and dolphins

blue whale
the largest animal that has ever lived

boiling point
the temperature at which a liquid changes to a gas

broadleaf [brôd′lēf′], *adj.*
having flat, broad leaves

brood [brōōd], *n.*
young birds that are hatched at the same time

C

camouflage [kăm′ōō·fläzh], *n.*
a disguise that causes people or animals to blend in with their surroundings

carbon dioxide [kär′bon dī·ŏk′sīd]
a gas which green plants absorb from the air during photosynthesis

chalk [chôk], *n.*
white, fine-grained limestone

chlorophyll [klōr′ô·fĭl], *n.*
the green coloring matter that green plants use to manufacture their own food

chrysalis [krĭs′ə·lĭs], *n.*
a hard case covering a butterfly larva

Glossary

circumference [sẽr·kŭm′fẽr·ens], *n.*
the distance around the outside of an object

cirrocumulus [sĭr′ō·kū′mû·lus], *n.*
piled-up whispy cirrus clouds

cirrostratus [sĭr′ō·strā′tus], *n.*
a very thin sheet of whispy cirrus clouds

cirrus [sĭr′us], *n.*
a very high, thin, featherlike cloud; means curly

clutch [klŭch], *n.*
a nest of bird eggs

cochlea [kŏk′lĕ·ə], *n.*
an organ in the inner ear that is filled with liquid

cocoon [ko·kōōn′], *n.*
a silk case covering a moth larva

coldblooded [kōld′blŭd′ĕd], *adj.*
having a body temperature that changes as the outside temperature changes

complete metamorphosis [mĕt′ə·môr′fō·sĭs]
of insects, four stages of growth—from egg to larva to pupa to adult

compound eye [kŏm′pound]
a large eye made up of many small eyes which allows insects (and certain other invertebrates) to see in almost all directions at one time

condensation [kŏn′dĕn·sā′shun], *n.*
the forming of tiny droplets of water as water vapor cools

conductor [kon·dŭk′tẽr], *n.*
of heat, a substance which carries heat to other objects

conglomerate [kon·glŏm′ẽr·ĭt], *n.*
sedimentary rock containing pebbles cemented together

conifer [kō′nĭ·fẽr], *n.*
a tree that produces seeds in cones instead of in flowers

conservation [kŏn′sẽr·vā′shun], *n.*
using natural resources wisely

constellation [kŏn′ste·lā′shun], *n.*
a picture made by stars

continent [kŏn′tĭ·nent], *n.*
a large area of land rising out of the oceans

continental shelf [kŏn′tĭ·nĕn′tal shĕlf]
underwater land along the edges of the continents

continental slope
the land between the continental shelf and the ocean floor

contract [kon·trăkt′], *v.*
to become smaller

core [kōr], *n.*
the innermost part of the earth

cotyledon [kŏt′i·lē′dun], *n.*
the tissue inside a plant seed which stores food

crater [krā′tẽr], *n.*
a hole

crest [krĕst], *n.*
of birds, a group of feathers on the head

crown [kroun], *n.*
of trees, the leaves and branches

crust [krŭst], *n.*
a solid layer of rock beneath the soil

crystal [krĭs′tal], *n.*
a substance with smooth, flat surfaces that meet in sharp edges and corners

cumulonimbus [kū′mû·lō·nĭm′bus], *n.*
a very tall cumulus cloud with dark undersides which brings quick, heavy downpours of rain

cumulus [kū′mû·lus], *n.*
a large, puffy cloud with a flat bottom; means piled up in heaps

current [kûr′ent], *n.*
a flowing stream within the ocean (that helps to moderate the earth's climate)

D

deciduous [dĕ·sĭd′ụ̄·us], *adj.*
shedding leaves each year, usually in the fall

delta [dĕl′tə], *n.*
a deposit of sand and soil found at the mouth of some rivers

dense [dĕns], *adj.*
closely packed together

dew [dū], *n.*
droplets of water that form on cool surfaces when water vapor from the air condenses; it is not a form of precipitation

dew point
the temperature at which water vapor condenses

diameter [dī·ăm′ē·tēr], *n.*
the distance across the center of a circle

dieffenbachia [dēf′en·băk′ĭ·ə], *n.*
a poisonous house plant

disk flowers
the flowers that form a disk in the center of a daisy (and other flowers in the daisy, sunflower, or composite family)

dolphin [dŏl′fĭn], *n.*
a toothed whale with a pointed snout

dormant [dôr′mænt], *adj.*
alive but not growing

down [doun], *n.*
a layer of small, fluffy feathers underneath the outer feathers of some birds

E

eardrum [êr′drŭm′], *n.*
a thin membrane which separates the outer ear from the middle ear

echo [ĕk′ō], *n.*
reflected sound that can be heard

embryo [ĕm′brĭ·ō], *n.*
the new plant inside a seed

energy [ĕn′êr·jĭ], *n.*
the ability to do work

entomologist [ĕn′tō·mŏl′ō·jĭst], *n.*
a scientist who specializes in the study of insects

equator [ē·kwā′tēr], *n.*
the imaginary line around the earth halfway between the North and South Poles

evaporation [ē·văp′ō·rā′shun], *n.*
the process by which liquid becomes water vapor

evergreen [ĕv′êr·grēn′], *adj.*
having green leaves all year

exoskeleton [ĕk′sō·skĕl′ē·tun], *n.*
an outside skeleton

expand [ĕks·pănd′], *v.*
to become larger

experiment [ĕks·pĕr′i·ment], *n.*
a planned way to test a hypothesis

F

fertilization [fûr′tĭ·lĭ·zā′shun], *n.*
the uniting of a sperm cell and an egg to form a new plant or animal

fertilize [fûr′tĭ·līz], *v.*
in plants, to make fruitful by uniting tiny sperm cells in the pollen with undeveloped seeds at the base of the pistil

field marks
distinctive markings which help in recognizing specific plants and animals

flatfish [flăt′fĭsh], *n.*
a flat fish that has both eyes on the same side of the head

flower [flou′êr], *n.*
the seed-producing part of a plant

Glossary

fog [fŏg], *n.*
a stratus cloud close to the earth's surface

force [fôrs], *n.*
a push or pull on an object

freezing point
the temperature at which a liquid changes to a solid

frequency [frē′kwen·sĭ], *n.*
the number of sound waves a vibrating object produces each second

frost [frôst], *n.*
tiny crystals of ice formed by frozen water vapor

fungus [fŭng′gus], *n.*
a plant which does not contain chlorophyll and cannot make its own food; *pl.* fungi [fŭn′jī]

G

galaxy [găl′ak·sĭ], *n.*
a large group of stars

gas [găs], *n.*
matter that has no shape and does not fill up a certain amount of space

gem [jĕm], *n.*
a rare, valuable mineral

geologist [jē·ŏl′ŏ·jĭst], *n.*
a scientist who studies the earth

germinate [jûr′mi·nāt], *v.*
to sprout

gill [gĭl], *n.*
the structure in a fish that removes dissolved oxygen from the water

gizzard [gĭz′ĕrd], *n.*
the part of a bird's stomach that grinds food

glacier [glā′shĕr], *n.*
a massive river of ice that moves very slowly

globe [glōb], *n.*
a sphere-shaped map of the world

granite [grăn′ĭt], *n.*
a rock which forms when liquid rock cools slowly, deep underground; most of the earth's crust is granite

gravity [grăv′i·tĭ], *n.*
the force which draws things down toward the center of the earth

grenadier [grĕn′ə·dêr], *n.*
a common deep-sea fish

Gulf Stream
a warm ocean current flowing from the Gulf of Mexico

H

habitat [hăb′i·tăt], *n.*
a particular area where an animal lives, such as a meadow, swamp, or forest

hail [hāl], *n.*
particles of ice which fall from the sky during some thunderstorms

hammer [hăm′ĕr], *n.*
a tiny bone in the middle ear

hemisphere [hĕm′i·sfêr], *n.*
a half of a sphere

hibernate [hī′bĕr·nāt], *v.*
to go into a long, deep sleep

Humboldt Current [hŭm′bōlt kûr′ent]
a cold ocean current flowing from the South Pole

humidity [hŭ·mĭd′i·tĭ], *n.*
the amount of water vapor in the air

humus [hū′mus], *n.*
the decayed material in soil

hydrogen [hī′drŏ·jen], *n.*
a gas which is combined with oxygen in water

hypothesis

hypothesis [hī·pŏth′ē·sĭs], *n.*
a reasonable explanation of something based on observations of that thing; a sensible guess; *pl.* hypotheses [hī·pŏth′ē·sēz]

I

idolatry [ī·dŏl′ə·trī], *n.*
the worship of false gods

igneous [ĭg′nē·us], *adj.*
fiery

igneous rock
rock formed from the cooling of magma

incomplete metamorphosis [mĕt′ə·môr′fō·sĭs]
three stages of insect growth—from egg to nymph to adult

insect [ĭn′sĕkt], *n.*
a small animal which has an outside skeleton, three body parts, and six jointed legs (in its adult state)

insecticide [ĭn·sĕk′tĭ·sīd], *n.*
a chemical used to kill insects

instinct [ĭn′stĭngkt], *n.*
a God-given ability or behavior that is inherited rather than learned

insulate [ĭn′sŭ·lāt], *v.*
to prevent loss or absorption of heat or sound

invertebrate [ĭn·vûr′tē·brāt], *n.*
an animal with no backbone

J

jet propulsion [jĕt prō·pŭl′shun]
the movement of an object in one direction by the movement of air or water in the opposite direction

luminous

K

key [kē], *n.*
the winged fruit of certain trees (such as maples) which contains a seed or seeds

L

larva [lär′və], *n.*
the second stage of complete metamorphosis of an insect; a caterpillar, grub, or maggot; *pl.* larvae [lär′vē]

larynx [lăr′ĭngks], *n.*
the voice box

lava [lä′və], *n.*
magma (hot, liquid rock) flowing onto the earth's surface

law of biogenesis [bī′ō·jĕn′ē·sĭs]
a scientific law which states that life can only come from other life

leaf [lēf], *n.*
the part of a plant that manufactures food

levee [lĕv′ē], *n.*
a high, man-made embankment along the edges of some rivers to control flooding

limestone [līm′stōn′], *n.*
sedimentary rock formed from the shells of sea creatures

liquid [lĭk′wĭd], *n.*
matter that takes up a certain amount of space but has no shape of its own

luminous [lū′mĭ·nus], *adj.*
able to give off its own light

Glossary

M

magma [măg′mə], *n.*
hot, liquid rock within the earth

mantle [măn′t'l], *n.*
the layer of earth beneath the crust

marble [mär′b'l], *n.*
metamorphic rock which may begin as limestone

Mariana Trench [mâr′ĭ·ăn′ə trĕnch]
the deepest known area in the sea

marine invertebrate [mə·rēn′ ĭn·vûr′tĕ·brăt]
an invertebrate (animal without a backbone) of the sea

marine mammal [mə·rēn′ măm′əl]
a mammal designed to live in the sea

matter [măt′ĕr], *n.*
anything that takes up space and has weight

Maury, Matthew F. [mô′rĭ]
the first man to make an orderly study of the sea

Mazzaroth [măz′ə·rŏth], *n.*
the Biblical name for the zodiac

melting point
the temperature at which a solid changes to a liquid

metamorphic rock [mĕt′ə·môr′fĭk]
rock which seems to have been changed by heat or pressure

metamorphosis [mĕt′ə·môr′fŏ·sĭs], *n.*
a change in form

meteorologist [mē′tĕ·ĕr·ŏl′ŏ·jĭst], *n.*
a scientist who studies the weather

migrate [mī′grāt], *v.*
to move from one place to another with the change in seasons

migration [mī·grā′shun], *n.*
moving from one place to another with the change in seasons

Milky Way
our galaxy, containing all the stars which are visible without a telescope

mimicry [mĭm′ĭk·rĭ], *n.*
the close resemblance of a harmless animal to a harmful one

mineral [mĭn′ĕr·əl], *n.*
a nonliving substance in the form of a crystal which is taken from the earth

molecule [mŏl′ĕ·kūl], *n.*
the smallest part of a substance that still has all the qualities of that substance

molting [mōl′tĭng], *n.*
the shedding of outer skin, scales, feathers, horns, or hair

monaural [mŏn·ô′rəl], *adj.*
having or producing one source of sound

N

narwhal [när′hwəl], *n.*
a toothed whale with a long tusk growing out the left side of its head; found only in the Arctic Ocean

natural resource [năt′ŭ·rəl rē′sōrs]
a material useful to man found in or on the earth

needleleaf [nē′d'l·lēf], *adj.*
having very narrow leaves that are needle-like or scalelike

nimbostratus [nĭm′bô·strā′tus], *n.*
a dark, gray sheet of rain clouds

nimbus [nĭm′bus], *n.*
a dark rain cloud

nitrogen [nī′trŏ·jen], *n.*
the gas that makes up most of the air

nocturnal [nŏk·tûr′nəl], *adj.*
active during the night

North Pole
the marking at the top of a globe

Understanding God's World

O

observation [ob′zĕr·vā′shun], *n.*
   looking carefully at something

observe [ob·zûrv′], *v.*
   to look carefully

obsidian [ob·sĭd′ĭ·an], *n.*
   a glassy, black, volcanic rock

ocean floor [ō′shan flōr]
   the bottom of the ocean

oceanic ridge [ō′shē·ăn′ĭk rĭj]
   an underwater mountain range

oceanographer [ō′shē·ə·nŏg′rə·fĕr], *n.*
   a scientist who studies the oceans

oceanography [ō′shē·ə·nŏg′rə·fĭ], *n.*
   the scientific study of the ocean

octopus [ŏk′tō·pus], *n.*
   the invertebrate with the largest brain; has eight tentacles

orbit [ôr′bĭt], *n.*
   the pathway which the earth follows; *v.* to travel in a path around an object

origin [ŏr′i·jĭn], *n.*
   the beginning

ovipositor [ō′vĭ·pŏz′ĭ·tĕr], *n.*
   the egg-laying part of some female insects

oxygen [ŏk′si·jen], *n.*
   a gas which green plants give off into the air during photosynthesis; necessary for life of people and animals

P

Pacific Ocean [pə·sĭf′ĭk ō′shan]
   the largest and deepest ocean

parasite [păr′ə·sīt], *n.*
   an animal or plant that attaches itself to another animal or plant and feeds on it

penicillin [pĕn′ĭ·sĭl′ĭn], *n.*
   a life-saving antibiotic produced by a green mold

petal [pĕt′l], *n.*
   the colorful part of many flowers which attracts pollinators

photosynthesis [fō′tō·sĭn′thē·sĭs], *n.*
   the process by which green plants use the energy of sunlight to change water and carbon dioxide into sugars (for food)

pistil [pĭs′tĭl], *n.*
   the center part of a flower which makes seeds

pitch [pĭch], *n.*
   the highness or lowness of a sound

planet [plăn′ĕt], *n.*
   a heavenly body which revolves around the sun

plankton [plăngk′ton], *n.*
   tiny plants and animals that float in the upper regions of the ocean

pointer stars
   two bright stars on the side of the cup of the Big Dipper which point in a straight line to the North Star

pollination [pŏl′i·nā′shun], *n.*
   the moving of pollen from a stamen to the pistil of a flower

porpoise [pôr′pus], *n.*
   a toothed whale with a blunt head

Portuguese man-of-war [pōr′tŭ·gēz]
   a poisonous jellyfish having tentacles up to 100 feet long

potential energy [pō·tĕn′shal ĕn′ĕr·jĭ]
   stored energy

precipitation [prē·sĭp′i·tā′shun], *n.*
   any form of water which falls from the clouds to the earth

predator [prĕd′ə·tĕr], *n.*
   an animal that feeds upon other living animals

Glossary

preen [prēn], *v.*
  to clean the feathers with the beak (said of birds)

pressure [prĕsh′ĕr], *n.*
  the measurement of force exerted against an object

primary root [prī′mĕr·ĭ rōōt]
  the root that grows from a plant seed when it germinates

pumice [pŭm′ĭs], *n.*
  a light, volcanic rock that is full of air holes

pupa [pū′pə], *n.*
  the third or resting stage of complete metamorphosis of an insect; *pl.* pupae [pū′pē]

Q

quill [kwĭl], *n.*
  the hollow stem of a feather

R

range [rānj], *n.*
  the part of a continent where a plant or animal can usually be found

range map
  a map which shows the range of an animal

ray flowers
  the flowers which radiate from the disk flowers of a daisy (and other flowers in the daisy, sunflower, or composite family)

reed [rēd], *n.*
  a thin piece of wood in the mouthpiece of some instruments

reflect [rĕ·flĕkt′], *v.*
  to bounce back

relative humidity [rĕl′ə·tĭv hŭ·mĭd′*i*·tĭ]
  the amount of water vapor in the air in relation to the temperature

resonance [rĕz′ô·nəns], *n.*
  the reinforcing of sound waves

revolve [rĕ·vŏlv′], *v.*
  to move in a circle around another object

rock [rŏk], *n.*
  the solid material which forms the earth's crust

root [rōōt], *n.*
  the part of a plant, usually underground, that anchors the plant, draws water and minerals from the soil, and stores food

rotate [rō′tāt], *v.*
  to spin around a center or axis

rotation [rŏ·tā′shυn], *n.*
  the spinning motion of the earth

sandstone [sănd′stōn′], *n.*
  sedimentary rock containing mostly sand

satellite [săt′e·līt], *n.*
  a smaller object that travels around a larger one

science [sī′ens], *n.*
  the study of the wonders of the universe

scientist [sī′en·tĭst], *n.*
  a person who spends time trying to learn about things God has made

sea wasp [sē wŏsp]
  an extremely poisonous jellyfish on the coast of Australia

seamount [sē′mount′], *n.*
  an isolated underwater mountain

sediment [sĕd′*i*·ment], *n.*
  matter that settles to the bottom or sides of a body of water

sedimentary rock [sĕd′*i*·mĕn′tə·rĭ]
  sediment that is pressed together until it hardens into rock

seed coat
the outer, protective covering of a plant seed

sensilla [sĕn·sĭl′ə], *n.*
tiny sense organs; *sing.* sensillum

sepal [sē′pəl], *n.*
a leaflike structure on the underside of a flower's head

shale [shāl], *n.*
sedimentary rock formed from mud or clay; the most common sedimentary rock

silt [sĭlt], *n.*
medium-sized particles of soil

simple eye
an insect eye with only one lens that is designed to sense light and movement

slate [slāt], *n.*
metamorphic rock which may begin as shale

sleet [slēt], *n.*
little balls of frozen rain or snow which fall from the sky during the winter

snow [snō], *n.*
ice crystals of frozen water vapor

social insects [sō′shəl ĭn′sĕks]
insects which live and work closely together

solar system [sō′lĕr sĭs′tem]
the part of the Milky Way galaxy which includes the sun and the nine planets with their satellites

solid [sŏl′ĭd], *n.*
matter that has a definite shape and takes up a certain amount of space

sonar [sō·när], *n.*
an ultrasonic device for sound navigation and ranging

sonogram [sŏn′ō·grăm], *n.*
a picture created by electrical impulses

sound wave
the movement of sound

soundproofing [sound′proof′ĭng], *n.*
the absorbing of unwanted sounds

South Pole
the marking at the bottom of the globe

spawn [spôn], *v.*
to lay eggs

sphere [sfêr], *n.*
a ball-like shape

spiracle [spī′rə·k′l], *n.*
a tiny opening through which air enters the breathing tubes of insects

stamen [stā′mĕn], *n.*
the center part of a flower which makes pollen

steam [stēm], *n.*
hot water vapor

stem [stĕm], *n.*
the part of a plant that carries water and minerals to the leaves and food to the roots

stereophonic [stĕr′ē·ō·fŏn′ĭk], *adj.*
having or producing two or more sources of sound

stirrup [stŭr′up], *n.*
the smallest bone in the body, located behind the eardrum

stratocumulus [strāt′ō·kū′mû·lus], *n.*
a low layer of puffy cumulus clouds

stratus [strā′tus], *n.*
a low, thick layer of clouds

submersible [sub·mûr′si·b′l], *n.*
a small submarine used by scientists to explore the ocean depths

subsoil [sŭb′soil′], *n.*
the soil beneath the layer of topsoil

sun [sŭn], *n.*
the closest star to Earth

surface tension [sûr′fĭs tĕn′shun]
the tight fitting together of water molecules near the water's surface

syrinx [sĭr′ĭngks], *n.*
the voice box of a bird

Glossary ■ 285

T

tension [těn′shun], *n.*
tightness

thorax [thôr′ăks], *n.*
the middle body part of an insect

thunderhead [thŭn′dĕr·hĕd′], *n.*
a thick, dark, heavy cumulus cloud

topsoil [tŏp′soil′], *n.*
the upper layer of soil

transparent [trăns·pâr′ent], *adj.*
clear; allowing light to pass through

trench [trĕnch], *n.*
the deepest part of the ocean (at the base of the continental slope)

trunk [trŭngk], *n.*
the stem of a tree

U

ultrasonic [ŭl′trə·sŏn′ĭk], *adj.*
high-frequency sounds that cannot be heard by the human ear

universe [ū′ni·vûrs], *n.*
all things which God created

V

vertebrate [vûr′tĕ·brăt], *n.*
an animal with a backbone

vibrate [vī′brāt], *v.*
to move rapidly back and forth

vibration [vī·brā′shun], *n.*
a rapid back and forth movement

vocal cord [vō′kəl kôrd]
the part of the throat which produces sound

W

water cycle [wô′tĕr sī′k′l]
the movement of water from the earth to the air and back again

water vapor [vā′pĕr]
water in its state of gas

Z

zodiac [zō′dĭ·ăk], *n.*
twelve constellations that encircle the earth; called Mazzaroth in the Bible

Index

Page numbers for illustrations are printed in *italic type*.

A

abdomen 22
absorption 263
Africa 202, *202, 203*
agriculture 93
air 147–156, 268
   layers of 148
   pressure of 150–151
   temperature of 152
   weight of 149
air mass 161
Aldrin, Edwin 265, *265*
altocumulus 160
altostratus 160
ambergris 238
American manual alphabet *174*
angler fish 227, *227*
animal tracks *10*
annual rings 65, *65*
ant *7*, 51–52, *51, 52, 178*
ant lion *7*
Antarctica 202, *202, 203*
antenna (of insects) 32, *32,* 61
anvil 176, *177*
aphid 50
Apollo 8 271–272
   Apollo 8 (postage stamp) *271*
Apollo 11 265
apple blossom *14*
aqualung 232, *232*
arbutus, trailing *19*
Arctic Ocean 200, 201, *203*
Arcturus 257 (*see also* Great Bear)
Armstrong, Neil 265
Asia 202, *202, 203*
asparagus *86*
aster 74, *74, 96*
astrology 254
astronomy 246–274, *254*
Atlantic Ocean 200, 201, *203*
atmosphere 147
atom 139
auditory canal 176, *177*
auditory nerve 176, *177*
auricle 176, *177*
Australia *202,* 203, *203*

avens, mountain *18*
axis 197
azalea *86*

B

baleen 237
barb 127, *127*
barbule 127, *127*
barnacle 241
bat 181, 185–186, *186*
beak 122–123, *122–123*
   (*see also* bill)
bean *12*
bedrock 208, *208*
bee 53, *53* (*see also* honeybee)
bee eater *122*
beehive (wooden) *53*
beetle *34,* 36, 37, *178*
   bombardier 41–42, *41*
   burying 48, *48*
   carrion 42, *42*
   Goliath 22, *23*
   Japanese 107
   milkweed 42, *42*
   sexton 48, *48*
   whirligig 33, *33*
Bell, Alexander Graham *174,* 190–191, *190*
Betelgeuse 260
Big Dipper 255, *255–259*
bill (of birds) 108, *108,* 122–123, *122–123,* 132
biogenesis 31
bird 97–133
   bills of 108, *108,* 122–123, *122–123,* 132
   bones of 126, *126*
   feet of 124–125, *124–125,* 133
   tails of 108, *108*
   wings of 125–127
birdbath 113, 116
bird feeder 111–112, *111, 112*
birdhouse 113–114, 116
birds, Canadian 16, 101
birds, state *14–15*
bitterroot *15*

black-eyed Susan *15,* 74, *74*
blow hole 237
blue jay 16, 101, *101, 102, 114*
   Steller's jay *101*
bluebird 117, *117*
   eastern *14,* 117
   mountain *14, 15,* 117
   western 117
bluebonnet *14*
boiling point 143
bones (of birds) 126, *126*
Boyle, Robert 163–164, 171
brood 99
bug, large milkweed *34,* 40
butter and eggs 74, *74*
butterfly 26–30, *26, 27, 34*
   black swallowtail 26, *26*
   cabbage 27, *27*
   dead leaf 43, *43*
   monarch 27, *27,* 30, 37, *43,* 47
   painted lady 26, *26,* 32, *32*
   viceroy 43, *43*

C

cactus blossom, saguaro *14*
caddis worm 47, *47*
camellia *14*
camouflage 43
Canadian birds 16, 101
Canadian floral emblems 17, *18–19*
carbon dioxide 64, 139, 148
cardinal *14, 15,* 85, *85,* 100, *100, 103, 114, 132*
cardinal flower 74, *74*
carnation, red *14*
carnivorous 229
Carver, George Washington 92, *92*
cat *179*
caterpillar *9,* 28, 29, *34*
   tiger swallowtail 42, *42*
centipede *7*
chalk 215, *215*
chickadee *15,* 114, 118, *118,* 121, *121, 132*

Index ■ 287

black-capped *14*
chicken 261
  blue hen *15,* 261
  Rhode Island red *15,* 261, *261*
chicory 75, *75*
chlorophyll 63
chrysalis 29
chrysanthemum 76, *76*
cicada 46, *46*
circumference 196
cirrocumulus 160
cirrostratus 160
cirrus 136
clam, giant *241*
clamworm *241*
clay 208
cloud 136, *136,* 160–161, *165*
  altocumulus 160, *160*
  altostratus 160, *160*
  cirrocumulus 160, *160*
  cirrostratus 160, *160*
  cirrus 136, *136, 165*
  cumulonimbus *160,* 161
  cumulus 136, *136, 165*
  nimbostratus cloud 160, *160*
  nimbus *160,* 161
  stratocumulus 160, *160*
  stratus 136, *136, 165*
cloud, storm 161
clover, red *14*
clutch 99
cochlea 176, *177*
coconut (*see* palm)
coconut plantation 69
cocoon 29
cod 225, *225*
coldblooded 39
columbine, Rocky Mountain *15*
compass 204
composite family (*see* daisy family)
conch *241*
condensation 157–158, *158*
conductor 116
cone 66, *67*
  white pine cone and tassel *15*
conglomerate 214, *215*
conifer 66
conservation 210, *211*
constellation 246, 255–260, *255–260*
continental shelf 224–225, *224*

continental slope 224, *224*
continents 202–203, *202, 203*
contract 143
copper 206
coral *241*
core (of the earth) 209, *209*
cosmos 76, *76*
cotyledon 78, *78*
cowrie *241*
crab, horseshoe *241*
creation 269–271
crest 109, *109*
cricket 22, *23, 34,* 38–39, *39, 177*
  Jerusalem *41*
crocus 85
  prairie *19* (*see also* pasqueflower)
crow 101
crown 65, *108*
crust 208, *208, 209*
crystal 206, *206, 207*
  alum 207, *207*
  salt 207
cucumber 12
cumulonimbus 161
cumulus 136
current (of oceans) 222–223, *222*

D

daffodil *86*
dahlia 76, *76*
daisy 73, *73, 74, 96*
daisy family 73–76
dandelion 75, *75*
Darwin, Charles 57
date (*see* palm)
day 197, 252, 253
deciduous 68
delta 211, *211*
Denebola 258, *258*
density 141, 235
dew 157–158, *158*
dew point 157
diameter 195, 196
diamond *206*
diatom 62
dieffenbachia 84, *85*
disk flower 73, *73*
dogwood, flowering *14, 15, 19*
dolphin 185–186, *186,* 239
dormant 82
down 127, *129*
dragonfly 33, *33, 36,* 44

dragonfly molting 22
duck *123*
dumbcane 84, 85

E

eagle 122, *122,* 179
ear 176–177, *177*
eardrum 176, *177*
  of a frog *178*
ears, animal 178–179
Earth 249, *249,* 251, *251*
earth 194–217
earthworm 7
earwig *41*
echo 185
Edison, Thomas 187
eggs (of insects)
  hera moth *58*
  honeybee *53*
  ladybug *50*
  large milkweed bug *40*
  monarch butterfly *29*
  mosquito *49*
elm 68, *68*
embryo (of plants) 78, *78*
emergency number 87
energy 144
  of sound 168–193
  of water 144–146
  of wind 153–154
energy, moving 145
energy, potential 145
entomologist 57
equator 195, *203*
erosion 210
Europe 202–203, *202, 203*
evaporation 156
evergreen 66
evolution 57
exoskeleton 21
expand 143
experiment 30
eye
  of birds 99
  of insects 33, *33, 54, 61*
eye, compound 33, *33, 61*
eye, simple 33, *54, 61*

288 ■ *Understanding God's World*

F

Fabre, Jean Henri 56–57
feathers *16*, 127–130, *127*
feet (of birds) 124–125, *124–125*, *133*
fertilize 72
field marks 109, *109*
finch, purple *15*, 91, *91*, *115*
fir 67, *67*
firefly 44, *44*
fireweed *18*
fish 225–231
    skeleton of *231*
flamingo *123*
flatfish 225
flea 36, *36*
flicker 123, *123*
    gilded 123
    red-shafted 123
    yellow-shafted (*see* yellowhammer)
flight 125–128
flood 212
Flood, Genesis 212
floral emblems of Canada 17, *18–19*
flounder 225
    winter 225, *225*
flowers 64, 70–76
    parts of 71, *71*, *94*
flowers, garden 76, *76*
flowers, provincial *18–19*, 72
flowers, state *14–15*, 72
fly (*see also* housefly)
    fairy fly 22, *23*
    syrphid fly *44*
flycatcher 118
    kingbird 119, *119*
    least flycatcher 118, *118*
    phoebe 119, *119*
    scissor-tailed flycatcher *15*, 57, *57*, 119
flying fish 228, *228*
fog *136* (*see also* cloud, stratus)
foot (*see* feet)
force 145, *145*
forget-me-not *14*
freezing point 143
    of salt water 235
frequency 181–182
frog *178*
frost 158
fruits *9*, 64
fungi 90

G

galaxy 248
gas 140, *140*, 141, 143, 270
gem 206, *206*
geode 205
geologist 205
geology 194–219
germination 82–84
gill (of a fish) 231
gizzard 128
glacier 211, *211*
globe 194, *195*
gnat 22, *23*
gold 206
goldenrod *15*, 75, *75*
goldfinch 79, *79*, *115*
    American *15*
    eastern *14*
goose, Hawaiian *14* (*see also* nene)
granite 214, *214*
graphite *206*
grasshopper 22, *22*, *23*, *34*, 38–39, *39*, *40*
gravity 145, 198
    on the moon 268
    on the sun 264
Great Bear 255, 257, *257–259*
Great Red Spot 250
grenadier 227, *227*
grouse
    ruffed *15*, 189, *189*
    sharp-tailed *16*
Gulf Stream 222, *222*
gull, California *14*, 147, *147*

H

habitat 109
hail 159
halibut 225, *225*
hammer 176, *177*
hatchet fish *226*, 227
hawk 122, *123*
hawthorn, red *14*
hearing 178
    of animals 178–179
    of birds 127, 179
    of insects 46, 178
    of man 176–178
    of reptiles 178
hearing aid 178

heat 263
    absorption of 263
    reflection of 263
hemisphere 195
hemlock 67, *67*
Herdsman 259, *259*
heron *123*
herring 225, *225*
hibernation 50
hibiscus *14*
holly *86*
honeybee 22, *23*, *34*, *35*, 53, *53*, *95*
hornet 22, *23*
housefly *22*, 32, *32*
Humboldt Current *222*, 223
humidity 155
hummingbird 105
    Anna's *106*
    ruby-throated 105, *105*
humus 205
hyacinth *85*
hydrogen 139
hypothesis 30

I

ice 140, *140*, 143
igneous 213
illuminate 266
Indian Ocean 200, 201, 203
Indian paintbrush *15*
insect 20–61
    body parts of 22, *22*
    characteristics of 21
    communication of 44–46
    eggs of *29*, *40*, *50*, *53*, *58*
    jointed legs of 35
    kinds of 20–21
    mouth parts of 34, *34*
    skeleton of 21
    wings of 26–27, *29*, 30, 32, 36–37, *36*, *37*, *42*, *44*, *46*, *48*, *61*
insecticide 49
insects, social 51–55
insect zoo 24–25, 51
instinct 47
insulate 127, 129
invertebrate 21
    marine invertebrates 240–243, *240–243*
iris *14*, *86*
ironweed 74, *74*

Index ■ 289

J

Jack Miner Bird Sanctuary 129–131
jay (*see* blue jay)
jellyfish *241,* 243, *243*
    Arctic jellyfish 243
    Portuguese man-of-war 243, *243*
    sea wasp 243
jessamine, Carolina 15
jet propulsion 242
jewelweed 75, *75,* 82
Jupiter 249, *249,* 250, *251*

K

katydid *46*
key 69, *69*
kingbird 119, *119*
krill 237

L

lacewing *42*
lady's slipper *19*
    showy lady slipper *14*
ladybug 22, *23,* 50, *50*
Landsat 195
lantern fish 227, *227*
lark bunting *15, 155, 155*
larva 28, 29, *29*
    carpenter ant *51*
    hera moth *58*
    honeybee *53*
    ladybug *50*
larynx 173
laurel, mountain *15*
lava 213
law of biogenesis 31
leaves *9,* 64, 66–69, *66–70*
leaves of three 88, *88*
Leo the Lion 258, *258, 259*
levee 212
lice (*see* louse)
lift 126
light 264, 266
lilac *15*
lily
    prairie *18*
    sego *14*
    white garden *18*
limestone 214, *215*

liquid 140, *140,* 141
Little Dipper 255, *255–257*
lobelia, scarlet 74, *74*
lobster *241*
locust 37, *37*
loon, common *14,* 137, *137*
louse 49, *49*
luminous 266

M

mackerel 225, *225*
magma 209
magnet 203
magnolia *14, 15*
mammal
    marine 237, *179*
mangrove tree, red 81, *81*
manta ray 227, *227*
mantle (of the earth) 209, *209*
maple 69, *69*
    flowers 71, *71*
    leaf 69, *69*
    seed *80*
marble 216, *216*
Mariana Trench 224
marigold *12*
marlin, blue 228, *228*
Mars 249, *249,* 250, *251*
martin, purple *114*
matter 138–139
Maury, Matthew F. 220–222, *221*
mayflower *14*
Mazzaroth 253
meadowlark 45, *45*
    western *14, 15*
melting point 142–143
Mercury 249, *249, 251*
metamorphic 216
metamorphosis 29–30, 40, 54
    complete 29–30, *29–30,* 53, 54, *58*
    incomplete 40, *40*
meteorologist 161
migrate 117
migration (of insects) 37
milkweed bug, large 34, *40*
Milky Way 248, *248*
millipede *7*
mimicry 43–44, *43*
minerals 205–206, *205–206*
mistletoe *15, 86*
mockingbird *14,* 25, *25,* 100, *102, 132*

mole cricket 35, *35*
molecule 138–139, *138*
molting 22
    of a dragonfly *22*
monaural 188
month 253
moon 265–268
    phases of 267
moon, full 267, *267*
moon, new 267, *267*
moonlight 265
morning glory *12, 86*
mosquito 32, *32,* 34, *34,* 49, *178*
moth 26, 27, 29
    fall webworm 27, *27*
    hera *58*
    Isabella 26, *26*
    measuring worm *43*
    polyphemus 32, *32, 36*
mouth parts (of an insect) 34, *34*
mushroom 87, *87*
mussel *241*

N

narwhal 238, *238*
natural resource 210, *211*
nautilus, chambered *241*
nene 245, *245*
Neptune 249, *249, 251*
nicotine 89
night 197, 252
nimbostratus 161
nimbus 161
nitrogen 148
nonluminous 266
North America 202, *202, 203*
North Pole 195, 203
North Star 255, *255,* 256, *256*
nuthatch *115,* 119, *119*
    red-breasted 119
    white-breasted 119
nymph 40, *40*

O

oak 68, *68*
oarfish *226,* 227
observation 6–13, 108–110, 115
obsidian 214, *214*
ocean floor 224, *226*
oceanic ridge 224, *226*
oceanographer 224, 232

oceanography 220–245, *222*
oceans *200*, 201
octopus 240, *240*, *241*
   blue-ringed 240
orange blossom *15*
orangutan *179*
orbit 198, 266
Oregon grape *15*
oriole, Baltimore *15*, 181, *181*
Orion 260, *260*
ostrich 124
   toes of *124*
ovipositor 22
owl 16, *17*
oxygen 64, 83, 139, 147
oyster *241*

P

Pacific Ocean *200*, 201, *203*
palm *66*, 69, *69*, *96*
parasite 48
pasqueflower *14*, 19
peach blossom *15*
pelican *123*
   brown *15*, 235, *235*
penicillin 90
peony *14*
petal 71, *71*
petunia 76, *76*
pheasant, ring-necked *14*, 267, *267*
philodendron *85*
phlox 76, *76*
phoebe *114*, 119, *119*
phonograph *187*
photosynthesis 63, 139
pig *179*
pine *67*, 67
   bristlecone 65, *65*
pistil 71, *71*
pistillate flowers 71, *71*
pitch 181, *182*
pitcher plant *18*
planet 249–251, *249*, *251*
plants 62–96
   poisonous 84–88, *84–88*
Pluto *249*, 249, *251*
poinsettia *86*
Pointer Stars *255*, 256, *256*
poison control center 87
poison ivy 88, *88*
poison oak 88, *88*
poisonous plants 84–88, *84–88*

Polaris 256 (*see also* North Star)
Pole Star 256 (*see also* North Star)
pollination 72, *72*, 95
pollinators 72, *72*, 95
poppy 79
   California poppy *14*
   seed capsule *79*
porpoise 239, *239*
Portuguese man-of-war *241*
potato, white 87
praying mantis 36, *36*, *43*, 49
precipitation 157, 159–160
predator 41
preen 127
pressure 150
   of air 150–151
   of water 233
primary root 83
ptarmigan, willow *14*, 271, *271*
pumice 214, *214*
pupa 28, 29, *29*
   hera moth *58*
   honeybee *53*
   ladybug *50*
   monarch butterfly *29*

Q

quail, California *14*, 199, *199*
Queen Anne's lace 75, *75*
quill 127, *127*

R

range map 16, *17*
rattail (*see* grenadier)
ray flower 73, *73*
Redi, Francesco 30–31
reflection 263, 266, *266*
regenerate 240
Regulus 258, *258*
revolution
   of the earth 198, *198*
   of the moon 266–267, *267*
revolve 198, *198*
Rhode Island red 261, *261*
rhododendron *15*
rhubarb *86*
Rigel 260
roadrunner *14*, 124, 219, *219*
robin *14*, *15*, 17, *17*, 99, *102*, 108, *132*

rock 10, 213–217, *214–217*
   formation of *213*, *215*, *216*
roots
   of plants 63
   of trees 65
   primary root 83
rose *14*
   Cherokee *15*
   wild prairie *14*
   wild *14*, 19
rotation 197
   of the earth 197–199, *198*, 252
   of the moon 267

S

sagebrush *15*
sailfish 228, *228*
salmon 225, *225*
salt *205*, 207
salt water 235
salvia 76, *76*
sand 208, 234
sand dollar *241*
sandstone 214, *215*
satellite 266
Saturn 249, *249*, 250, *251*
scallop *241*
scientist 4, 5
scuba diver 232, *232*
sea anemone *241*
seamount 226
seas 220–245
sea slug *241*
sea snail *241*
seasons 198–200, *199*, 253
sea urchin *241*
sea wasp 243
sediment 211, 214
sedimentary 214
seed 11, 63, 77–84, *96*
   germination of *83*
   kinds of
     bush bean *12*
     coconut *81*
     cucumber *12*
     dandelion *80*
     jewelweed *82*
     maple tree *80*
     marigold *12*
     milkweed *80*
     morning glory *12*

orchid 79
pine cone *80*
pumpkin *12*
pussy willow 81
red mangrove tree 81, *81*
squash *12*
squirting cucumber 82
tumbleweed 80, *80*
wisteria 82
zinnia *12*
  parts of 78, *78*
  purpose of 77
seed coat 78, *78*
seeds, airborne 79, *80*, 96
seeds, hitchhiking 81, *81*
seeds, traveling 79–82, *80–81*
sense of hearing
  of animals 178–179
  of birds 127, 179
  of insects 46, 178
  of man 176–178
sense of sight
  of birds 99
  of insects 33, *33*, 44, *54*, 61
sense of smell
  of insects 45
sense of touch
  of insects 45
sensilla 33, *54*
sepal 71, *71*
sequoia, giant 62
shale 215, *215*
shark 229–230
  whale shark 229, *229*
  white shark 229, *229*
shells 9
  conch *241*
  cowrie *241*
shrimp *241*
sign language 173–174
silt 208
silver *206*
silverfish *37*
skeleton (of a fish) *231*
slate 216, *216*
sleet 157, 159
snake *178*
snow 157, 159, *159*
snowflake *159*
soil 205–212, *205*
  layers of 208–209, *208*
solar system *248*, 249–251, *249, 250*
solid 140, *140*

sonar 186
sonogram 186
sound 168–193
  of animals 175
  speed of 171
soundproofing 184
sound waves 170, *170*, 181
South America 202, *202, 203*
Southern Cross 255, *255*
South Pole 195, 203
sow bug *7*
Spallanzani, Lazarro 181
sparrow 105, *105, 108, 132*
  chipping *102*
  English *102*
  Eurasian tree *103*
  house *102*
  savannah *127*
  song *115*
  tree *102*
spawn 225
speaking 173–174
sphere 194
spiracle 22, *22*
sponge *241*
spruce 67, *67*
squid *241*, 242, *242*
squirrel *81*
stamen 71, *71*
staminate flowers 71, *71*
starfish *241*
starling *102, 103, 104, 132*
star viewer 260, *260*
steam 146 (see also water vapor)
stems 64
stereophonic 188
stinkbug *42*
stirrup 176, *177*
stratocumulus 160
stratus 136
submersible 232, *232*
subsoil 208, *208*
sulfur *205*
sun 251, *251*, 262–264
sunbird, orange-breasted *72*
sunfish, ocean 228, *228*
sunflower *15*, 76, *76*
sunflower family (see daisy family)
surface tension 141, 142
swim bladder 231
swordfish 228, *228*
syringa *14*
syrinx 106

T

tansy 75, *75*
telephone 192
  tin can 180
temperature 83
  of the moon 268
tentacle
  of jellyfish 243
  of octopuses 240
  of squids 242
termite *41*, 55, *55*
termite mound *55*
thorax 22, 35
thrasher, brown *15*, 211, *211*
thrush 117, 175, *175*
  hermit *14*, 177
  wood 177
thunderhead 136
Titan 281
toadflax 74, *74*
tobacco 89
tomato (plant) 87, *87*, 96
tongue (of a woodpecker) *120*
topsoil 208, *208*, 210
touch-me-not 75, *75*
tree 65–70
trees, broadleaf 68–69
trees, deciduous 68–69
trees, needleleaf 65–67
trees, state 70
trench 224, *224*
trillium, white *18*
trunk 65, *65*
tsunami 226
tumbleweed 80, *80*
tuna 227, *227*
twilight zone 226

U

ultrasonic 185
ultrasound 185–186
undersea lab 232, *232*
universe 248, *249*
  origin of 269–272
Uranus 249, *249, 251*

V

Venus 249, *249, 250, 251*
vertebrate 21
vibrate 141, 168

vibrations 168–169, 180
vines 12, *12*
violet *14*, 15
  purple *19*
  wood *15*
viper fish 227, *227*
vocal cord 173, *173*
volcano *224,* 226

W

walking stick 22, *23*
wasp
  hornet 22, *23*
  mud dauber wasp 48, *48*
  parasitic wasp 48
  yellow jacket 22, *23*, 54, *61*
wasps, social 54
water 82, 134–146, 154–160, 210–212
water boatman 35, *35*
water bug, giant *41,* 49, *49*
water cycle 154–155, *155*
water, fresh 235
water, salt 235
water, sea 233, 235
water vapor 140, *140,* 155 (*see also* steam)
water wheel 146, *146*
waves
  ocean 236
  sound 170, *170,* 181
weather 157–163
  hail 159
  humidity 155
  sleet 159
  snow 159, *159*
  wind 152–154
weather forecasting 161–162
weeds 73
weck 253, 254
weevil 34, *34*
  acorn weevil 47
whale 237–239
whales, baleen 237–238
  blue 237, *237*
  humpback 238, *238*
whales, toothed 238–239
  beluga whale 238, *238*
  dolphin 239, *239*
  killer whale 239, *239*
  narwhal 238, *238*
  pilot whale 239, *239*
  porpoise 239, *239*
  sperm whale 238, *238*
wildflowers 74–75, *74–75*
wind 152–154
windmill *153*
wings
  of birds 125–127
  of insects *29, 32,* 36–37, *36, 37, 42, 44, 46, 48, 61*
wisteria 82, *86*
woodpecker *115,* 119–120
  downy woodpecker 121, *121*
  flicker 123, *123*
  hairy woodpecker 121, *121*
  pileated woodpecker *120*
  yellow-shafted flicker (yellowhammer) *14,* 120
woodpecker's foot *125*
woodpecker's tongue *120*
woolly bear 26, *26*
wren 104, *104,* 107, *107, 132*
  cactus *14*
  Carolina *15*
  house *103,* 104, *115*
  long-billed marsh *106*

Y

year 252, 253
yellowhammer *14,* 120
yellow jacket 22, *23,* 54, *61*
yellow jacket nest 54
yucca *14*

Z

zinnia *12*
zodiac 253

Scripture Index

Genesis
1:1 269, 272
1:2 134
1:9 215
1:9, 10 212
1:10 272
1:11 78
1:14 252
1:16 262
1:21 237
1:24–31 270
1:28 226
1:29 93
6–8 215
7 212
7:11 135
8:22 83
9, 10 213
10:25 215

Exodus
11:12–15 37
20:9–11 271
20:11 253

Leviticus
11:9–12 231

Job
5:8a, 10 134
9:9 257, 260
12:8b–9 231
26:7 194, 195
26:14 4, 5
28:9 213
28:10 210
28:24–25 149
38:22 159
38:31 260
38:32 253, 257

Psalms
8 220
8:3, 4 246
19:1 254
19:3 247
19:6 264
65:9 157
95:5 201
95:5a 221
102:25 213
104:24 2, 23
147:4 248

Proverbs
6:6–8 52
30:27 37

Ecclesiastes
1:6 152
1:7 154

Isaiah
40:22 194
47:13, 14 254

Daniel
2 254

Amos
5:8 260

Matthew
5:8 272

Mark
5:36 131

John
4:24 138
12:24 82

1 Corinthians
6:19, 20 89

Hebrews
1:3 269

1 Peter
5:7 131

294 ■ *Understanding God's World*

Credits

Illustrations and photographs not credited below were provided by the publisher. Credits are listed left to right from top to bottom on each page. For clarification, sometimes a photo number from the text is given, or a location is described. The following abbreviations have been used: ABB–A Beka Book Publications; FPG–FPG International Corporation; HAR–H. Armstrong Roberts; PR–Photo Researchers, Inc.; WF–William E. Ferguson.

Cover–birds–FPG, sun over water–Ulf Sjostedt/FPG, lightning–D. Gleiter/FPG, squirrel–WF, wave–J. Divine/FPG, clown fish–C. Roessler/FPG, butterflies–WF, nest–H. Abernathy/HAR, moon and stars–FPG; **iii**–E. R. Degginger/HAR, WF; **iv**–D. Muench/HAR, Bob and Ira Spring/FPG; **v**–Ralph Wetmore/PR, WF, **vi**–John Giannicchi/Science Source/PR (bottom); **vii**–C. Roessler/FPG (top); **viii**–FPG, earth–NASA; **2**–J. Divine/FPG, WF, L. West/FPG, E. R. Degginger/HAR; **2–3**–D. Muench/HAR (background photo); **5**–Stephanie Ferguson/ WF, Jack Jones/PR, WF, WF, WF, ABB, NASA/FPG (background photo); **14–15**–U.S. Postal Service, F. Stein/FPG (background photo); **18–19**–Canadian Postal Corporation (stamps); **18**–Stephanie Ferguson/WF, J. Swietlik/Canada's Northwest Territories, Jane Latta/PR, Saskatchewan Economic Development and Tourism, John Bova/PR, WF; **19**–Scott Camazine/PR, D. Mohrhardt/PR, New Brunswick, Manitoba Culture, Heritage, and Recreation, WF, WF; **20–21**–WF; **22**–WF (top); **29**–WF; **30**–WF; **32**–WF (top, left); **33**–WF; **34**–WF; **35**–WF (top, bottom right); **36**–WF; **37**–WF (top), Gianni Tortoli/ PR (bottom right); **39**–WF; **40**–WF; **41**–WF; **42**–WF; **43**–WF; **44**–WF; **45**–WF (center); **46**–WF; **47**–WF; **48**–WF; **49**–WF; **50**–WF; **51**–WF; **52**–WF; **53**–WF; **54**–WF; **55**–WF; **56**–The Granger Collection; **58**–WF; **61**–WF; **62–63**–D. Muench/HAR (background photo); **65**–WF; **66**–Stephanie Ferguson/WF, WF, Stephanie Ferguson/WF; **67**–Alfred B. Chaet, WF, WF, Virginia P. Weinland/PR, WF, V. P. Weinland/PR; **69**–WF (center, bottom); **70**–WF, WF, WF, Alvin E. Staffan/National Audubon Society/PR, S. P. Krasemann/PR; **71**–WF (both bottom); **72**–WF; **73**–Angelina Lax/PR (top); **76**–Stephanie Ferguson/WF, WF, WF, WF, WF, WF, George B. Jones III/PR, WF; **77**–WF (top); **79**–WF (bottom); **80**–WF, WF, WF, WF, Tom McHugh/PR; **81**–WF; **83**–WF (left); **85**–WF (2, 4), Karlene Schwartz/PR (3); **86**–Stephanie Ferguson/WF (12), WF (all others); **87**–WF; **88**–WF; **92**–The Granger Collection; **95**–WF; **96**–WF, WF, WF, WF, Jeff Lepore/PR, Angelina Lax/PR; **97**–Calvin Larsen/PR; **98–99**–Bob and Ira Spring/FPG; **100**–L. West/PR, Gregory K. Scott/PR; **101**–Steve Maslowski/PR, Leonard Lee Rue III/PR; **104**–G. C. Kelley/PR, Leonard Lee Rue III/PR; **105**–Gregory K. Scott/PR, Steve Maslowski/PR; **106**–Richard R. Hansen/PR, G. C. Kelley/PR; **111**–Harold Hoffman/PR (left), John Bova/PR (right); **112**–Stephen J. Krasemann/PR (left); **118**–Pat and Tom Leeson/PR, Bill Dyer/PR; **119**–Ken Brate/PR, G. C. Kelley/PR, Rod Planck/PR; **120**–Gregory K. Scott/PR (top); **121**–Rod Planck/PR (center), Richard R. Hansen/PR (bottom); **122**–Helen Williams/PR, E. Hanumantha Rao/PR, Paul Banko/WF, Leonard Lee Rue III/PR; **123**–Tom McHugh/PR (5), Joseph J. Oliver/PR (6), WF (7), Mason Rutherford/PR (8), Gregory J. Dimijian/PR (9); **124**–WF, Patrick Grace/PR, WF, WF, WF, WF; **125**–WF (6, 7); **127**–WF (center), Anthony Marcieca/PR (right); **129**–L. West/PR (top); **130**–The Jack Miner Foundation; **131**–The Jack Miner Foundation; **134–135**– Ralph Wetmore/PR; **140**–WF, WF, ABB; **145**–WF (bottom); **146**–WF (top); **148–149**–F. Stein/ FPG (background photo); **153**–WF; **158**–WF (top); **159**–Caroline W. Coleman/WF; **163**–The Granger Collection; **165**–WF; **166**–WF; **175**–WF (bottom); **178**–WF (wood frog); **185**–WF (top); **186**–WF; **190**–The Granger Collection; **194–195**–John Giannicchi/Science Source/PR (background photo); **205**–WF; **206**–WF (all except ring); **208**–WF; **211**–WF (top left), F. Gohier/PR (bottom left); **214**–WF; **215**–WF (4, 5, 8), Stephanie Ferguson/WF (7); **216**–WF (except top); **220–221**–C. Roessler/FPG (top); **239**–WF (6); **246–247**– J. Zehrt/FPG; **248**–© California Institute of Technology 1959, 1965; **250**–NASA; **265**–NASA; **271**–U.S. Postal Service.

A Beka Book Publications, a division of Pensacola Christian College, is a Christian textbook ministry designed to meet the need for Christian textbooks and teaching aids. The purpose of this publications ministry is to help Christian schools reach children and young people for the Lord and train them in the Christian way of life.

If we can be of further help to your ministry, please write *A Beka Book Publications,* Box 18000, Pensacola, Florida 32523-9160.